Public Employee Unions

A Study of the Crisis in
Public Sector Labor Relations

Edited by

A. Lawrence Chickering
Institute for Contemporary
Studies

Lexington Books
D.C. Heath and Company
Lexington, Massachusetts
Toronto

Published simultaneously in Canada.

International Standard Book Number: 0-669-00980-6

Library of Congress Catalog Card Number: 76-17444

The Institute of Contemporary Studies, founded in 1972, is a publicly supported, nonpartisan research and educational foundation. Its purpose is to
distribute research and information on national and international issues to
the opinion-making institutions, especially the mass media. Views expressed in the Institute's publications are those of the authors and do not
necessarily reflect the views of the staff, officers, or directors of the Institute.

TABLE OF CONTENTS

CONTRIBUTORS

Jack D. Douglas
Professor of Sociology, University of California, San Diego

Raymond D. Horton
Professor of Business, Columbia Business School
Staff Director, Temporary Commission on City Finances

Theodore W. Kheel
Battle, Fowler, Lidstone, Jaffin, Pierce & Kheel

David Lewin
Professor of Business, Columbia Business School

Seymour Martin Lipset
Professor of Political Science and Sociology, Stanford University
Senior Fellow, Hoover Institution on War, Revolution and Peace

Harvey C. Mansfield, Jr.
Chairman, Department of Government, Harvard University

George Meany
President, AFL-CIO

Robert A. Nisbet
Albert Schweitzer Professor in the Humanities, Columbia University

Daniel Orr
Professor of Economics, University of California, San Diego

A. H. Raskin
Labor Columnist, New York Times

The Honorable Wes Uhlman
Mayor, City of Seattle

Harry H. Wellington
Edward J. Phelps Professor of Law, Yale University
Dean, Yale Law School

The Honorable Charles B. Wheeler, Jr.
Mayor, City of Kansas City

Ralph K. Winter, Jr.
Professor of Law, Yale University

Jerry Wurf
President, American Federation of State, County, and
Municipal Employees

PREFACE

Public employee unions in the United States have caused growing concern since the mid-1960s when wages in the public sector began to rise more rapidly than those of private employees. Strikes became significant for the first time in 1966 and tension has continued to mount, particularly in the older industrial cities.

The economic problems and financial collapse of New York City in 1975—admittedly influenced by the unions—intensified public concern with the role of organized government employees. As this is the fastest growing segment of the labor movement, with responsibility for protecting public health and safety—particularly in major urban areas—the problem of satisfying its requirements is critical.

The authors in this volume therefore have been asked to examine the role of public sector unions in political, economic, and social life, and to discuss those facts, issues, and strategies which may lead to a cooperative understanding of the crisis. All the articles were commissioned by the Institute except that by Harry H. Wellington and Ralph K. Winter, Jr., which was reprinted with permission of the authors and of the Brookings Institution, and presents a classic statement of the differences between bargaining in the public and private sectors. Other contributors include union leaders, elected city officials, lawyers and economists involved in the analysis of labor relations, and scholars familiar with the background and philosophy of the subject in order to offer a broader perspective than that which ordinarily governs public discussions of labor problems.

> H. Monroe Browne
> President
> Institute for Contemporary Studies

June 1976
San Francisco, California

I

INTRODUCTION: BACKGROUND AND HISTORY

THEODORE W. KHEEL
Battle, Fowler, Lidstone, Jaffin, Pierce & Kheel, New York

Public employees and civil rights laws. Collective bargaining and civil service. Pensions and social security. New York transit strike 1966. Organized labor and public employees. Collective bargaining and collective negotiation. The right to strike.

Public sector labor relations are not working well, certainly not as well as in the private sector. Some commentators say the reason is because the private sector's experience hasn't been followed closely enough. Others argue it has been followed too closely.

The most fundamental issue is the nature of public employment itself. The argument that public employees should enjoy the same rights as their fellow workers in the private sector is deceptively simple, and is based on the observation that they are often doing the same work and have the same living problems to face. On the other hand, government is not an enterprise for profit. Government has particular standards and obligations, such as public accountability and the problem of sovereignty, which private sector employers never face. From

1

these questions follows the issue of the suitability of private
sector labor relations as a model for labor relations in the public sector.

HISTORICAL PERSPECTIVE

The responsibility for setting wages and working conditions in
the public sector historically has been thought to lie solely with
the government. In 1947 the Taft-Hartley Act rounded out the
national commitment to collective bargaining in the private
sector begun by the Wagner Act of 1935. Public employees
were specifically excluded from the jurisdiction of both acts.
Also in 1947 New York passed the Condon-Wadlin Act which
banned public employees' strikes, yet established no collective
bargaining procedures for employee participation in setting
working conditions. Governor Thomas E. Dewey, the law's
principal sponsor, emphasized that setting wages, working
conditions, and hours was the prerogative of the government,
and that the proper course for public workers dissatisfied with
the decisions was not collective bargaining but the traditional
political channels of lobbying and electioneering.

Civil Rights Legislation

"Labor movements" in the United States initially represented
simply the conscious, united, and persistent efforts of wage
earners to improve their economic and social conditions.
These efforts were sometimes conducted on the economic
level, sometimes on the political plane, and at other times on
both. They were part of a civil rights movement to correct the
injustices precipitated by the industrial revolution, and sought
to remove the impediments to correction imposed by the courts
with the support of legislative and executive initiative.

In the early years of the nineteenth century, the U.S. courts
frequently found that unions constituted combinations in restraint of trade. Later they concluded that the Sherman Anti-
Trust Act, designed to prevent monopolistic restraints of trade
by capital, applied its treble damage provisions to the acts of
labor unions and their members as well as to business. When

damage suits proved ineffective, the courts were ready with injunctions to prevent union organization and activities.

The Clayton Act of 1914, hailed by Samuel Gompers as labor's Magna Carta, was designed to remove the labor of human beings from the restraints imposed by the Sherman Act on commodities and articles of commerce. It was also intended to ban injunctions against union formation and related union activities such as strikes, picketing, boycotts, and the like. However, the Clayton Act was silent on collective bargaining or the making of collective bargaining agreements. Despite these reforms, the courts continued to hand down injunctions impeding worker efforts to improve their social and economic conditions.

The use of injunctions was not effectively eliminated until the passage of the Norris-LaGuardia Act in 1932. For the first time, a general law of the United States mentioned the right of workers to bargain collectively. It was still civil rights legislation, however, and had no application to public workers. In a policy statement in the act, Congress noted that the individual unorganized worker was commonly helpless to exercise liberty of contract and to protect his freedom of labor, thereby to obtain acceptable terms and conditions of employment. It attributed the worker's helplessness to the prevailing economic conditions which allowed owners of property to organize in corporate and other forms of ownership association with the aid of governmental authority.

The Wagner Act, passed three years after Norris-LaGuardia, was also civil rights legislation. It decried the "denial by employers of the right of employees to organize and the refusal by employers to accept the procedure of collective bargaining." It paved the way for the modern era of the collective bargaining agreement by preventing employer interference with employee organization, by providing means for determining the employees' choice of representatives, by enacting the doctrine of exclusive recognition of the majority agent, and by commanding employers to bargain collectively with that agent.

The modern era of collective bargaining did not bloom until 1947 with the passage of the Taft-Hartley Act which completed the legal prescription for bilateral agreements by requiring unions as well as employers to bargain collectively. Taft-Hartley also defined the duty of collective bargaining as the mutual obligation of both employers and unions. They are obligated to meet at reasonable times and to confer in good faith with respect to wages, hours, and other terms and conditions of employment. It also called for the "negotiation of an agreement, or any question arising thereunder, and the execution of a written contract incorporating any agreement reached."

Like the Wagner Act, Taft-Hartley exempted the United States or any wholly owned government corporation, or any state or political subdivision thereof, from the definition of employer. There were legal reasons embedded in the separation of powers for the exclusion, but there were practical reasons as well. When these laws were adopted, the pressure for collective bargaining and the making of agreements was not yet developing among public employees, as it was in the private sector.

Collective Bargaining and Civil Service

Collective bargaining agreements are legally enforceable, but their strength lies more in their mutual advantage to companies and unions. For companies, they provide a period of stability during which planning for production and marketing can take place with reasonable assurance that the employees will not interfere by refusing to work. They contain grievance and arbitration machinery which effectively resolves disputes during the term the contract. For unions, they enable the workers to mobilize their full strength at the termination of an agreement, to work for substantial improvements in wages and conditions for the ensuing term.

The organization of public employees for the purpose of collective bargaining lagged behind the private sector. One important reason was that public employment tended to be steady and without the seasonal and cyclical fluctuations that can produce frequent layoffs in the private sector. The other reason was the civil service system.

Job protection for public employees was gained through legislation much earlier than for their counterparts in the private sector. The civil service system, by which selection for positions is required by law to be based on merit and fitness of applicants, spread rapidly in this and other western democracies in the latter half of the nineteenth century. In 1868 the United States Congress adopted a law providing that eight hours shall constitute a day's work in all government employment. With civil service came safeguards against discrimination in promotions or dismissals, a form of protection later obtained by private sector employees through the grievance and arbitration provisions of collective bargaining agreements.

Pensions were granted public employees long before they were considered for those in private employment. Of the various public and private systems prior to social security, by far the largest—applicable to about 90 percent of all federal employees—is the civil service retirement system established by congressional act in 1920. In the same year the New York City Employees' Retirement System became effective. Together with other employee pension systems in New York, it had sufficient funds to invest more than $3 billion in city bonds in 1975 to help prevent the city from defaulting on its obligations.

THE NEW YORK TRANSIT STRIKE, 1966

Despite an initial reluctance to apply the private model to the public sector, certain forces made comparisons between the two sectors unavoidable. Governments at all levels were entering new fields of endeavor, many in place of companies in the private sector or in competition with them. Public employment was growing by leaps and bounds. Organized labor began to look with considerable interest at this expanding field of employees at the same time that machine politics in cities was declining.

The experience of the Transport Workers Union, AFL-CIO, in New York exemplifies some of the problems in the transition to collective bargaining in the public sector. The TWU came into the public service out of the private sector. It had gained bargaining rights in 1934 while the subways and buses in New York City were still privately owned; they were purchased that year by the city. The private owners could not operate it at a 5-cent fare, and the public would not pay more.

Mayor La Guardia, coauthor of the Norris-La Guardia Act, ironically took the position that since public workers were protected by civil service, they were not entitled to a collective bargaining agreement. The TWU did not resist at the time the city assumed its ownership. The union remained quiescent until the war ended, when it threatened the first of a series of city-wide transit strikes, thus commanding the attention of the mayor and the city's principal decisionmakers.

At that time there were employee associations, but no collective bargaining agreements with the city. The Civil Service Forum, no longer in existence, was one of the major associations. It specifically eschewed the right to strike, relying instead upon lobbying and electioneering to further the interests of its members. The TWU wanted a written collective bargaining agreement, with the same provisions for exclusive recognition and arbitration it had won in the private sector. Racing the deadline the union had set for a strike, an all-night meeting at City Hall resulted in the appointment of a five-member fact-finding board to make recommendations.

The board's report—hailed at the time as pioneering—is more noteworthy for what it did not recommend than for its affirmative proposals. The principal issue was that of exclusive recognition, which is a troublesome concept in the public sector. The board recommended that the TWU be recognized as the first among competing unions because of its numerical advantage. The city opposed a written contract as illegal. The board recommended a memorandum of understanding to memorialize the results of the negotiations. As for grievances, it recommended advisory arbitration so as not to challenge the city's right to make the final decision. In addition, it recommended against a union shop, a provision the union had won in the private sector.

The union persisted in the years that followed. Eventually, it achieved exclusive recognition, a signed agreement, binding arbitration of grievances, and a revocable check-off, but not the union shop. With these benefits the union also won significant across-the-board increases. These gains proved attractive to other city employees, whose organizations—mostly called associations—had followed the traditional paths of political activity. The strategy to be followed obviously was the one that offered the greatest gain for the employees and their organizations. Changing course did not call for any fundamental reorganization of the association, only a change in tactics. The Policeman's Benevolent Association thus declared itself a union. The National Educational Association learned a lesson when it lost out to the United Federation of Teachers, principally because the NEA did not seek all of the perquisites of a labor union. In other localities it was able to remain the dominant organization without changing name simply by adopting the tactics of its rival. The firemen, who had previously been affiliated with an AFL union, likewise took on all of the characteristics of a private sector labor union.

In 1965 the Transport Workers Union again demonstrated the unique problems facing public employee unions in their struggle to achieve collective bargaining rights, when a new mayor, John V. Lindsay, was to take office at the very moment the old contract was due to expire. The union's deadline to reach a new agreement was barely five hours after Lindsay's inauguration. When no contract appeared, the TWU went out on strike, one which proved to be the most calamitous in U.S. municipal history.

Three major problems faced the union and the city. The first—and most influential for the course of municipal collective bargaining during Lindsay's administration—was the mayor's unfamiliarity with bargaining procedures and the union's claims. Lindsay was guided by advice from political sources and editorial commentators, a natural predilection for a leader selected by popular vote.

The second problem has been generally overlooked in post-mortem analysis of the strike. The hidden issue was the narrowed pay differential between skilled and unskilled workers in the TWU, which had been produced by the across-the-board increases of the preceding contracts. This issue was exacerbated by the ability of other employees, who were not represented in collective bargaining, to increase the differential on the basis of New York State's doctrine of paying its public employees the rate prevailing in private industry.

The final issue is one that is unique to public employee labor relations. Who, among the municipal leaders, has the authority to bargain with the union? This became a major block to progress in the TWU strike. Legally the strikers' employer was the Transit Authority, an autonomous agency created by the legislature to take transit out of politics. Transit Authority members had the legal right to make the final decision. Actually, the decision was made by the mayor—not pursuant to his legal authority, but by force of his personality and because the public expected him to make the decision. In subsequent negotiations, decisions were made by the chairman of the Transit Authority, sometimes with and sometimes without consulting the mayor. At times the governor was a behind-the-scenes participant, especially when state action was required in connection with the settlement.

In order to end the strike, the mayor offered a wage settlement in violation of the state's Condon-Wadlin law, which prohibited striking public workers from receiving an increase pursuant to a work stoppage. To avoid a second strike, the governor persuaded the legislature to repeal retroactively the penalties of the law, a repeal which applied to this dispute alone. He then appointed George W. Taylor, the renowned collective-bargaining expert, to head a committee to study public employee bargaining and to recommend changes in the law.

The report of the Taylor Committee found fault with Condon-Wadlin's failure to provide employees with rights granted by the Wagner and Taft-Hartley acts to employees in the private sector. These included principally the rights to organize and to be represented in negotiations with their employers. The law codifying the Taylor Committee's recommendations established procedures for assuring these rights through prohibitions on unfair interference with them and through the designation of representatives. But the ban on strikes was continued, and by using the term "collective negotiation" instead of "collective bargaining" the committee implicitly noted that it was not recommending rights to collective bargaining comparable to those given private sector employees.

The committee never explained the precise difference. The term "negotiation" was embodied in the new law and remains to this day. Both commentators and courts have tended to use the terms "collective negotiation" and "collective bargaining" interchangeably. It is unfortunate that the distinction was not defined.

ISSUES AND PROSPECTS

The evidence is now conclusive that it is impossible to establish collective bargaining in the public sector in precisely the form that it has developed in the private sector. It would be better if a term other than "collective bargaining" could be used to describe the process by which employee organizations and governmental units arrive at determinations of wages, hours, and working conditions.

The similarity to the private sector system could be better understood if "collective bargaining" were applied only in situations where public employees had the right to strike and the public employer had the right to take a strike. The term "collective negotiation" would then clearly refer to those relationships in which the determination of wages, hours, and working conditions was reached through procedures that precluded the strike.

It is important that the impact of a strike ban on any form of bargaining not be overlooked. The strike enables employees, through their representatives, to participate in the decisions setting their wages, hours, and working conditions. In the absence of the right to strike, an alternative system of determination is required when negotiating parties reach an impasse. The search for such an alternative has produced an extensive body of law and practice on impasse procedures. Methods vary from state to state between and among the views that there should be ultimate decisionmaking either through the limited use of strikes, compulsory arbitration, or legislative determination. There is still no consensus on the appropriate course to follow.

A strike ban precipitates another question not faced in the private sector. What penalties should be imposed for violations? This in turn has provoked the tantalizing question of ascertaining the culprit: Is it the union, the leader of the union, or the employees who participate in the strike who should be penalized? All three have been the subject of varying penalties. The employee may be denied wage benefits or deprived of job rights. The union official is sometimes put in jail, especially if an injunction against striking is obtained. The union is subject to loss of check-off and the dues that would otherwise flow into its treasury, thereby damaging its capacity to serve its members. It may also be fined. Ironically, a bargaining atmosphere often is created despite the strike ban because of an implied or express threat of the union to strike. But this is hardly the desired way to produce collective bargaining.

Most laws on public sector relations speak of a collective bargaining agreement. But they cannot readily include subjects regulated by policies in other enactments which the agency or department must administer. What are the permissible and mandatory subjects of bargaining under these circumstances? The decisions of the National Labor Relations Board obviously cannot be used as the yardstick of determination when the question is related more to the powers of the agency or department than to its proximity to wages, hours, and working conditions.

Can collective bargaining exist if the legislature can supersede a contract by freezing wages, as New York has done during the recent fiscal crisis? What if, for example, the legislature precludes or regulates bargaining on pensions because of cost, as it has also done in New York? Can collective bargaining prevail if the voters restrict the powers of their negotiators? Above all, who is the decisionmaker on the employer's side? Can collective bargaining exist in the manner of the private sector without an identifiable decisionmaker with appropriate authority on both sides of the bargaining table?

These questions are not about to be answered conclusively in the near future. Experimentation is bound to continue. New insights will appear and new procedures will be tried. But employee organization in the public sector will continue, and there will be no return to the simplistic days of lobbying and electioneering as the sole and final determinants of employee relationships in the public sector. Negotiation will continue, whether it is collective bargaining as developed in the private sector, or a system called "collective negotiation." The private sector experience will continue to be a useful measuring rod, but it is no longer nor has it ever been a model for ready adoption without modification.

This book will examine differences between the private and public sectors and thereby point towards solutions. The system of labor relations in the public sector is still developing, and major changes are clearly indicated. The system needs careful reexamination. The present book provides timely new insights and fresh analyses by leading students and commentators on this difficult and frustrating field of employee relations.

II

PUBLIC UNIONS AND THE DECLINE OF SOCIAL TRUST

ROBERT A. NISBET
Albert Schweitzer Professor in the Humanities, Columbia University

Social roots of public unions. State and community: the patterns of allegiance and trust—Egypt, Athens, Rome. 16th century: decline of community and rise of the national state. French Revolution. 19th century: industrial revolution and rebirth of community. Rise of cooperatives and trade unions. Public unions. The uncertain future.

Two fundamental propositions underlie what follows in this chapter. First, public unions are at bottom *social structures* and hence responsive in their activities to the same basic needs, interests, and loyalties which we find in the relationships of individuals to all major groups: family, kindred, neighborhood, church, guild, university, and the like. Irrespective of whether the purpose of a group is economic, educational, procreative, or charitable, its social character is vital, and is made manifest by the degree of cohesion or solidarity which accompanies pursuit of purpose.

The second proposition is closely related to the first. The actual authority or significance public unions have in their members' lives is closely related to the *trust* that is reposed in them by their members. Such trust, as I shall argue, is in turn strongly influenced by the degree of trust that is reposed in the surrounding political community, in the state and its agencies of government. When trust in political government is strong, there is correspondingly less trust placed by individuals in groups such as guild or labor union. As I shall indicate, history reveals itself in changing patterns of trust. There are ages when the state is strong, with human trust going in substantial degree to the state rather than to competing social groups such as kindred, guild, local community or trade union. But there are other ages in history when the state is manifestly weak, unable to inspire trust or confidence, and it is in such ages that we find a strong efflorescence of nonpolitical groups seeking to meet individual needs and desires not met by the political process.

THE SOCIAL ROOTS OF PUBLIC UNIONS

That labor unions, like all groups including the family, have an economic, rational, and contractual character in some degree is beyond dispute. But we cannot understand these groups in terms of the rational factor alone. G. K. Chesterton once wrote: "The rational lover would never marry; the rational soldier would never fight." To which I add: the rational worker would not organize. If he were purely and exclusively rational, he would know or quickly learn how much farther he travels who travels alone. He would most certainly discover that, propaganda from union headquarters notwithstanding, the rise in wages and improvement in working conditions during the last two centuries has had little to do with the activities of labor unions and a great deal to do with efficiencies and motivations which cannot possibly be located in any spread of unionism. He would discover, in short, that just as the rational lover would not marry or the rational soldier go into combat, the rational worker would not become enmired in a labor union.

But men do marry, soldiers do fight, and workers do organize into unions. So do businessmen form chambers of commerce and join Rotary Clubs no matter how competitive with one another they may be. The vaunted individualist ethic of the eighteenth and nineteenth centuries is correct to a point; but the point is quickly reached. For, as John Dewey observed in his classic *Individualism Old and New,* the kind of individual conceived by the economists of the nineteenth century, whether classical or Marxist, for purposes of economic theory, is in truth a monstrosity. From the sociological point of view individualism in the literal sense is a pathological condition. Men live in groups. Communities, associations, groups, and unions are not externalities, much less superfluities; they are as much parts of our human lives as are the organs, tissues, and reflexes we inherit biologically. From the point of view of man the cultural animal, *homo sapiens,* what we inherit socially is just as important as what comes to us from the germ plasm, if not more important.

Human culture apart from groups is inconceivable. It is strange in many ways that we give as much attention as we do in Western writing to the "individual." When we look out at the world of humanity, we do not really see individuals as such, but, rather, human beings as members of groups, communities, and associations. For as far back in evolutionary time as we can look, man was living in families, clans, kindreds, and tribes; later in villages, towns, and, gradually, forming cooperatives, mutual-aid groups, guilds, trade unions, churches, and other kinds of associations. Long before the political state made its appearance in the form of kingdom and empire, countless human beings lived their lives—meeting problems of survival, maintenance of order, procreation, and production—solely in the context of such associations. No political state founded upon the use of force, upon sovereignty, was necessary. To this day, or until very recently, such groups have sufficed for many people.

THE STATE AND COMMUNITY: PATTERNS
OF ALLEGIANCE AND TRUST

The fact is, however, that the political state did come into existence approximately five thousand years ago in the form we have known it in the history of civilization, and once it did, the status of the older forms of association was significantly changed. For the West, the political state began in the Mediterranean area, probably in Egypt, and from the beginning it was characterized by a military-derived form of authority that was bound to affect the authorities and existences of the older, pre-political associations. Where the state was strong and commanded trust and respect, the authorities of the groups intermediate to individual and state became diminished in some degree. Conflict of authority was inalienably involved.

If we look back on Western history during the past three thousand years, it is possible to see a very interesting alternation, an almost rhythmic alternation, in the respective capacities of the political and the social spheres to command individual allegiance and trust. We may indeed state a proposition: The stronger the political state in subjects' or citizens' lives, the weaker the social order: that is, family, kindred, village, church, guild, and the like. But the reverse is equally true! Wherever these and related groups are powerful in human lives, attracting individual loyalties and inspiring trust, we may assume that the political state together with its varied assemblies and bureaucracies tend to be weak in what they are able to command or inspire in human allegiance. Over and over in history the political state and the social order are in competition over, in conflict for, the loyalties of human beings. The triumph of the one means necessarily the subjugation or subordination in some degree of the other.

For our purposes it suffices to stay with Western society as it comes into being in ancient Greece. My brief remarks will illustrate, I think, a point that has a great deal of significance to the relation at the present moment between labor unions and the political state.

Prior to the fifth century BC in Athens, the political state, to the degree that it existed at all, was weak. Far stronger were the ancient tribes of Athens and within them the clans, kindreds, households, and social classes. These, not the state, were the major influences in Athenian lives. In them was reposed the Athenian's trust. But all of this changed with the famous Cleisthenean Revolution at the end of the sixth century BC. Then the city-state came into existence, and from the beginning the status of the older groups, kinship and other, was substantially affected. With the new loyalty to city-state there went a measurable loss of allegiance to the ancient loyalties of tribe, clan, and household—attested to amply by the philosophy and the literature of the great fifth century BC. Nor was this changed by the rise of the Alexandrian Empire. The sheer power of Alexander and his successors in the political-military realm is testimony to the diminished authority of the social.

Turn to Rome. Prior to the rise of the Empire under the Caesars at the beginning of the first century AD, the major authority in Roman lives was the *patria potestas*, that is, the authority long embedded in the kinship group—household as well as extended family. Even the famous Roman Senate under the Republic was known officially as the Conscript Fathers. The political tie was, and had to be, weak, for tradition and customary law placed all major functions and authorities in the kinship-social realm. Included in this realm was a great variety of voluntary associations, including guilds of workers.

The onset of the Empire changed all this. We see a centralization of political power and administration, the expansion of the state into every aspect of society and economy, and a gradual transfer of individual allegiance from the kinship to the political authority. The state was powerful; the social order weak. This condition, this balance, lasted until about the fifth century. Again, the balance of power changed. In direct proportion to the decline of the political state in the West, there occured a recrudescence of intermediate society: of kindred and clan, mutual-aid group and village community, monastery and other religious community, guild and cooperative, and many another kind of association at all levels, within which human beings gained a sense of security and membership. The decline of political power could only result in a decline of trust in the capacity of the state to maintain security. There had to be a turning of human attention to other means of achieving security. And these means were found in the whole sphere of intermediate society. To family, household, guild, and monastery were given the kind of trust that had once been given in this very same territory to the political state. There was no alternative. The vital point here, though, is the fact that the Middle Ages was rich in social groupings, in social experiments, in the uses of social initiative, simply because the central political power was virtually absent from the West for many centuries.

Tradition, custom, folkway—what has been so well called "the inner order of associations"—triumphed over law in the strict sense of the word, and this came from the fact of the law's weakness. If self-styled king or emperor could not provide security through law, the social group could. Every social group, ranging from household or manor or walled town to guild, monastery, or university, demanded and commonly received respect based upon its claim of corporate right rising from the very nature of the group. As stressed by such historians of the era as von Gierke, Maitland, and Vinogradov, the ideas of political state and individualism were dim in exact proportion to the brightness of the whole intermediate area of association. What Athens had known prior to the fifth century BC, and what Rome had known prior to the first century BC, Western Europe during the Middle Ages knew once again: the vitality of all those groups founded upon kinship, mutual-aid, common residence, and work. But such vitality existed— could only exist—in the presence of central power as weak as the political state's power was during the period from about 600 to 1500 AD in the West.

THE DECLINE OF COMMUNITY AND
THE RISE OF THE NATIONAL STATE

The rise of the modern national state, absolute in theory, in the sixteenth century changed the picture substantially. Increasingly, it is the state, represented by the king—a Henry VIII, a Louis XIV—that begins to receive the kind of trust from populace that had for so long gone to Church as well as to so many other kinds of medieval association. Too many of these had become corrupt and oppressive. More and more people found monastery, guild, manor, and other medieval associations repugnant, the more so as a developing economy and polity offered a degree of freedom that was, or could be, intoxicating. It is a point worth stressing that the absolute monarchies of the early-modern era could never have come into being, or become so quickly powerful, had it not been for the protection they offered to enlarging numbers of persons. The "king's peace," as it had been known in the late Middle Ages, steadily widened to become the national-public law of a Henry VIII or an Elizabeth. Almost everywhere in Western Europe, though at different rates of speed, the political state was reborn, and with it the modern idea of citizenship—an idea that was of course born of the individual's gradually enhanced sense of trust in state rather than in other, competing, forms of association. More and more we find the state engaging in activities unknown to it in the medieval era—charitable, religious, and educational, as well as legal and political.

Hence the conflict between state and intermediate association. How could there not have been conflict? We ordinarily think in terms of conflict between *individual* and state, and while this view is sanctionable, there is another view to be reckoned with, one that puts the real conflict—and, as I shall indicate in this essay, the lasting conflict—between, not individual and state, but *social group* and state.

The true enemies faced by political sovereigns and their advisers in the period of Renaissance and Reformation were communal and corporate: preeminently the Church, of course, more than a millennium old in its vast ascendancy over so many areas of society, but also such groups or associations as the monasteries, guilds, universities, village communities, walled towns, and even great, extended families which had for so long known the kind of freedom and autonomy that can only exist when the central power in society is weak or nonexistent.

What we have, in short, is a triangular relationship: one formed by state, individual, and social group. Only by keeping our eyes on the fate in the long run of the social group can we properly appreciate what happened, commencing in the sixteenth century, to state and individual. Rightly did the constitutional historian Maitland declare: "At the end of the Middle Ages, a great change in men's thoughts about groups of men was taking place." Rightly too does Maitland refer to the "pulverizing" and "macadamizing" forces exerted upon the social order by the advance of the centralized state. For how could the state take power to itself—that is, become strong, sovereign—except by taking to itself functions and authorities previously resident in the great profusion of social groups that covered the Western landscape during the medieval era? For very good reason—so far, that is, as the aggrandizement of the national state is concerned—did the new monarchs seek, and commonly succeed in their effort, to subordinate, nationalize, even extinguish such historic groups in the West as the guilds, monasteries, towns, and other kinds of social union. All of these, by virtue of their intermediation between state and individual were bound to serve as buffers to the state's power, to limit the capacity of the state to enter the lives of individuals. Thus the same age in which Henry VIII expropriated the monasteries in England saw in the same country the nationalization of guilds, the destruction of hundreds of village communities, and even the subordination of the once-powerful aristocratic families to whom earlier kings had been forced to go on occasion for very permission to rule. Nor was the matter different in the France of the Bourbons.

With the practical reduction in power of the intermediate sphere of association in the West went a reduction theoretical in character that was hardly less spectacular: the rise of the modern theory of political sovereignty. The roots of this theory lie in Roman Law—or, rather, in the revival of the principles of Roman Law that we find first in the universities of the twelfth and thirteenth centuries, then in spreading areas of political and economic life. Apart from the principles of Roman Law with their stress upon absolute sovereignty in the head of state alone, upon citizenship, contract, and, far from least, upon the right of any association to exist solely by "concession" of the sovereign, it is unlikely that the modern theory of political sovereignty would ever have come into being in the West.

But it did come into being, and from Bodin's *Commonweale* (1576) through Hobbes' *Leviathan* (1651), Rousseau's *Social Contract* (1762), to Jeremy Bentham's *Fragment on Government* (1776), we find a constantly increasing emphasis upon the absolute power of the national state and, closely related, a constantly increasing hostility toward all forms of association intermediate to individual and this absolute state. If Bodin was reluctant to cut such association out altogether from his society, Hobbes, Rousseau, and Bentham assuredly were not. Hobbes likened intermediate groups—religious, economic, educational and other—to "worms in the entrails of natural man." Rousseau banned all "partial associations" from his ideal state, which must be governed by an omnipotent General Will, monolithic in character. And Bentham became notorious for his hatred of all forms of particular or partial association, including juries, households, universities, guilds, labor unions, boroughs, and voluntary associations. It was John Austin, later in the nineteenth century, who gave final, definitive statement to the unitary theory of absolute sovereignty of political state, but his classic work on the subject would never have been written had he not studied Bentham—and through Bentham, Rousseau and Hobbes—intently. I am inclined to think that the modern national state reached its zenith during the period 1776-1876, and although it remained visibly powerful down through World War I, the acids of dissolution may be seen at work throughout the nineteenth century: evidenced by the turning once again to the social sphere by large numbers of people.

THE FRENCH REVOLUTION

Something should be said, though, about the French Revolution and intermediate groups if only because this revolution, from any intellectual point of view, is the key event in modern history. We know it for its nationalism, democracy, and individualism. It must be known also for its destructive impact upon social groups. Whether as power or freedom, we are obliged to note the effects of the Revolution, or, rather, of its successive assemblies and conventions in their lawmaking, upon family, local community, monastery, university, school, and, far from least, guild.

The guilds—products of the Middle Ages, objects of monarchical nationalizing policy in later centuries—had suffered the hatred of countless ministers of state—who saw in them barriers to easy taxation—and, by the eighteenth century, of the great majority of the philosophes. Turgot, prior to the Revolution, probably came the closest, under Louis XIV, to a genuine dissolution of these historic economic-social bodies. But the opposition of the guilds was too great, and Turgot's resignation was demanded by the king in considerable degree as a result of this opposition.

Very different was the fate of the guilds under the Revolution. In 1791 a law was passed that dissolved utterly and permanently the guilds. Moreover, a few months later, another law was passed which forbade the creation of any forms of association whatever (chambers of commerce alone excepted) which would number more than eighteen persons. Liberty of work, freedom of contract, equality of individual talents, these were some of the phrases used by the legislators in the preambles to the laws on guilds and other associations. Much the same prohibition against association would be incorporated later in the Napoleonic Code. It was this codified prohibition of so many types of association under the Napoleonic Code that stimulated a great deal of the special form of liberalism we see in France throughout the nineteenth century, a form that affected the minds of individuals as diverse as Tocqueville, Proudhon, and La Tour du Pin, a form of liberalism that made the group or association its object.

Revolutionary legislation was by no means confined to the guilds. The patriarchal family was deeply affected. The ancient rights of primogeniture and entail were abolished, thus serving to individualize property inheritance. Divorce was made legal. Sons were emancipated from paternal authority at age twenty-one. Not the family but the state was declared the proper repository of education.

So were other groups affected. The village community, the commune, the town, the university, the province, and of course the Church were all dealt with in specific and uncompromising statutes. Whether from the point of view of the individual and his freedom or from the point of view of the nation and its declared sovereignty, these groups were regarded by legislators as inherently antagonistic to the kind of France —une et indivisible—that the Jacobins prized as an ideal. The Declaration of the Rights of Man had explicitly stated that the individual—not the group, not the corporation—is the true unit of the social order; and it also stated that from the nation alone sprang all legitimate authority. From the point of view of internal, intermediate associations, in short, individualism and étatisme were like two great millstones, capable of crushing between them all that seemed to threaten either individual or state.

It is no wonder that the French Revolution excited the mind of Western Europe—and indeed other parts of the world as well, though less forcefully—whether in hope or fear. The conservatives, beginning with Edmund Burke, were entirely correct in seeing this event, or complex of events, as without precedent in history so far as destruction of the organic nature

of society was concerned. Burke was only the first who saw
the depredations of the Revolution upon intermediate structures such as province, commune, church, family, class, and
guild, and whose animosity to the Revolution was built upon
fear of what would happen to masses of alienated, atomized,
individuals.

But there were nationalists, centralists in politics, radicals
eager to remake the entire social order, liberals devoted to individual freedom, businessmen restive under quasi-feudal restrictions, and others who saw something almost redemptive in
the French Revolution. And the nineteenth century history of
Western Europe, indeed in many respects of the United States,
was in very large measure given its course, its pattern of
changes, by the different interpretations which the Revolution
invited. To the Revolution may be traced a great deal of the
individualism and the nationalism alike which are so prominent in nearly all European countries during the century. Both
its symbolic and its concrete legislative influence upon the
European political mind were vast.

INDUSTRIAL REVOLUTION AND
THE REBIRTH OF COMMUNITY

From our point of view, however, what is chiefly important
about the impact of the Revolution—and also of the
Napoleonic order that arose out of it—is the powerful stimulus
that was given to the organizing of new associations to replace
those which the Revolutionary combination of individualism
and nationalism had destroyed or weakened. I do not want to
leave the impression that the French Revolution was alone in
this impact. After all, we are dealing with the age in which not
one but two revolutions were remaking the European landscape: the democratic and the industrial. What the French Revolution, in the name of popular sovereignty, had done to ancient intermediate organizations, the industrial revolution was,
in its own way, doing throughout the ninetheenth century: aid-
ing in the tearing-up of old villages and towns, social classes,

kindreds, and other groups, and in the process wrenching human beings in ever-enlarging numbers from their historically-developed contexts of life and feeling.

This is what historians, from both the left and the right, refer to as the modern rise of the masses. When we refer to the masses, we have in mind not so much mere numbers—least of all those of base, ignoble character—but, rather, enlarging aggregates of people which have become separated in substantial degree from traditional allegiances to family, village, social class, guild, and church. The masses result, in short, from alienation of individuals from those groups and communities which most commonly endow lives with the sense of identity, of meaning, and purpose. Edmund Burke referred to these groups and communities as "the inns and resting-places of the human spirit," and so they are.

It would be a mistake to think that the vision of the masses, of the horde of unattached, helpless, insecure individuals, was limited to intellectuals in the nineteenth century—to Burke, Tocqueville, Burckhardt, Carlyle, Arnold, and so many others. For apart from some more popular sense of the mass, however dim, it would be difficult to account for the sudden, widespread, efflorescence of new associations. It is as though from every sector, representing almost every creed or interest, human beings suddenly found themselves starved for society—that is, for the sense of community, of association, that was so signally missing. The old groups had vanished or been reduced to irrelevance or impotence by the new political and economic forces; nothing sprang naturally into existence to relieve individuals from the feeling of the social void.

Thus the extraordinary profusion in the nineteenth century of new forms of association, created to meet economic, urban, and material needs, yes, but created also to meet social needs. There were the cooperatives, consumer and producer; so-called assurance societies, many of which would become over a period of time major insurance companies or banking institutions; a large number of utopian-communal associations, many of them in the United States, most of them inspired by the writings of such men as Saint-Simon, Fourier, Cabet, and Comte. Mutual aid groups of every kind flourished. Anarchist-syndicalism as a revolutionary movement came into being, its roots deep in proposed *syndicats* and similar groups in which workers could know fulfillment of social and spiritual as well as economic needs.

There were many such groups. The nineteenth century, despite its conventional stereotyping as the age of individualism and nationalism—which indeed it was—must be seen as one of the greatest ages in Western history so far as the formation of social groups is concerned. It is extraordinary, looking back on the age, how diverse the philosophies were which helped spawn this great profusion of groups and associations. I have mentioned the utopians and the anarchists. But there were also the so-called Social Catholics, a movement, particularly in France, Germany, and the Low Countries, that had so much to do with the establishment of cooperatives and labor unions. Conservatives were hardly less interested than radicals in the creation of intermediate groups which would be at one and the same time buffers against state power and protections of individuals from economic and social insecurity. The *French Action,* although monarchist, aristocratic, and devoutly Catholic in inspiration, was critical of mass democracy, capitalism, and what it called anarchic individualism as was any syndicalist group.

THE RISE OF TRADE UNIONS

It is in these circumstances that we have to see some of the most powerful incentives to the rise of trade unions everywhere in the West in the nineteenth century. If a few had actually taken root in the late eighteenth century, it is nevertheless in the nineteenth that they and many others developed and spread. It is incorrect, of course, to equate trade union and guild. Guilds in the Middle Ages had been associations of masters and apprentices in the crafts. No division between "owner" and "worker" existed or could have existed. Very different is the trade union—from the beginning an association of workers designed to afford protection against owners, managers, and where necessary against elements of the public. Whatever their diverse, specific points of origin, all such unions must be seen, however, as parts of the much larger associative movement in the nineteenth century, one that included cooperatives, assurance societies, burial associations, utopian communities, friendly societies, and lodges—also structures of what came to be known as the social gospel in the Christian churches. In this fact lay a great deal of the unions' strength.

Strength was required. There was not only the predictable opposition to unions, craft and industrial, of the owners and managers of the great, increasingly impersonal corporations. The laws of governments also militated frequently against the unions. There were statutes of "conspiracy" or "combination" going back many centuries, not only in countries where Roman Law principles dominated but even in those where common law or its analogue existed. The doctrine of unitary sovereignty, of national unity, has never been stronger than it was in the nineteenth and early twentieth centuries, if as strong.

It is in this light, indeed, that we may understand the rise of the legal and political pluralists in France, Germany, and England, numbering such names as Otto von Gierke, Leon Duguit, Roger Salleilles, J. N. Figgis, F. W. Maitland, and the youthful Harold Laski. These men saw the position of social groups—families, churches, parishes, localities, and regions, as well as trade unions and cooperatives—as inherently precarious in any society where absolute authority existed in unitary fashion in political state alone, where society was conceived as a mass of discrete individual particles, with rights granted individuals alone, not to groups, and where all associations intermediate to individual and state tended to be regarded with suspicion. Hence the advocacy by Figgis, Maitland, Duguit, and others of a plural state, one in which a monopoly of power by the state succeeded by division of power among state and other major social and economic institutions.

In short, the upsurge of labor unions as well as other forms of association in the nineteenth century can indeed be seen as a response to the kind of atomism that had been created by the new industrial system, with its large, impersonal factories, its rigid division between "owners" and "workers," and by the sudden loss of traditional, communal contexts of village, parish, and extended family by so many thousands of workers. But this same upsurge can also be seen politically as a response to a kind of legal atomism that had been a fixed aspect of the Western state since the breakup of the Middle Ages.

But there is one, too-little realized, too-dimly perceived, overwhelming conclusion to be drawn from the rise of associations in the nineteenth and early-twentieth centuries. Although they were obliged to cope with an often harsh political order in their efforts at recognition and acceptance, the blunt fact is, the heyday of the Western national state was already drawing to an end. The height was reached during the century 1776-1876, but events such as the Civil War in America, the Franco-Prussian War, and for Britain the Crimean War were all, I would argue, symbolic of an inner fragmentation, a *stasis* in Western civilization that would reveal itself much more dramatically in the two world wars of the twentieth century. The power of the Western state, its capacity to generate trust and allegiance and patriotism among its subjects or citizens—which had been so great under the monarchies of the sixteenth and seventeenth centuries, which remained great through the nineteenth century in external appearance—this power was beginning to decline after the French Revolution, and the decline has continued, constantly intensifying, to the present moment.

The fierce drive of peoples all over the West to form new associations, religious, communal, economic, and other, must be seen as a harbinger of the collapsed confidence in the state that is so evident in the West today. The crisis of the political community began, in sum, when enlarging numbers of people in the West turned, or returned, to religion in all its doctrinal and social shapes, to cooperatives, utopias, and—far from least—to trade unions. In these rather than the state individuals reposed their trust.

PUBLIC UNIONS AND THE DECLINE OF SOCIAL TRUST

These are the essential social and historical terms in which the public sector union has to be perceived. In their sphere—the public domain—they are reflections of precisely the same diminished confidence and trust in the political state and its governing bureaucracy. They have appeared, grown, spread, become powerful in almost exact proportion to the diminution of political power in the contemporary world. The inescapable fact is, the contemporary democratic state does not really know how to deal with them and even if it did, I doubt very much that there is sufficient authority left in the state, sufficient confidence in the state by its citizens, to do anything about it. I do not say the national government, or state or municipal government, is as yet moribund, or if moribund actually *in extremis*. Its continuing functional importance is attested to by the interactions between public union heads and governmental officials. I have no doubt that under sufficient provocation—say a combination of convulsive economic recession-inflation and widespread fear of terrorism—the Western state *could* become, at least theoretically, the military state modelled upon a Soviet Union or a Nazi Germany where public and private unions and all other intermediate associations would become arms of the state—a state governed by the military as is the case right now in both China and the Soviet Union, with all visible bodies including the Politburo, as Solzhenitsyn has told us, mere facades, trappings.

But this notwithstanding, the governments we currently find in the West—for all of their vast bureaucratic apparatuses, for all their multifold penetration of human lives from cradle to

grave, for all their huge budgets—are actually weak governments. And I doubt that there is an important union leader in
the United States today who does not understand this fact. On
a constantly widening scale the confidence and the trust of
workers have gone to unions rather than to the governments
—municipal, state, and national—which actually employ
them.

These public unions came into existence in circumstances
analogous to those in which private unions appeared. As government agencies became larger and more impersonal, more
dominated by civil service regulations and boards, with the
older forms of intimacy vanishing, with the kind of personal
touch that even (and especially) political bosses could offer
through patronage disappearing along with the political
machine—as these conditions became more and more widespread, with elected councils, mayors, governors, and con-
gresses seemingly powerless to do anything about them, the
soil of public unionism was being prepared. It is no exaggera-
tion, I believe, to say that the public union is the successor in
many ways to the old political machine. Just as that machine
offered in its way security to countless Americans, mostly of
lower class, many of them insecure immigrants recently ar-
rived, so does the large public union today, along with its
complex of locals, offer the same kind of security. To it has
gone, I repeat, a degree of trust that our contemporary democratic government finds it increasingly hard to inspire.

Let me offer one example here in an area I am familiar with:
the university. When I joined the Berkeley faculty in 1939,
any thought of a faculty union anywhere in the United States
was abhorrent to professors—and students too if they thought
about the matter. True, there was the AAUP, but it was much
more like a gentleman's club than a bargaining, protective
agency. One's only real community was the university, or the
college, itself—its faculty, its administration, its students. I
am not idealizing or exaggerating. The American university or
college commanded trust: among its own members and also in
the public outside. That trust began to dissolve in the 1950s,

and the process of dissolution has continued to the present moment. It will only accelerate. And side by side with the dissolution of trust in academia has grown a constantly increasing desire on the part of faculty to organize, to become members—as so many elementary and secondary teachers have (and for precisely the same reasons)—of trade unions, public unions or private. Without doubt, we shall see unions grow and spread faster in the public colleges and universities, as well as public schools, than in the private, but I believe that before the century is over, almost the whole of the American teaching profession will be union-organized.

Precisely the same appears to be the future of the public employee union. Based fundamentally upon the same desire for group-making we find in kinship, local community and church, like these groups, it is a form of protection. If on occasion its demands, financial and other, upon members seem great, the larger record of the unions—like the long historical record of family and neighborhood and village—is one of providing a sense of security and protection that political government cannot and in my judgment should not seek to offer.

This is particularly true, I suggest, at the present time when the state and its agencies have come to lose so widely the confidence and trust of citizens. Without this trust, the state can only proceed repressively, coercively, if it tries to interpose itself between individuals and their diverse social organizations — public unions included. It is difficult for the state (the more so when it has lost the respect of its citizens) to act through negotiation, compromise, and adaptation in the achievement of the equilibrium that society as well as economy requires. There is a strong tendency for the state at such times to make use of sheer force, with something approximating totalitarianism often in prospect.

THE UNCERTAIN FUTURE

I do not know how long the present system, the present balance of powers, in American society will continue. It is always possible that the circumstances around us will continue indefinitely, with the political order occasionally winning out at the expense of unions—as in wage freezes, prohibitions on strikes, pension reductions, and the like—and, conversely, the social-economic order containing the unions winning out. To be sure it is not always clear-cut. We are used to liaisons between the unions—private and public—and the political order at every level which suggest a form of feudalism.

With the inflationary pressures presented by unions, and the power to cripple the entire city, state, or nation through utilization of the strike, people will demand greater control of the unions. But such control, even if mandated by vote, is much easier to prescribe than it is to execute. In any event, assuming its full-blown success, the loss of social trust—and the loss of the informal accommodation that goes with it—would have to bring political domination, which means ever-greater bureaucracy and centralization. Industrial, economic, social life is too complex, too diverse and fluctuating ever to be handled by political commands. The experience of Rome during its century or two of extreme domination of the economic order—a wholly abortive and crippling experience—should serve for all time.

We are living in what I have elsewhere referred to as an age of twilight—twilight of authority. There are no easy solutions. The onset of the political and industrial revolutions brought an intolerable degree of atomism in the social order—or perceived atomism. Unions are among the widespread responses in the nineteenth and twentieth centuries to this atomism. Man will not, cannot, live in what he sees as the void, as a vacuum. Unions, along with the great corporations, now multinational in scope and power, may be revealed in the decades ahead to be the real possessors of power in the Western world. Plainly, the historic national state is showing signs of moribundity. To assume that any single kind of structure is eternal is of course belied by history. Prior to the sixteenth century the state was weak, had been weak for more than a thousand years. Then it became strong, capable down through the French Revolution of making as many depredations upon the social sphere as it cared to. Such strength no longer exists in the political state in the West today. It no longer inspires popular respect, trust, confidence. Its clerisy—politicians, bureaucrats, and political intellectuals—are either derided or hated by large sections of the public.

As I say, it is impossible to predict the future. But if I were to speculate on the future, it would be to this effect: either the national state becomes the military state, as it has become in the Soviet Union, Cuba, China, and elsewhere, or else the West is in for a period of a new feudalism, one rooted in corporations and in large unions precisely as the old feudalism was rooted in manors, fiefs, and comparable organizations. I don't see how the present increasingly unstable, bankruptcy-prone condition can last very much longer.

III

THE PRESTIGE OF
PUBLIC EMPLOYMENT

HARVEY C. MANSFIELD, JR.
Professor of Government, Harvard University

Rethinking liberalism. Hobbes and the abandonment of public spirit. From the state of nature to absolute sovereignty. The right of self-preservation and the problem of a soldier's obedience. John Locke and the American political system. Individual rights and majority rule: the importance of property as a whole. Rousseau and democratic socialism. Rediscovering public spirit in liberal society.

THE DECLINE OF PUBLIC SPIRIT

There is an old story, not funny enough to be called a joke, about the divorced wife of a municipal street cleaner who went to court to ask that her former husband be required to take another job so that he could earn more money and pay her more alimony. "Madam," said the judge as he denied her petition, "you underrate the prestige of public employment."

That old story is now obsolete. Public employees in America have made startling gains in wages and benefits in recent years. They have made these gains while increasing greatly in number, and so much more is now paid to so many more that public employment has become attractive to lovers

35

of lucre as well as to those with heavy expenses. The old canard that civil servants lack ambition and seek security has been shown to understate their ambition for comfort and their militancy in self-promotion.

In achieving these—to say truly—rather easily won gains, public employees have abandoned or transformed "the prestige of public employment." Using the private-sector analogy, they have established the right to form public employee unions like unions of private employees and have immediately begun to behave like them. While they have not yet received general legal recognition of the right to strike, they have pulled off many illegal strikes with relative impunity and have succeeded in creating the impression that the right to strike for public employees will in time inevitably be granted.

Public employees appeal to the indispensability and to the dignity of their jobs—policemen and firemen to the security they provide, teachers to the responsibility of education. But in making such implicit comparisons they do not rest satisfied with their own importance: they want to be paid for it. In urging the superiority of public to private employment they adopt the standards and values of private employment, as if a public job were different in degree but not in kind from a private job. For them, the prestige of public employment is something to trade on, not live by. And that prestige has been transformed, in some cases, into the charisma of successful rapacity. Who could deny the partisan satisfactions, both material and moral, of being a teacher in Albert Shanker's union in New York City? Who could deny, also, that these are not the satisfactions of being a teacher? We—meaning the rest of us who are not public employees—seem to be suffering from a decline in public spirit, that spirit from which "the prestige of public employment" derives. [In Chapter II Robert Nisbet addresses the decline of public spirit in terms of the decline of public confidence in political government.] As an economist might put it, the decline of public spirit is extremely costly: reduced prestige now requires that we pay a *premium* for public service.

But is it correct to say that public spirit is limited only to public employment? Isn't it true that some kind of public spirit can also be found in private employment? Teachers, for example, are no different as teachers when their employer is private; so when they fail in professional dedication, this is not a decline of public spirit. And in general, it might be said, anyone today who works *in* a bureaucracy, whether it is public or private, works *for* that bureaucracy in a bureaucratic spirit that is neither public spirit nor private gain merely, but some kind—good or bad—of corporate pride.

In *The Republic* Plato offered the model for the public-spirited man as the practitioner of an art who as such is professionally dedicated to the good of his subject or client, and not to his own good. But while professional dedication and organizational loyalty do exist in private employment, and these may be versions of public spirit, the decline of public spirit may therefore be a perversion of public spirit into unionism.[1] At any rate, motives involving public spirit cannot be interpreted as simply motives of private gain or self-interest, and so some distinction between private and public or private and social is necessary.

A second, more fundamental, objection to making a distinction between public and private is that it is not required. Everything hoped for from public spirit can be achieved more neatly and easily by calculation of private advantage. If there is danger from public employee unions, it is because private advantage is not being calculated correctly—by public employees or by the rest of us or by both. The trouble is not lack of public spirit but a defect of sovereignty, or a failure to insist on the rule of law, or a skewing of the normal American political process. In this view, by the standard of private advantage, the problem of public employee unions is no more than our failure to control them.

Sovereignty and rule of law have an old-fashioned legalistic ring, and indeed it was to them that judges used to refer in the days when they used to rule against the claimed rights of public unionism.[2] But these problems remain troublesome. For in a representative democracy, the problem of sovereignty raises the question of public accountability: How do strong public employee unions affect the accountability of elected representatives to the voters? It has been argued that these notions now need to be reasserted and their obvious merits appreciated.[3]

It has also been argued, with reliance on contemporary political science, that the normal American political process is distorted when a group such as public employees, by being well-placed to exert pressure, can get more than its number or needs or merits would justify.[4]

Both arguments of sovereignty and fairness—quite reasonably—avoid resting their case with an appeal to the public spirit of public unions, but both imply that the solution is in a general recognition of everyone's long-term self-interest. This solution gives full recognition to the power of the private-sector analogy, since it assumes that whatever is public can be derived from private advantage, from "self-interest well-understood," in Tocqueville's phrase. This approach therefore implies the abandonment of a special place for public spirit, and of a distinction between public and private.

We become aware that both the problem of public unions and the solution proposed for it have their root in the political philosophy of liberalism. By examining liberal political philosophy, we may look for the distinction between public and private, and examine the characteristic thesis of liberalism that the public can be derived from private interest without reliance upon public spirit.

RETHINKING LIBERALISM

Hobbes and the Abandonment of Public Spirit

In reconsidering liberal philosophy, we shall examine particularly its founders, Hobbes and Locke, who led the movement away from public spirit to reliance on individual rights and the individualism inherent in private interest.* And we shall also consider Rousseau because he attempted, reacting against Hobbes and Locke, to rediscover public spirit—or rather to find for it a substitute spirit that anticipated modern democratic socialism.

Unions as we have them today presuppose the right of collective bargaining in which the representative of a majority bargains for all. Unions thus presuppose a society committed to free association in which workers have an equal legal status with other men, allowing them to associate with each other, so that a majority can decide for all. When workers form a "union," they make something like the "social contract" of liberal political philosophy; and the free and (legally) equal society out of which they make it resembles Thomas Hobbes's "state of nature" which precedes all society. Liberal society presupposes the state of nature even more than it resembles it, in order to explain why men should be legally equal in liberal society.

According to Hobbes, men should be free to associate in society because they are free and equal outside society. In the state of nature men are seen as they really are—stripped of all advantages and superiorities—before anything artificial (in civilization) has been added. What they really are is equal, roughly equal in strength and prudence as measured by the ability to kill each other: no man—or woman—is so much stronger or cleverer than another that he does not have to fear being killed. From this equality proceeds equality of hope in attaining our ends, or equal pretensions. But if two men desire the same thing with equal pretensions the result is "diffidence" and then war. The state of nature is therefore a state of war, the war of every man with every man, where the life of

---

*In considering liberal philosophy, it is important to be aware that we shall use the word "liberal" in the expanded (nineteenth century) sense that liberal individualism (avoiding reliance on public spirit) underlies the positions of both modern liberals and conservatives. As a result, neither Hobbes nor Locke can be identified as either liberal or conservative in the terms of today's political usage.

man, in Hobbes's famous phrase, is "solitary, poor, nasty, brutish and short."

This is man's beginning, which reveals each man as an individual, standing alone. In man's beginning, all men are equally endangered and sorely beset, because all are equal and no one is the natural ruler of anyone. In the beginning, according to Hobbes, man's end must be self-preservation.

Hobbes's view of man as isolated individuals is the basis of modern liberal philosophy, and it departed from the prior view that man is a social being with public spirit—"a political animal" in Aristotle's phrase, whose existence can only be understood in terms of his community and group associations.

In opposing Aristotle's view, Hobbes took man's beginning for his "state of nature"—and in fact was the first to do so—because he believed that society in his time and in other times suffered from vain men of too much ambition. They had been allowed to divide up the government and interfere when they liked without accepting responsibility, and had been encouraged to do this by the traditional notion that ambition was justified when it was combined with public spirit.

Hobbes thought that the idea of public spirit, or the ambition to do public good, did infinite mischief in politics because whatever was conceived to be the "public good" constituted a standard of action independent of the actual and visible government. This invisible public good was personified by ambitious men and endowed with powers greater than those possessed by human governments, who sought to satisfy their own vanity by manipulating the people's "fear of invisible spirits."

The ambitious men Hobbes feared were of course priests, together with the scholars in universities who aided and abetted them. With his idea of equality in the state of nature, Hobbes intended to give these men a cold shower—to cool their pretensions and quench their ambition, as well as to counter, with fear for self-preservation, the "fear of invisible spirits" which they spread. Thus the liberal principles first conceived by Hobbes have their very origin in hostility to the notion of public spirit.

According to Hobbes, men are not by nature public-spirited, but rather in a state of war with each other. Fortunately, men are supplied with rules of reason to enable them to escape from their predicament. These rules tell men to seek peace, and men are impelled to listen to natural law by fear for their own self-preservation.

Reason makes science possible. With science man can conceive a common power or sovereign which has never existed before, and thus free himself from the state of nature in which each man must anticipate the hostility of every other. While other desires may prompt men to obey the sovereign, the passion to be reckoned on, Hobbes says, is fear.

Instead of relying on positive qualities of human sociability or public spirit—indeed, as we have seen, precisely to *avoid* relying on them—Hobbes relies on science, motivated by sub-human *fear;* and his reliance on fear as the dominant motivating force has important consequences for politics.

Since Hobbes puts human faculties in the service of a sub-human end, he removes—or attempts to remove—all pride in being a man. Men are not men when resisting their submergence in nature or when claiming a special status, such as the capacity for public spirit—or special rights in creation. They are most human, Hobbes argues, when accepting their unprivileged place in the scheme of things, using their human talents to make the best of it. They are most human, in other words, when they give up the pretense of public spirit and consign themselves to the pursuit of private advantage.

This attempt to level human pride has the consequence of leveling those men who are remarkable for their pride—the public-spirited. Hobbes thoroughly disposes of public-spirited men with a theory that subdues human pride generally. To secure society against the risks and inconveniences of such men, he does away with any principle for which public-spirited mn might sacrifice themselves and in which ordinary men might take pride.

The human problem, for Hobbes, is selfishness; but his cure is not to renounce selfishness and invoke public spirit. On the contrary, the cure for selfishness is more selfishness—indeed, ultimate selfishness. Only when everyone realizes that no independent principle outside his own preservation is possible or viable, will he yield to the sovereign, so as to take himself out of the state of nature. "The public," or the state, is thus created by calculating one's private good while expecting that others in the same pickle will do the same. There is no higher principle to serve as the basis for public duty or spirit, only a "common power" created by generalizing everyone's private good. The "common power," therefore, is not a "higher power." It has our consent and commands our unlimited obedience, but without public spirit it does not have our respect or admiration.

Hobbes's system sounds strange to us: "The state of nature" is by now an antique phrase—though we cannot dismiss the idea as easily as the name—and we do not accept the arbitrary power of Hobbes's absolute sovereign. I have dwelt on Hobbes, however, because in his system the liberal principle of self-interest is carried to an extreme where we can understand it better than in its more familiar setting.

In particular, Hobbes's difficulties resemble ours. For although he is the most extreme advocate of absolute sovereignty that ever was, he is also—ironically—the source of our doubts and hesitations regarding sovereignty. For Hobbes, sovereignty must be absolute to assure everyone that everyone else will obey. But the artificial sovereign made by men derives from the natural right of self-preservation, *and this private right is therefore more fundamental than the public duty,* and thus denies public spirit.

Even though the sovereign's power is unlimited, the private right of self-preservation is unalienable. A man threatened by execution under a sovereign he has consented to can justly attempt to escape, though his execution is also just. Similarly, a soldier may justly disobey his officer to save himself. To suggest how little an absolute sovereign, without recourse to public spirit, can command someone to risk his life, Hobbes jocularly defines a battle of such soldiers as a "running away on both sides."

What is the source and extent of a soldier's obligation to obey orders, if any? In our day there is talk of establishing unions in the U.S. armed forces; and in Germany, Sweden, Belgium, and the Netherlands such unions already exist. Clearly, soldiers' unions are a threat to sovereignty, but clearly too, in a system based on individual rights and the right of self-preservation, soldiers' unions thrive on the very right that authorizes sovereignty. One cannot successfully appeal to the principle of "sovereignty" against these unions when sovereignty is justified merely by calculation of self-interest, for as we see even by Hobbes's rigorous calculation, sovereignty cannot always be to one's interest. Without a concept of public spirit, private interest may legitimate a soldier's disobedience. Common sense would have concluded the same thing much sooner, but in the modern world we live by principles and therefore sometimes need to be excused from principle by principle.

It is important to note, of course, that Hobbes's principle of absolute sovereignty is not ours; our principle is the rule of law or democratic accountability or the "normal American political process." But these principles, like Hobbes's, do not rely on public spirit. And the question remains whether the problem of public employee unions can be solved without a concept of public spirit. We may understand how the principles underlying the American political system attempt to deal with the problem by investigating the political philosophy of John Locke.

John Locke: Individual Rights and Majority Rule

Though Locke has many points of similarity with Hobbes, especially his use of "the state of nature" and his support for individual rights, he presents himself in contrast to Hobbes. In one passage particularly, he seems determined to answer Hobbes's difficulty in getting soldiers to obey.[5] He says that the preservation of the army, and with it the whole commonwealth, "requires an absolute obedience to the command of

every superior officer," even "the most dangerous or unreasonable of them"; yet the same sergeant, "with all his absolute power of life and death," cannot dispose of one penny or
even one *farthing* of that soldier's goods.

Why this difference? The soldier's "blind obedience" is
necessary to the "preservation of the rest," but his goods are
not. We see that the preservation of "the rest," that is, of the
majority, has a standing in Locke's thought which it does not
have in Hobbes's. Government is made accountable to the majority and it is thereby put under the "rule of law"; perhaps
these will substitute for public spirit and achieve Hobbes's end
by different means.

Locke develops his notions of government accountable to
the majority out of his theory of property. For him, men join
or are driven into society less out of fear of one another's ambition, as with Hobbes, than out of anxiety for one's own property. Society is formed to protect life and liberty as well as
property, but property is the touchstone: when one's property
is safe— that is, cannot be taken without one's consent—then
so are life and liberty safe. And when the majority's property
is safe —not merely that of the rich—then the majority is safe
and the society is safe.

Property is more than a need; it is what later was called an
"interest," a stake of each individual in the whole that each
will be anxious to protect. But property is a whole that depends on society. And since each man's property, though private, has value only as others' property has value, the majority
may authorize taxation or even confiscation of any individual's
property to protect "property" as a whole. In the above example of the soldier, his property could have been taken and his
life spared if he were considered as a taxpayer. For Locke, the
character of property as a whole is the basis for shifting the
weight of his politics from the individual to the majority, and
permits him—when necessary—to justify sacrifice of the
individual's right to the majority's preservation.

In Locke's thought as in Hobbes's, the individual is the important unit and he consents to government by considering the plight of every individual and is thus, as we say, "humanitarian." But after society is formed Locke, unlike Hobbes, introduces a sum of human beings, the majority of a society, who are between each individual and all humanity, and to whom each of these individual rights may be justly sacrificed. For Locke, all rights of the members of society must be consistent with the preservation of society, which is the majority. No one can have a right which would destroy society, in the opinion of the majority.

The critical point is that in setting forth the principles that came to underlie American constitutional democracy, Locke did not make preservation of the majority an effect of public spirit; preservation of the majority is based rather on individual commitments to protect property as a whole. But unlike Hobbes, Locke does permit society to enjoin obedience—as in the armed forces—by making government accountable to the majority rather than to every individual acting as private judge of his own preservation.

How is government made accountable to the majority? By the rule of law, in Locke's version. Actually Locke speaks of the supremacy of the legislative power which, to avoid the possibility of an all-powerful parliament, becomes what we call "the legislative process," a series of stages in lawmaking, no one of which is sovereign. These stages, as in English practice in Locke's day and American practice today, include participation by both the legislature and executive. When elections and political parties are added to constitute the government, and administration and the courts to execute the laws, we have the "normal American political process" to which no one is denied access, by which no minority can dominate, from which no one can appeal.

As with Hobbes's system, without an appeal to public spirit, Locke allows the individual's rights to corrode all authority. When sovereignty does not suit them, those rights justify men in challenging it. For even if sovereignty is expressed in a nonarbitrary process—such as that provided in the U.S. Constitution—the result may still be unacceptable to any individual or group. And though the majority may have an interest in enforcing the result so as to preserve society, it may compromise that interest for reasons of convenience or comfort, or to avoid danger. Thus, in the case of public employee labor relations, the public may often buy public labor peace with costly settlements, rather than endure the inconveniences of a strike.

In the Lockean system, no sense of public spirit holds the majority together or directs it to its public duty. As a result, the balance of private interests often makes the public prey to the leverage of specially placed interest groups and elites. One might suppose that obstreperous public unions can be kept in check without appealing to public spirit by making them accountable to the taxpaying majority, and sometimes this has worked. But it is easy to exaggerate the resistance of taxpayers: if they are so reluctant, why are taxes so high? Nor is it convincing to claim that the majority is fooled by complicated budgets. The dodges of politicians are not difficult to penetrate. Everyone knew that New York City's budget was dishonest, but the majority did not object. An economist might say that the absence of public spirit has been extremely expensive for New York taxpayers—but one must note it is precisely the habit of calculating in economists' terms that makes for the absence of public spirit.

From these arguments one might say that the difficulty is in the notion of a natural right of self-preservation for the individual. As long as this natural right is thought to exist, individuals will have an arguable basis for challenging the sovereign, whether the sovereign is arbitrary or constitutional. The trouble with the unalienable right of self-preservation, it might be said, is that it does you no good to keep it (for then you have insecurity and war), but you cannot give it away (so sovereignty is always suspect). Could we solve the problem of public unions, then, by abandoning the notion of natural, unalienable rights, as in the political philosophy of Rousseau?

Rousseau and Democratic Socialism

According to Rousseau, men form a society by total alienation of all the rights of each individual to the community so as to produce a moral, collective unity to which all belong without reservation. Men then receive all their rights from the community, and the rights they have in the state of nature are left behind them, never to disturb the sovereignty of the community created by a free act of all together. This free creation is expressed in the General Will, a will that has no particular content or end such as self-preservation or the preservation of the majority in Hobbes and Locke. Since Rousseau's free society lacks a specific natural end, its sovereign cannot be criticized for failing to achieve that end. Although the General Will is not a form of public spirit—for it is an evident advantage to men, not a sacrifice—it is designed to avoid the defects of a collectivity based on self-interest.

To adopt Rousseau today would be to follow the way of democratic socialism. Rousseau resolves the problem of distinguishing private from public—and of the loss of public spirit in Hobbes and Locke—by giving all rights a public origin. Thus democratic socialism resolves the problem of public and private unions by making all unions public, in effect if not in law.[6] But there is reason to doubt the viability of making all men citizens by taking away their natural, private rights.*

Rousseau himself states stringent conditions for his social contract: the society must be small and homogeneous so that the citizens can trust each other. Clearly they must trust each other if they are going to alienate everything to the community and receive back from the community what is theirs privately.

For that reason it is useless to appeal to "fraternity" in a large society divided by many separate, conflicting interests where, as in the United States, the belief in private rights has

---

*In Chapter VII, S. M. Lipset discusses this problem in terms of persistent resistance in socialist and communist countries to governmental efforts to bring about equality of condition.

long flourished. In such a society, "socialism" has come to mean little more than the private rights of workers pursued with partisan intent in an adversary situation. On the basis of experience up to now, it seems very unlikely that appeals to a General Will or democratic socialism will change partisan habits of public unions in America and restore the sense of public spirit that Hobbes and Locke discarded.

REDISCOVERING PUBLIC SPIRIT IN LIBERAL SOCIETY

In considering the problem of public employee unions, most people assume that the principles of liberal individualism, without public spirit, are sufficient. They assume either that public unions can do what they want—following the private-sector analogy—or, also on liberal principles, that unions must be forced to bow to sovereignty and be made accountable to the majority.

From the brief survey in this chapter, however, it should be clear that liberal principles are as much the problem as the solution. For the real question is whether we can solve the problem of public employee unions without a concept of public spirit. And that problem leads in turn to the question whether public spirit can be resurrected in a large society like America, based on liberal principles.

Our discussion of public employee unions needs a new standpoint. It is time to look beyond the current liberal-conservative pro- and anti-union debate for a standpoint from which we can become aware of both the strengths and weaknesses of liberalism. In particular, it is time to recognize that liberal principles, in deriving the public good from private interests, may have taken for granted a public spirit in ambitious men and an uncalculating affection in the citizens at large which cannot be derived from self-interest. We may have been living off the moral capital—meaning the public spirit—of pre-liberal times, so that we now face a crisis from the exhaustion of this human resource.

To clarify the nature of the problem, no one in modern times can be preferred to Tocqueville. For Tocqueville appreciated both the strengths and weaknesses of "democracy" —as he called the liberal principle of private interest—and without encouraging false hopes for easy reconciliation, he looked for points of compatibility between democracy and "aristocracy"—which embodied pre-liberal principles, including the principle of public spirit.

Tocqueville stressed the aristocratic aspects of the right of free association. Free, individual association is important in democratic societies, because it enables individuals to come out of their isolation and unite. Yet at the same time, free association *depends on the initiative of a few*—on their willingness to sacrifice comfort and interest for recognition and principle—the principle of public spirit. The principle applies to the leaders of public employee unions no less than to the leaders of other associations.

And as for ordinary union members, their behavior too is hard to understand simply as self-interest. They are attached to their "standard of living," which is less an amount of goods or money than a comparison with others—and thus a matter of honor. They do not want to "give up their gains" even when that might be in their interest, because to do so would be to admit defeat. But what they demand in money terms will depend at least in part on the value and honor they—and we— place on public service.

By calling attention to "aristocratic" aspects of "democratic" or self-interested organizations—and by reinvoking the concept of public spirit—one does not solve the problem of public unions in our society. But one can at least begin to see the problem for what it is—a decline in the prestige of public employment, which results from a perversion of public spirit.

IV

THE LIMITS OF COLLECTIVE COLLECTIVE BARGAINING IN PUBLIC EMPLOYMENT*

HARRY H. WELLINGTON
Edward J. Phelps Professor of Law, Yale University

RALPH K. WINTER, JR.
Professor of Law, Yale University

Claims for collective bargaining in the private sector. Claims in the public sector. The private sector model. The public sector model: monetary issues. Nonmonetary issues. Public employee unions and the political process.

Writing in the March 1969 issue of the *Michigan Law Review,* Mr. Theodore Kheel, the distinguished mediator and arbitrator, placed the weight of his considerable authority behind what is fast becoming the conventional wisdom. In the public sector, as in the private, Mr. Kheel argues, "the most effective technique to produce acceptable terms to resolve disputes is voluntary agreement of the parties, and the best system we have for producing agreements between groups is collective bargaining—even though it involves conflict and the possibility of a work disruption."[1] Clearly for Kheel, as for others, the

*Adapted from *The Unions and the Cities* (1971), chap. 1. Reprinted with permission from the Brookings Institution. ©1971 by the Brookings Institution, Washington, D.C.

51

insistence upon a full extension of collective bargaining—including strikes—to public employment stems from a deep commitment to that way of ordering labor-management affairs in private employment. While such a commitment may not be necessary, a minimal acceptance of collective bargaining is a condition precedent to the Kheel view. Those skeptical of the value of collective bargaining in private employment will hardly press its extension. But even if one accepts collective bargaining in the private sector, the claims that support it there do not, in any self-evident way, make the case for its full transplant. The public is *not* the private, and its labor problems *are* different, very different indeed.

THE CLAIMS FOR COLLECTIVE BARGAINING IN THE PRIVATE SECTOR

Four claims are made for private-sector collective bargaining. First, it is said to be a way to achieve industrial peace. The point was put as early as 1902 by the federal Industrial Commission:

> The chief advantage which comes from the practice of periodically determining the conditions of labor by collective bargaining directly between employers and employees is that thereby each side obtains a better understanding of the actual state of the industry, of the conditions which confront the other side, and of the motives which influence it. Most strikes and lockouts would not occur if each party understood exactly the position of the other.[2]

Second, collective bargaining is a way of achieving industrial democracy, that is, participation by workers in their own governance. It is the industrial counterpart of the contemporary demand for community participation.[3]

Third, unions that bargain collectively with employers represent workers in the political arena as well. And political representation through interest groups is one of the most important types of political representation that the individual can have. Government at all levels acts in large part in response to the demands made upon it by the groups to which its citizens belong.[4]

Fourth, and most important, as a result of a belief in the unequal bargaining power of employers and employees, collective bargaining is claimed to be a needed substitute for individual bargaining.[5] Monopsony—a buyer's monopoly,[6] in this case a buyer of labor—is alleged to exist in many situations and to create unfair contracts of labor as a result of individual bargaining. While this, in turn, may not mean that workers as a class and over time get significantly less than they should—because monopsony is surely not a general condition but is alleged to exist only in a number of particular circumstances[7]—it may mean that the terms and conditions of employment for an individual or group of workers at a given period of time and in given circumstances may be unfair. What tends to insure fairness in the aggregate and over the long run is the discipline of the market.[8] But monopsony, if it exists, can work substantial injustice to individuals. Governmental support of collective bargaining represents the nation's response to a belief that such injustice occurs. Fairness between employee and employer in wages, hours, and terms and conditions of employment is thought more likely to be ensured where private ordering takes the collective form.[9]

There are, however, generally recognized social costs resulting from this resort to collectivism.[10] In the private sector these costs are primarily economic, and the question is, given the benefits of collective bargaining as an institution, what is the nature of the economic costs? Economists who have turned their attention to this question are legion, and disagreement among them monumental.[11] The principal concerns are of two intertwined sorts. One is summarized by Professor Albert Rees of Princeton:

> If the union is viewed solely in terms of its effect on the economy, it must in my opinion be considered an obstacle to the optimum performance of our economic system. It alters the

wage structure in a way that impedes the growth of employment in sectors of the economy where productivity and income are naturally high and that leaves too much labor in low-income sectors of the economy like southern agriculture and the least skilled service trades. It benefits most those workers who would in any case be relatively well off, and while some of this gain may be at the expense of the owners of capital, most of it must be at the expense of consumers and the lower-paid workers. Unions interfere blatantly with the use of the most productive techniques in some industries, and this effect is probably not offset by the stimulus to higher productivity furnished by some other unions.[12]

The other concern is stated in the 1967 Report of the Council of Economic Advisers:

Vigorous competition is essential to price stability in a high employment economy. But competitive forces do not and cannot operate with equal strength in every sector of the economy. In industries where the number of competitors is limited, business firms have a substantial measure of discretion in setting prices. In many sectors of the labor market, unions and managements together have a substantial measure of discretion in setting wages. The responsible exercise of discretionary power over wages and prices can help to maintain general price stability. Its irresponsible use can make full employment and price stability incompatible.[13]

And the claim is that this "discretionary power" too often is exercised "irresponsibly."[14]

Disagreement among economists extends to the quantity as well as to the fact of economic malfunctioning that properly is attributable to collective bargaining.[15] But there is no disagreement that at some point the market disciplines or delimits union power. As we shall see in more detail below, union power is frequently constrained by the fact that consumers react to a relative increase in the price of a product by purchasing less of it. As a result any significant real financial benefit, beyond that justified by an increase in productivity, that accrues to workers through collective bargaining may well cause significant unemployment among union members. Because of this employment-benefit relationship, the economic costs imposed by collective bargaining as it presently exists in the private sector seem inherently limited.[16]

THE CLAIMS FOR COLLECTIVE BARGAINING IN THE PUBLIC SECTOR

In the area of public employment the claims upon public policy made by the need for industrial peace, industrial democracy, and effective political representation point toward collective bargaining. This is to say that three of the four arguments that support bargaining in the private sector—to some extent, at least—press for similar arrangements in the public sector.

Government is a growth industry, particularly state and municipal government. While federal employment between 1963 and 1970 increased from 2.5 million to 2.9 million, state and local employment rose from 7.2 to 10.1 million,[17] and the increase continues apace. With size comes bureaucracy, and with bureaucracy comes the sense of isolation of the individual worker. His manhood, like that of his industrial counterpart, seems threatened. Lengthening chains of command necessarily depersonalize the employment relationship and contribute to a sense of powerlessness on the part of the worker. If he is to share in the governance of his employment relationship as he does in the private sector, it must be through the device of representation, which means unionization.[18] Accordingly, just as the increase in the size of economic units in private industry fostered unionism, so the enlarging of governmental bureaucracy has encouraged public employees to look to collective action for a sense of control over their employment destiny. The number of government employees, moreover, makes it plain that those employees are members of an interest group that can organize for political representation as well as for job participation.[19]

The pressures thus generated by size and bureaucracy lead inescapably to disruption—to labor unrest—unless these pressures are recognized and unless existing decision-making procedures are accommodated to them. Peace in government employment too, the argument runs, can best be established by making union recognition and collective bargaining accepted public policy.[20]

Much less clearly analogous to the private model, however, is the unequal bargaining power argument. In the private sector that argument really has two aspects. The first, just adumbrated, is affirmative in nature. Monopsony is believed sometimes to result in unfair individual contracts of employment. The unfairness may be reflected in wages, which are less than they would be if the market were more nearly perfect, or in working arrangements that may lodge arbitrary power in a foreman, that is, power to hire, fire, promote, assign, or discipline without respect to substantive or procedural rules. A persistent assertion, generating much heat, relates to the arbitrary exercise of managerial power in individual cases. This assertion goes far to explain the insistence of unions on the establishment in the labor contract of rules, with an accompanying adjudicatory procedure, to govern industrial life.[21]

Judgments about the fairness of the financial terms of the public employee's individual contract of employment are even harder to make than for private sector workers. The case for the existence of private employer monopsony, disputed as it is, asserts only that some private sector employers in some circumstances have too much bargaining power. In the public sector, the case to be proved is that the governmental employer ever has such power. But even if this case could be proved, market norms are at best attenuated guides to questions of fairness. In employment as in all other areas, governmental decisions are properly political decisions, and economic considerations are but one criterion among many. Questions of fairness do not centrally relate to how much imperfection one sees in the market, but more to how much imperfection one sees in the political process. "Low" pay for teachers may be merely a decision—right or wrong, resulting from the pressure of special interests or from a desire to promote the general welfare —to exchange a reduction in the quality or quantity of teachers for higher welfare payments, a domed stadium, and so on. And the ability to make informed judgments about such political decisions is limited because of the understandable but unfortunate fact that the science of politics has failed to supply either as elegant or as reliable a theoretical model as has its sister discipline.

Nevertheless, employment benefits in the public sector may have improved relatively more slowly than in the private sector during the last three decades. An economy with a persistent inflationary bias probably works to the disadvantage of those who must rely on legislation for wage adjustments.[22] Moreover, while public employment was once attractive for the greater job security and retirement benefits it provided, quite similar protection is now available in many areas of the private sector.[23] On the other hand, to the extent that civil service, or merit, systems exist in public employment and these laws are obeyed, the arbitrary exercise of managerial power is substantially reduced. Where it is reduced, a labor policy that relies on individual employment contracts must seem less unacceptable.

The second, or negative, aspect of the unequal bargaining power argument relates to the social costs of collective bargaining. As has been seen, the social costs of collective bargaining in the private sector are principally economic and seem inherently limited by market forces. In the public sector, however, the costs seem economic only in a very narrow sense and are on the whole political. It further seems that, to the extent union power is delimited by market or other forces in the public sector, these constraints do not come into play nearly as quickly as in the private. An understanding of why this is so requires further comparison between collective bargaining in the two sectors.

THE PRIVATE SECTOR MODEL

Although the private sector is, of course, extraordinarily diverse, the paradigm is an industry that produces a product that is not particularly essential to those who buy it and for which dissimilar products can be substituted. Within the market or markets for this product, most—but not all—of the producers must bargain with a union representing their employees, and this union is generally the same throughout the industry. A price rise of this product relative to others will result in a decrease in the number of units of the product sold. This in turn will result in a cutback in employment. And an increase in price would be dictated by an increase in labor cost relative to output, at least in most situations.[24] Thus, the union is faced with some sort of rough trade-off between, on the one hand, larger benefits for some employees and unemployment for others, and on the other hand, smaller benefits and more employment. Because unions are political organizations, with a legal duty to represent all employees fairly,[25] and with a treasury that comes from per capita dues, there is pressure on the union to avoid the road that leads to unemployment.[26]

This picture of the restraints that the market imposes on collective bargaining settlements undergoes change as the variables change. On the one hand, to the extent that there are nonunion firms within a product market, the impact of union pressure will be diminished by the ability of consumers to purchase identical products from nonunion and, presumably, less expensive sources. On the other hand, to the extent that union organization of competitors within the product market is complete, there will be no such restraint and the principal barriers to union bargaining goals will be the ability of a number of consumers to react to a price change by turning to dissimilar but nevertheless substitutable products.

Two additional variables must be noted. First, where the demand for an industry's product is rather insensitive to price —that is, relatively inelastic—and where all the firms in a product market are organized, the union need fear less the employment-benefit trade-off, for the employer is less concerned about raising prices in response to increased costs. By hypothesis, a price rise affects unit sales of such an employer only minimally. Second, in an expanding industry, wage settlements that exceed increases in productivity may not reduce union employment. They will reduce expansion, hence the employment effect will be experienced only by workers who do not belong to the union. This means that in the short run the politics of the employment-benefit trade-off do not restrain the union in its bargaining demands.

In both of these cases, however, there are at least two restraints on the union. One is the employer's increased incentive to substitute machines for labor, a factor present in the paradigm and all other cases as well. The other restraint stems from the fact that large sections of the nation are unorganized and highly resistant to unionization.[27] Accordingly, capital will seek nonunion labor, and in this way the market will discipline the organized sector.

The employer, in the paradigm and in all variations of it, is motivated primarily by the necessity to maximize profits (and this is so no matter how political a corporation may seem to be). He therefore is not inclined (absent an increase in demand for his product) to raise prices and thereby suffer a loss in profits, and he is organized to transmit and represent the market pressures described above. Generally he will resist, and resist hard, union demands that exceed increases in productivity, for if he accepts such demands he may be forced to raise prices. Should he be unsuccessful in his resistance too often, and should it or the bargain cost him too much, he can be expected to put his money and energy elsewhere.[28]

What all this means is that the social costs imposed by collective bargaining are economic costs; that usually they are limited by powerful market restraints; and that these restraints are visible to anyone who is able to see the forest for the trees.[29]

THE PUBLIC SECTOR MODEL: MONETARY ISSUES

The paradigm in the public sector is a municipality with an elected city council and an elected mayor who bargains (through others) with unions representing the employees of the city. He bargains also, of course, with other permanent and ad hoc interest groups making claims upon government (business groups, save-the-park committees, neighborhood groups, and so forth). Indeed, the decisions that are made may be thought of roughly as a result of interactions and accommodations among these interest groups, as influenced by perceptions about the attitudes of the electorate and by the goals and programs of the mayor and his city council.[30]

Decisions that cost the city money are generally paid for from taxes and, less often, by borrowing. Not only are there many types of taxes but also there are several layers of government that may make tax revenue available to the city; federal and state as well as local funds may be employed for some purposes. Formal allocation of money for particular uses is made through the city's budget, which may have within it considerable room for adjustments.[31] Thus, a union will bargain hard for as large a share of the budget as it thinks it possibly can obtain, and even try to force a tax increase if it deems that possible.

In the public sector, too, the market operates. In the long run, the supply of labor is a function of the price paid for labor by the public employer relative to what workers earn elsewhere.[32] This is some assurance that public employees in the aggregate—with or without collective bargaining—are not paid too little. The case for employer monopsony, moreover, may be much weaker in the public sector than it is in the private. First, to the extent that most public employees work in urban areas, as they probably do, there may often be a number of substitutable and competing private and public employers in the labor market. When that is the case, there can be little monopsony power.[33] Second, even if public employers occasionally have monopsony power, governmental policy is determined only in part by economic criteria, and there is no assurance, as there is in the private sector where the profit motive prevails, that the power will be exploited.

As noted, market-imposed unemployment is an important restraint on unions in the private sector. In the public sector, the trade-off between benefits and employment seems much less important. Government does not generally sell a product the demand for which is closely related to price. There usually are not close substitutes for the products and services provided by government and the demand for them is relatively inelastic. Such market conditions are favorable to unions in the private sector because they permit the acquisition of benefits without the penalty of unemployment, subject to the restraint of non-union competitors, actual or potential. But no such restraint limits the demands of public employee unions. Because much government activity is, and must be, a monopoly, product competition, nonunion or otherwise, does not exert a downward pressure on prices and wages. Nor will the existence of a pool of labor ready to work for a wage below union scale attract new capital and create a new, and competitively less expensive, governmental enterprise.

The fear of unemployment, however, can serve as something of a restraining force in two situations. First, if the cost of labor increases, the city may reduce the quality of the service it furnishes by reducing employment. For example, if teachers' salaries are increased, it may decrease the number of teachers and increase class size. However, the ability of city government to accomplish such a change is limited not only by union pressure but also by the pressure of other affected interested groups in the community.[34] Political considerations, therefore, may cause either no reduction in employment or services, or a reduction in an area other than that in which the union members work. Both the political power exerted by the beneficiaries of the services, who are also voters, and the power of the public employee union as a labor organization then combine to create great pressure on political leaders either to seek new funds or to reduce municipal services of another kind. Second, if labor costs increase, the city, like a private employer, may seek to replace labor with machines. The absence of a profit motive, and a political concern for unemployment, however, may be deterrents in addition to the deterrent of union resistance. The public employer that decides it must limit employment because of unit labor costs will likely find that the politically easiest decision is to restrict new hirings rather than to lay off current employees.

Where pensions are concerned, moreover, major concessions may be politically tempting since there is no immediate impact on the taxpayer or the city budget. Whereas actuarial soundness would be insisted on by a profit-seeking entity like a firm, it may be a secondary concern to politicians whose conduct is determined by relatively short-run considerations. The impact of failing to adhere to actuarial principles will frequently fall upon a different mayor and a different city council. In those circumstances, concessions that condemn a city to future impoverishment may not seem intolerable.

Even if a close relationship between increased economic benefits and unemployment does not exist as a significant deterrent to unions in the public sector, might not the argument be made that in some sense the taxpayer is the public sector's functional equivalent of the consumer? If taxes become too high the taxpayer can move to another community. While it is generally much easier for a consumer to substitute products than for a taxpayer to substitute communities, is it not fair to say that, at the point at which a tax increase will cause so many taxpayers to move that it will produce less total revenue, the market disciplines or restrains union and public employer in the same way and for the same reasons that the market disciplines parties in the private sector? Moreover, does not the analogy to the private sector suggest that it is legitimate in an economic sense for unions to push government to the point of substitutability?

Several factors suggest that the answer to this latter question is at best indeterminate, and that the question of legitimacy must be judged not by economic but by political criteria.

In the first place, there is no theoretical reason—economic or political—to suppose that it is desirable for a governmental entity to liquidate its taxing power, to tax up to the point where another tax increase will produce less revenue because of the number of people it drives to different communities. In the private area, profit maximization is a complex concept, but its approximation generally is both a legal requirement and socially useful as a means of allocating resources.[35] The liquidation of taxing power seems neither imperative nor useful.

Second, consider the complexity of the tax structure and the way in which different kinds of taxes (property, sales, income) fall differently upon a given population. Consider, moreover, that the taxing authority of a particular governmental entity may be limited (a municipality may not have the power to impose an income tax). What is necessarily involved, then, is principally the redistribution of income by government rather than resource allocation,[36] and questions of income redistribution surely are essentially political questions.[37]

For his part, the mayor in our paradigm will be disciplined not by a desire to maximize profits but by a desire—in some cases at least—to do a good job (to implement his programs), and in virtually all cases by a wish either to be reelected or to move to a better elective office. What he gives to the union must be taken from some other interest group or from taxpayers. His is the job of coordinating these competing claims while remaining politically viable. And that coordination will be governed by the relative power of the competing interest groups. Coordination, moreover, is not limited to issues involving the level of taxes and the way in which tax moneys are spent. Nonfinancial issues also require coordination, and here too the outcome turns upon the relative power of interest groups. And relative power is affected importantly by the scope of collective bargaining.

THE PUBLIC SECTOR MODEL:
NONMONETARY ISSUES

In the private sector, unions have pushed to expand the scope of bargaining in response to the desires of their members for a variety of new benefits (pension rights, supplementary unemployment payments, merit increases). These benefits generally impose a monetary cost on the employer. And because employers are restrained by the market, an expanded bargaining agenda means that, if a union negotiates an agreement over more subjects, it generally trades off more of less for less of more.

From the consumer's point of view this in turn means that the price of the product he purchases is not significantly related to the scope of bargaining. And since unions rarely bargain about the nature of the product produced,[38] the consumer can be relatively indifferent as to how many or how few subjects are covered in any collective agreement.[39] Nor need the consumer be concerned about union demands that would not impose a financial cost on the employer, for example, the design of a grievance procedure. While such demands are not subject to the same kind of trade-off as are financial demands, they are unlikely, if granted, to have any impact on the consumer. Their effect is on the quality of life of the parties to the agreement.

In the public sector the cluster of problems that surround the scope of bargaining are much more troublesome than they are in the private sector. The problems have several dimensions.

First, the trade-off between subjects of bargaining in the public sector is less of a protection to the consumer (public) than it is in the private. Where political leaders view the costs of union demands as essentially budgetary, a trade-off can occur. Thus, a demand for higher teacher salaries and a demand for reduced class size may be treated as part of one package. But where a demand, although it has a budgetary effect, is viewed as involving essentially political costs, trade-offs are more difficult. Our paradigmatic mayor, for example, may be under great pressure to make a large monetary settlement with a teachers' union whether or not it is joined to demands for special training programs for disadvantaged children. Interest groups tend to exert pressure against union demands only when they are directly affected. Otherwise, they are apt to join that large constituency (the general public) that wants to avoid labor trouble. Trade-offs can occur only when several demands are resisted by roughly the same groups. Thus, pure budgetary demands can be traded off when they are opposed by taxpayers. But when the identity of the resisting group changes with each demand, political leaders may find it expedient to strike a balance on each issue individually, rather than as part of a total package, by measuring the political power of each interest group involved against the political power of the constituency pressing for labor peace. To put it another way, as important as financial factors are to a mayor, political factors may be even more important. The market allows the businessman no such discretionary choice.

Where a union demand—such as increasing the disciplinary power of teachers—does not have budgetary consequences, some trade-offs may occur. Granting the demand will impose a political cost on the mayor because it may anger another interest group. But because the resisting group may change with each issue, each issue is apt to be treated individually and not as a part of a total package. And this may not protect the public. Differing from the private sector, nonmonetary demands of public sector unions do have effects that go beyond the parties to the agreement. All of us have a stake in how school children are disciplined. Expansion of the subjects of bargaining in the public sector, therefore, may increase the total quantum of union power in the political process.

Second, public employees do not generally produce a product. They perform a service. The way in which a service is performed may become a subject of bargaining. As a result, the nature of that service may be changed. Some of these services—police protection, teaching, health care—involve questions that are politically, socially, or ideologically sensitive. In part this is because government is involved and alternatives to governmentally provided services are relatively dear. In part, government is involved because of society's perception about the nature of the service and society's need for it. This suggests that decisions affecting the nature of a governmentally provided service are much more likely to be challenged and are more urgent than generally is the case with services that are offered privately.

Third, some of the services government provides are performed by professionals—teachers, social workers, and so forth—who are keenly interested in the underlying philosophy that informs their work. To them, theirs is not merely a job to be done for a salary. They may be educators or other "change agents" of society. And this may mean that these employees are concerned with more than incrementally altering a governmental service or its method of delivery. They may be advocates of bold departures that will radically transform the service itself.

The issue is not a threshold one of whether professional public employees should participate in decisions about the nature of the services they provide. Any properly run governmental agency should be interested in, and heavily reliant upon, the judgment of its professional staff. The issue rather is the method of that participation.

Conclusions about this issue as well as the larger issue of a full transplant of collective bargaining to the public sector may be facilitated by addressing some aspects of the governmental decision-making process—particularly at the municipal level —and the impact of collective bargaining on that process.

PUBLIC EMPLOYEE UNIONS AND
THE POLITICAL PROCESS

Although the market does not discipline the union in the public sector to the extent that it does in the private, the municipal employment paradigm, nevertheless, would seem to be consistent with what Robert A. Dahl has called the " 'normal'

American political process," which is "one in which there is a high probability that an active and legitimate group in the population can make itself heard effectively at some crucial stage in the process of decision," for the union may be seen as little more than an "active and legitimate group in the population."[40] With elections in the background to perform, as Mr. Dahl notes, "the critical role . . . in maximizing political equality and popular sovereignty,"[41] all seems well, at least theoretically, with collective bargaining and public employment.

But there is trouble even in the house of theory if collective bargaining in the public sector means what it does in the private. The trouble is that if unions are able to withhold labor— to strike—as well as to employ the usual methods of political pressure, they may possess a disproportionate share of effective power in the process of decision. Collective bargaining would then be so effective a pressure as to skew the results of the " 'normal' American political process."

One should straightway make plain that the strike issue is not simply the importance of public services as contrasted with services or products produced in the private sector. This is only part of the issue, and in the past the partial truth has beclouded analysis.[42] The services performed by a private transit authority are neither less nor more important to the public than those that would be performed if the transit authority were owned by a municipality. A railroad or dock strike may be more damaging to a community than "job action" by police. This is not to say that governmental services are not important. They are, both because the demand for them is inelastic and because their disruption may seriously injure a city's economy and occasionally impair the physical welfare of its citizens. Nevertheless, the importance of governmental services is only a necessary part of, rather than a complete answer to, the question: Why be more concerned about strikes in public employment than in private?

The answer to the question is simply that, because strikes in public employment disrupt important services, a large part of a mayor's political constituency will, in many cases, press for a quick end to the strike with little concern for the cost of settlement. This is particularly so where the cost of settlement is borne by a different and larger political constituency, the citizens of the state or nation. Since interest groups other than public employees, with conflicting claims on municipal government, do not, as a general proposition, have anything approaching the effectiveness of the strike—or at least cannot maintain that relative degree of power over the long run— they may be put at a significant competitive disadvantage in the political process.

The private sector strike is designed to exert economic pressure on the employer by depriving him of revenues. The public employee strike is fundamentally different: its sole purpose is to exert political pressure on municipal officials. They are deprived, not of revenues but of the political support of those who are inconvenienced by a disruption of municipal services. But precisely because the private strike is an economic weapon, it is disciplined by the market and the benefit/unemployment trade-off that imposes. And because the public employee strike is a political weapon, it is subject only to the restraints imposed by the political process and they are on the whole less limiting and less disciplinary than those of the market. If this is the case, it must be said that the political process will be radically altered by wholesale importation of the strike weapon. And because of the deceptive simplicity of the analogy to collective bargaining in the private sector, the alteration may take place without anyone realizing what has happened.

Nor is it an answer that, in some municipalities, interest groups other than unions now have a disproportionate share of political power. This is inescapably true, and we do not condone that situation. Indeed, we would be among the first to advocate reform. However, reform cannot be accomplished by giving another interest group disproportionate power, for the losers would be the weakest groups in the community. In most municipalities, the weakest groups are composed of citizens who many believe are most in need of more power.

Therefore, while the purpose and effect of strikes by public employees may seem in the beginning designed merely to establish collective bargaining or to "catch up" with wages and fringe benefits in the private sector, in the long run strikes may become too effective a means for redistributing income; so effective, indeed, that one might see them as an institutionalized means of obtaining and maintaining a subsidy for union members.[43]

As is often the case when one generalizes, this picture may be considered overdrawn. In order to refine analysis, it will be helpful to distinguish between strikes that occur over monetary issues and strikes involving nonmonetary issues. The generalized picture sketched above is mainly concerned with the former. Because there is usually no substitute for governmental service, the citizen-consumer faced with a strike of teachers, or garbage men, or social workers is likely to be seriously inconvenienced. This in turn places enormous pressure on the mayor, who is apt to find it difficult to look to the long-run balance sheet of the municipality. Most citizens are directly affected by a strike of sanitation workers. Few, however, can decipher a municipal budget or trace the relationship between today's labor settlement and next year's increase in the mill rate. Thus, in the typical case the impact of a settlement is less visible—or can more often be concealed—than the impact of a disruption of services. Moreover, the cost of settlement may fall upon a constituency much larger—the whole state or nation—than that represented by the mayor. And revenue sharing schemes that involve unrestricted funds may further lessen public resistance to generous settlements. It follows that the mayor usually will look to the electorate that is clamoring for a settlement, and in these circumstances the union's fear of a long strike, a major check on its power in the private sector, is not a consideration.[44] In the face of all of these factors other interest groups with priorities different from the union's are apt to be much less successful in their pursuit of scarce tax dollars than is the union with power to withhold services.[45]

With respect to strikes over some nonmonetary issues— decentralization of the governance of schools might be an example—the intensity of concern on the part of well-organized interest groups opposed to the union's position would support the mayor in his resistance to union demands. But even here, if the union rank and file back their leadership, pressures for settlement from the general public, which may be largely indifferent as to the underlying issue, might in time become irresistible.[46]

The strike and its threat, moreover, exacerbate the problems associated with the scope of bargaining in public employment. This seems clear if one attends in slightly more detail to techniques of municipal decision making.

Few students of our cities would object to Herbert Kaufman's observation that:

> Decisions of the municipal government emanate from no single source, but from many centers; conflicts and clashes are referred to no single authority, but are settled at many levels and at many points in the system: no single group can guarantee the success of any proposal it supports, the defeat of every idea it objects to. Not even the central governmental organs of the city —the Mayor, the Board of Estimate, the Council—individually or in combination, even approach mastery in this sense.

> Each separate decision center consists of a cluster of interested contestants, with a "core group" in the middle, invested by the rules with the formal authority to legitimize decisions (that is to promulgate them in binding form) and a constellation of related "satellite groups" seeking to influence the authoritative issuances of the core group.[47]

Nor would many disagree with Nelson W. Polsby when, in discussing community decision making that is concerned with an alternative to a "current state of affairs," he argues that the alternative "must be politically palatable and relatively easy to accomplish; otherwise great amounts of influence have to be brought to bear with great skill and efficiency in order to secure its adoption."[48]

It seems probable that such potential subjects of bargaining as school decentralization and a civilian police review board are, where they do not exist, alternatives to the "current state of affairs." If a teachers' union or a police union were to bargain with the municipal employer over these questions, and were able to use the strike to insist that the proposals not be adopted, how much "skill and efficiency" on the part of the proposals' advocates would be necessary to effect a change? And, to put the shoe on the other foot, if a teachers' union were to insist through collective bargaining (with the strike or its threat) upon major changes in school curriculum, would not that union have to be considerably less skillful and efficient in the normal political process than other advocates of community change? The point is that with respect to some subjects, collective bargaining may be too powerful a lever on municipal decision making, too effective a technique for changing or preventing the change of one small but important part of the "current state of affairs."

Unfortunately, in this area the problem is not merely the strike threat and the strike. In a system where impasse procedures involving third parties are established in order to reduce work stoppages—and this is common in those states that have passed public employment bargaining statutes—third party intervention must be partly responsive to union demands. If the scope of bargaining is open-ended, the neutral party, to be effective, will have to work out accommodations that inevitably advance some of the union's claims some of the time. And the neutral, with his eyes fixed on achieving a settlement, can hardly be concerned with balancing all the items on the community agenda or reflecting the interests of all relevant groups.

THE THEORY SUMMARIZED

Collective bargaining in public employment, then, seems distinguishable from that in the private sector. To begin with, it

imposes on society more than a potential misallocation of resources through restrictions on economic output, the principal
cost imposed by private sector unions. Collective bargaining
by public employees and the political process cannot be separated. The costs of such bargaining, therefore, cannot be fully
measured without taking into account the impact on the allocation of political power in the typical municipality. If one assumes, as here, that municipal political processes should be
structured to ensure "a high probability that an active and
legitimate group in the population can make itself heard effectively at some crucial stage in the process of decision,"[49] then
the issue is how powerful unions will be in the typical municipal political process if a full transplant of collective bargaining
is carried out.

The conclusion is that such a transplant would, in many
cases, institutionalize the power of public employee unions in
a way that would leave competing groups in the political process at a permanent and substantial disadvantage. There are
three reasons for this, and each is related to the type of services
typically performed by public employees.

First, some of these services are such that any prolonged
disruption would entail an actual danger to health and safety.

Second, the demand for numerous governmental services is
relatively inelastic, that is, relatively insensitive to changes in
price. Indeed, the lack of close substitutes is typical of many
governmental endeavors.[50] And, since at least the time of
Marshall's *Principles of Economics,* the elasticity of demand
for the final service or product has been considered a major
determinant of union power.[51] Because the demand for labor
is derived from the demand for the product, inelasticity on the
product side tends to reduce the employment-benefit trade-off
unions face. This is as much the case in the private as in the
public sector. But in the private sector, product inelasticity is
not typical. Moreover, there is the further restraint on union
power created by the real possibility of nonunion entrants into
the product market. In the public sector, inelasticity of demand
seems more the rule than the exception, and nonunion rivals

are not generally a serious problem.

Consider education. A strike by teachers may never create an immediate danger to public health and welfare. Nevertheless, because the demand for education is relatively inelastic, teachers rarely need fear unemployment as a result of union-induced wage increases, and the threat of an important non-union rival (competitive private schools) is not to be taken seriously so long as potential consumers of private education must pay taxes to support the public school system.

The final reason for fearing a full transplant is the extent to which the disruption of a government service inconveniences municipal voters. A teachers' strike may not endanger public health or welfare. It may, however, seriously inconvenience parents and other citizens who, as voters, have the power to punish one of the parties—and always the same party, the political leadership—to the dispute. How can anyone any longer doubt the vulnerability of a municipal employer to this sort of pressure? Was it simply a matter of indifference to Mayor Lindsay in September 1969 whether another teachers' strike occurred on the eve of a municipal election? Did the size and the speed of the settlement with the United Federation of Teachers (UFT) suggest nothing about one first-rate politician's estimate of his vulnerability? And are the chickens now coming home to roost because of extravagant concessions on pensions for employees of New York City the result only of mistaken actuarial calculations? Or do they reflect the irrelevance of long-run considerations to politicians vulnerable to the strike and compelled to think in terms of short-run political impact?

Those who disagree on this latter point rely principally on their conviction that anticipation of increased taxes as the result of a large labor settlement will countervail the felt inconvenience of a strike, and that municipalities are not, therefore, overly vulnerable to strikes by public employees. The argument made here, however—that governmental budgets in large cities are so complex that generally the effect of any particular labor settlement on the typical municipal budget is a matter of very low visibility—seems adequately convincing. Concern over possible taxes will not, as a general proposition, significantly deter voters who are inconvenienced by a strike from compelling political leaders to settle quickly. Moreover, municipalities are often subsidized by other political entities —the nation or state—and the cost of a strike settlement may not be borne by those demanding an end to the strike.

All this may seem to suggest that it is the strike weapon— whether the issue be monetary or nonmonetary—that cannot be transplanted to the public sector. This is an oversimplification, however. It is the combination of the strike and the typical municipal political process, including the usual methods for raising revenue. One solution, of course, might well be a ban on strikes, if it could be made effective. But that is not the sole alternative, for there may be ways in which municipal political structures can be changed so as to make cities less vulnerable to strikes and to reduce the potential power of public employee unions to tolerable levels.

All this may also seem to suggest a sharper distinction between the public and private sectors than actually exists. The discussion here has dealt with models, one for private collective bargaining, the other for public. Each model is located at the core of its sector. But the difference in the impact of collective bargaining in the two sectors should be seen as a continuum. Thus, for example, it may be that market restraints do not sufficiently discipline strike settlements in some regulated industries or in industries that rely mainly on government contracts. Indeed, collective bargaining in such industries has been under steady and insistent attack.

In the public sector, it may be that in any given municipality —but particularly a small one—at any given time, taxpayer resistance or the determination of municipal government, or both, will substantially offset union power even under existing political structures. These plainly are exceptions, however. They do not invalidate the public-private distinction as an analytical tool, for that distinction rests on the very real differences that exist in the vast bulk of situations, situations exemplified by these models. On the other hand, in part because of a recognition that there are exceptions that in particular cases make the models invalid, it is important that the law regulating municipal bargaining be flexible and tailored to the real needs of a particular municipality.

When our work on collective bargaining and public employment was first published, more than a few labor relations specialists greeted it with skepticism, for it was at odds with what was then the conventional wisdom that "government was just another industry."

Recent events, to say the least, have not shaken our conviction that collective bargaining in the public sector raises problems of a different order than in the private sector and is radically restructuring the allocation of political power in our large cities. We believe that the evidence of the last five years demonstrates that a number of factors all contribute to making municipal unions far more powerful than those in the private sector. These include the complexity of municipal budgets, the difficulty in laying off public employees, the availability of funds from other branches of government to pay the costs of settlements, the ability to defer those costs to later administrations (as in pensions), and the need of municipal officials to give undue attention to the short-run inconveniences caused by public employee strikes.

The real limit we now discern on the power of those unions merely bolsters our conclusion, since that limit appears to be the impairment of municipal credit or municipal bankruptcy itself. Unless our cities are "just another business," public employee labor relations is not "just another industry."

V

TWO MAYORS
AND MUNICIPAL
EMPLOYEE UNIONS

SEATTLE
THE HONORABLE WES UHLMAN, *Mayor*

Union-municipality confrontation. Firefighters' union. Recall petition. Linemen's union. Rights and obligations of public employees. Municipal financial problems. Fair Labor Standards Act. Public sector productivity. Negotiation and arbitration.

There are two ways that public employees can make things uncomfortable for elected officials in the State of Washington, and Seattle has experienced them both in the last twelve months.

In December of 1974 I angered Seattle's firefighters by dismissing their popular, convivial, personable, and totally ineffectual chief. I looked upon this action as exercising one of my most important responsibilities as Mayor. The firefighters, on the other hand, viewed it as an intrusion by a politician into the internal affairs of their department. Police officers and

77

firefighters are prohibited by state law from striking, but found a very effective tool for demonstrating their unhappiness through another state law: the right of citizens to petition to recall any elected official for virtually any offense.

The petitions were filed, the finely tuned political machine of the Firefighters' Union went to work, the signatures were collected, and I found myself facing a special recall election on July 1 of last year. Fortunately, the antipathy of the fire-fighters was surpassed by the insistence of our residents upon sound fiscal control and good management in city govern-ment. I won the election by nearly a 2-1 margin.

But before that election was even over, we were in the midst of negotiating a new contract with our linemen at Seattle City Light, our municipal electric utility. They insisted on a salary increase that was far beyond what other city employees had reasonably agreed to. And they refused even to discuss changes in work rules and scheduling to increase productivity. Because we would not give in to their demands, they went on strike in October and remained off the job for three full months. Management personnel were able to maintain power to our residents, but a couple of special situations caused some temporary disruptions. In November a gasoline truck over-turned and burning fuel cut electric cables to several down-town buildings, including City Hall. And on New Year's Eve a self-proclaimed revolutionary underground group blew up one of our major transformers, interrupting service to a major Seattle community.

Despite these and other problems, we held out, and in January the strikers came to terms. Our terms. In fact, they settled for less than we had originally been prepared to offer.

Having survived the recall election and the strike, I suppose I have earned some sort of right to address the issues of public employee rights and responsibilities, and the rights and re-sponsibilities of elected officials in dealing with them.

I believe that public employees should have the right to col-lective bargaining. Mayors and city managers should not be afraid to face organized employee groups at the bargaining table. I think we have a responsibility to discuss with them the issues of salaries, benefits, and working conditions. And we also have a responsibility to our constituents to maintain control over policymaking decisions. We must, therefore, have the courage to keep policymaking free from the bargaining process.

Union leaders have responsibilities as well. They must have the authority to speak for their membership and to maintain the respect and confidence of the rank and file. Where we have generally had difficulties with employee groups in Seattle, it has not been because the leadership of those groups was too strong, but rather because they were too weak to lead. Furthermore, I believe that responsible union leaders must consider the impacts of their demands on government's ability to serve the public. Demands which ultimately weaken the financial fiber of cities and which weaken government's ability to perform are not in the interests of our citizens nor in the long-term interests of public employees themselves.

The cities of this nation face very serious financial problems. New York has been the symbol of that, but it does not stand alone. In talking with my fellow mayors, I find that many of them face the very same problems which we face in Seattle—rapidly rising inflation, militant demands from citizen groups for services and facilities, higher and higher wage demands from our public employees, and, of course, a very limited, inelastic, and insufficient tax base.

Tax reform in most states and municipalities is urgently needed. A recent study indicates that the State of Washington has the most regressive tax structure in the nation. But tax reform in most states and municipalities is far, far away. So while mayors and public employees should work together to press for that tax reform, we must also face the world as it exists until we are able to change it.

Public employees deserve a fair wage. But public employees must consider the ability of government to pay when they make their demands. In Seattle, we have virtually no authority to raise taxes. So when the wages of one group of employees rises too fast, another group bears the burden by losing their jobs. We have to set the priorities for services on the basis of public needs rather than as a reaction to the most powerful or vocal local labor union.

In that context, the context of real cities fighting to survive in a real world, I believe every public employee deserves a fair day's pay for a fair day's work. In fact, I was frankly amazed to hear some labor leaders suggest that the National League of Cities sought an injunction against the Fair Labor Standards Act in order to avoid paying minimum wage to police and firefighters. I'd like to know where a professional police officer or firefighter does not make two dollars an hour? In Seattle, the starting salary for our uniformed employees is fourteen thousand dollars a year. In virtually every other major city in the country, starting salary for uniformed personnel is between ten and twenty thousand dollars a year. In terms of public employees in Seattle—and I submit in most cities across this country—the minimum wage issue is really a red herring.

The real reason we did not want to see the national Fair Labor Standards Act applied to public employees is that it would have interfered with the collective bargaining process on the local level. When we sit down with our unions to negotiate, we do not want the federal government telling us what we can or cannot agree to. And our unions do not want that either. Some local union requests for comp time (compensation time) instead of overtime—which we agreed to at the bargaining table—would have been precluded by this act. Local union representatives should have the greatest range of flexibility possible in making their proposals.

If cities are going to be able to respond to those proposals in a positive way, they are going to have to be adequately financed.

But the real message that mayors and city managers are trying to voice across the country is this: Regardless of our funding sources, cities still have a responsibility to our taxpayers to manage our employees efficiently, to use their time and their talents in the most effective way possible.

That is what the whole issue of productivity is all about. It does not mean cramming more and more people into public hospital wards, jamming overcrowded classrooms with more and more students, or piling more paperwork on law enforcement officers. Any good manager knows that those kinds of actions are clearly counterproductive. What we do mean by productivity is making certain that our work force is organized and managed efficiently so that people are not sitting around with nothing to do. Productivity means eliminating any inefficient use of an employee's time. It means revising work rules which prevent an employee from getting his or her work done. It does not mean making hard-working employees work harder still, but rather allowing them to work more usefully. It is simply another way of expressing the concept of good management.

The private sector has long been involved in trying to increase productivity, and I think it's time for the public sector to catch up. A recent study of trash collection by the Columbia University Graduate School of Business, for example, found that on the national average, it costs 69 percent more for public employees to collect garbage than for private companies to do the same job. Public employees are simply not being managed as effectively as private employees. And that is frustrating not only to us in administration, it is frustrating for our taxpayers and frustrating for our employees themselves.

In fact, every union which has signed an agreement with the City of Seattle in our latest round of contracts has agreed to very specific productivity language in that contract. Our union leadership realizes that unless we are able to use their members to the fullest of their abilities and potentials, we will not be able to provide the salaries and benefits which they will ask for at the bargaining table.

I believe that public employees do have the right to form collective bargaining units. They are not second-class citizens just because they serve the public. I know that the thought of dealing with organized labor frightens some mayors and city managers, but our experience in Seattle has been a positive and productive one.

I believe that the scope of those negotiations with collective bargaining units should be as broad and encompassing as possible. As an elected official, I have a responsibility to maintain control over the management of my city. I will not give away management prerogatives at the bargaining table. But I don't want any legislation telling me or the unions what we can or cannot discuss. In 1971 we included a union security clause in all of our contracts. I think that is the kind of issue which should be available for discussion when contract time comes around. As a lawyer, I personally prefer putting our relationship—all our rights and obligations—down in black-and-white in a written contract. Then we each know where we stand and can enforce those rights, in court if necessary.

When bargaining breaks down, we should be prepared to face a strike. I know it may not be popular with some of my colleagues, but I think that—where the health or safety of the public is not jeopardized—public employees should have the right to strike. That is the only way that they can exert any real leverage to assure fair and careful consideration of their labor demands. If management can simply refuse to negotiate and public employees have no recourse, then you really do not have negotiations at all. You have a sort of paternalism which is not healthy for the workers and not healthy for the city.

Again, I emphasize that a strike can be tolerated only where the public health or safety is not affected. In such cases I think a city can withstand a strike. That was our experience with the City Light strike. Our citizens were inconvenienced by the strike, but they indicated their strong support for the city's position even though it meant some hardship.

The issues involved in this strike underscore the fact that we mayors and city managers simply have to exhibit more back-bone in dealing with public employees. Knowing that the strike is the ultimate weapon which can be used against us, we have to have the courage to confront that, and we have to be prepared to deal with it. Public employees should not have to leap up and accept the first offer that management may make, nor should management be intimidated by the political power of public employees nor by their ability to make our jobs uncomfortable. That's what we get paid for. When we feel that it would be irresponsible to accept a union's demands—and that's how I felt about our electrical workers' demands—then we have to stick to our principles and prepare to endure it.

The other side of the issue is when the public health and safety is jeopardized by a strike. We give our police and firemen what is for all practical purposes a monopoly on protecting the life of our cities. For such special categories of public service, there can be no right to strike.

Yet there must be some way of resolving an impasse in the bargaining process here as well. In the state of Washington we have binding arbitration for our uniformed personnel. If we cannot reach an agreement, we call in a third party to settle the matter for us. In theory, this deprives elected officials of some of their power to set city policy. It gives an outsider an opportunity to greatly impact our city budget—a budget which we must then live with. I do have these reservations about it. And the state law, lobbied through the state legislature by the police and fire unions, does not contain one important basic criterion —the ability of the city to pay. I would hope that the local jurisdiction's tax structure and ability to pay would become a mandatory consideration in any arbiter's award.

Of course, the best alternative to strikes and binding arbitration is to avoid them in the first place. I do not like confrontation with public employees. Such confrontation is not the key to political popularity. Public employees are a force to be reckoned with—politically—in any city. In some, they are the largest single organized voting group. As Victor Gotbaum said of his public employees in New York this summer, "We have the power, in effect, to elect our own boss." Few politicians want to go out of their way to antagonize a large group of voters unless it's necessary in the responsible management of the city.

But more to the point, confrontation is simply poor management. With every strike, and to a limited extent with binding arbitration, the public suffers. There is much more for both sides to gain through honest bargaining and a reasonable agreement.

We have been extremely fortunate in Seattle to develop positive relationships with most of our thirty-three unions, to assure that this kind of process takes place. The union leadership in Seattle is in large part responsible for that relationship. They understand our problems and limitations, and have a clear and forthright way of expressing their own needs. Our discussions are sincere, and do not encompass the hot rhetoric which some union leaders have taken to using.

In fact, if I were going to suggest one way of improving the relationship between city government and city employees, I would recommend stronger, better leadership on the part of public employee unions. Where we have had problems in Seattle, they have been in large part the result of the failure of the union leadership's ability to lead its membership, to represent them adequately, and to act in their behalf. We cannot negotiate with fifteen hundred or two thousand individuals; we can only negotiate with representatives who know what their members want and have their support in getting it.

So I would encourage my fellow mayors as well as the leaders of public employee unions to regard the collective bargaining process as a useful and healthy tool in establishing salaries, benefits, and working conditions. But only if both sides go in with an attitude of cooperation, and each makes an effort to understand the needs and problems of the other side.

We're long past the era of sweatshops, strikebreakers, and dollar-an-hour civil servants. And we're long past the era when government can use the security of the civil service system as an excuse for low wages or poor working conditions. And the sooner both sides recognize the real world we live in, the sooner other cities will be able to achieve the kind of positive approach we've developed in Seattle.

KANSAS CITY

THE HONORABLE CHARLES B. WHEELER, JR., *Mayor*

Confrontation: teachers, firefighters. Mediation. Municipal finances. Congressional intervention. Union responsibility.

Until a few years ago Kansas City was not under the direct threat of strikes by its public employees. While it is true that the city's firefighters had staged several work slowdowns in the years before my administration began in April 1971, an actual strike was not thought to be imminent. The police department is run by an independent Police Board appointed by the governor of Missouri with wage rates fixed by the General Assembly; members of the department have an organization to represent them, but state law does not grant it bargaining power. The American Federation of State, County and Municipal Employees had not then succeeded to any great degree in convincing City Hall employees of the benefits of joining Local No. 500.

But the rather serene climate changed radically. In April 1974, eager to test their newly found strength, Local No. 691 of the American Federation of Teachers staged a strike which lasted forty-five days. The firefighters walked off their jobs on October 3, 1975, in a four-day strike. The American Federation of State, County and Municipal Employees has increased rapidly in numbers and now represents about 2,000 municipal employees in Kansas City.

My first experience in dealing with striking public employees was with the teachers. Despite a court order declaring the strike illegal and the ten-day sentencing of the union local president, the teachers persisted. The strike continued in the face of opposition by city officials, the media, and the general public. What I saw during that strike were things which would be repeated in the firemen's strike less than two years later. I saw threats, sometimes overt and sometimes not, against lives and property. I saw our citizens unable to resume their normal life patterns. I saw local labor leaders egged on by their superiors who flew into Kansas City to oversee the strike.

Settlement finally was reached on the teachers' major salary and non-salary demands. However, it was clear the union was far from satisfied. It adopted a "just wait until next year" attitude, and in 1975 and again this year during contract negotiations the union threatened to call a strike vote. Fortunately, union members have not voted to strike the last two years. But the specter of another prolonged strike hangs over the school district, and this has promoted the reputation that Kansas City schools are unstable—which in turn has discouraged families with school-age children from locating in the older part of the city and has driven them to the more suburban areas.

Although the firefighters' strike lasted only four days, unlike the teachers' strike it directly affected the public safety of the citizens of Kansas City. By putting the citizens in jeopardy, the firemen broke faith with the city and the people they had pledged to serve.

About 850 of the city's 891 firefighters of Local No. 42 walked off the job in defiance of a court order. The main issue was pay parity with the city's police; the two other major demands were increased manpower and cost of living increases for three consecutive years.

Less than thirty minutes after the strike began, a vacant house burned to the ground. A makeshift crew of National Guardsmen and public works department employees was assembled to fight what turned out to be a record number of fires—three times the normal rate. Plans called for having two police officers and two National Guardsmen at each of the city's 59 fire stations, but only two fire engines were available to handle the barrage of calls. Police reported widespread arson and sabotage. Pickup orders issued to stop and question "suspicious looking" people resulted in several arrests, although criminal charges or arson were not proved before a grand jury. A circuit court judge in Kansas City set a hearing on a show cause order the following week. The judge claimed he was satisfied there had been violations of state statutes by the firemen and that the lives and property of the citizens were in jeopardy. The show cause order was not dissolved even after the firemen returned to the jobs, and the suit is still pending. Another suit has been filed by the Attorney General seeking $300,000 for National Guard expenses.

On the second day of the strike the attorney for the firemen demanded that the City Council (which was unanimous in its opposition to the strike) and I, as Mayor, apologize for insinuating that the firemen were responsible for the turmoil. We refused. We also rejected the union's offer to put the firemen back on the job that night in exchange for the city's agreement to submit to binding arbitration on the issue of pay parity with the police.

The next two days the situation shifted in favor of the city as Governor Bond sent more and more National Guardsmen in relief. Finally, on the night of the fourth day, the firefighters agreed to return to work immediately while terms were being negotiated with the help of a federal mediator, the Reverend Leo Brown of St. Louis. Fifty firemen who had been fired were rehired as part of the truce.

Seven months have passed and no settlement has been reached. Father Brown's recommendations were not acceptable to the city. The union, in turn, has refused to accept the city's proposals. The impasse continues, but agreement on a new three-year contract seems close.

Had the city accepted the mediator's proposal, the result would have been an almost insurmountable fiscal problem. In effect, it would have been the first step toward bankruptcy because the law requires that Kansas City have a balanced budget—must remain solvent.

I am unequivocally opposed to strikes by public employees in which the health and safety of our citizens are directly involved. I am not going to capitulate to the exorbitant demands of some labor leaders who are out to bankrupt our cities. I am not going to turn over the fiscal management of Kansas City to striking employees and will resist such management by "experts" in compulsory arbitration over public employees' salaries.

Compulsory arbitration, in my opinion, is not an alternative to a strike and would aggravate the pressing financial problems of our cities. To turn over the public budgetary process to a person not responsible to the electorate would be disastrous. Arbitration awards, in recent years, have been excessively high. In addition, the City Charter specifically designates to elected officials the legislative function of managing the budget.

In Kansas City, the mediator rendered a non-binding award. Had it been binding, the city would be in dire straits. As it happened, the award served to undermine peaceful labor relations rather than promote them. There is no doubt in my mind that the firemen's strike would have been successfully concluded by now if there had been no outside interference. City governments are managed by professional, highly qualified people who understand what it means to be fiscally sound and know how to write a balanced budget.

I fault our Congress for meddling with city wage structures. This is a matter which local officials can competently handle without federal intervention. It is irresponsible for Congress to sell out the cities each year to a few labor leaders.

Perhaps the best solution for settling disputes involving public unions would be impasse procedures such as mediation or fact finding. Mediation and, if successful, non-binding arbitration by a neutral person may be a workable combination. In this process, the neutral party may want to select item-by-item from the last best offer of the parties. A proposal of this type is pending in the Missouri General Assembly. Submitting a disputed wage package to public referendum is a possibility which offers little hope for the unions in these days of taxpayer revolt.

In my experience with striking employees, I am certain the solution lies in the city providing good wages and working conditions within the bounds of fiscal responsibility. Most cities have been fair, even generous, to their public employees. Reasonable demands, and some unreasonable ones, have been met. City governments have held up their end of the bargain. In Kansas City, for example, the major issue during the strike was pay parity with the police. Yet the average fireman currently makes more per month ($1,055) than the average police officer ($1,034) because of the longer length of service. If an inequity exists in the wages paid to firemen, it favors them in relation to other city employees. Salaries paid to public employees in Kansas City are comparable to those paid in other cities throughout the country.

A solution to current problems in public sector labor relations will come when we realize that the cities, the states, and the nation are strapped for funds. There is a limit to what we can spend. There is a limit to what we can logically demand from government at any level. All of us—and the leaders of public employee unions in particular—must learn these are the facts of life and act accordingly.

VI

URBAN POLITICS AND PUBLIC EMPLOYEE UNIONS

JACK D. DOUGLAS
Professor of Sociology, University of California, San Diego

The urban problem—social trust and order. Moralism and rationalism in urban politics. The urban political cycle: payoffs, reform, and rationalism. Mayor Daley and Chicago's machine politics. The Lindsay experience in New York and urban Götterdämmerung. Recalling Boss Tweed. Collective bargaining as politics. The Wagner record. Conclusion.

Politics has become a dirty word to most Americans. They see it as immoral and irrational. They wonder why decisionmakers can't simply do what is rational and right, rather than what is politic. Nowhere is this view more evident than in public sector labor relations.

Social thinkers of many persuasions increasingly conclude that both the rationalist and moralist conceptions are simplistic and mistaken. Both view society monolithically; and both are therefore unable to accommodate the major social and moral problems in a complex society. The point is particularly true of American society which, more than almost any other, ac-

91

commodates basic and vast conflicts over morality, values, and culture.

Politics is a process that attempts to solve conflicts—a process of deciding what is moral and rational, as well as what is workable and just. Rationality that does not consider the political process and its efforts to resolve social conflict is therefore irrational and self-defeating. For when the political process fails, especially when it is swept aside by moralism or the myth of rationalism, then social trust and order—which are essential to democracy—become severely threatened.

In recent years both moralism and rationalism have exercised an increasing influence on the American style of public sector labor relations, especially of dealing with public employee unions. This approach may have worked reasonably well when America was a collection of small and homogenous towns and villages, but it cannot work in the society which grew up as a vast mosaic of complex and conflicting cultural, ethnic, and racial groups.

The problem is particularly evident in the heterogeneous and conflict-ridden cities of the northeast and midwest. And to deal with it, creative politicians fashioned what became the uniquely American way of building trust and cooperative order among the many ethnic and interest groups—the infamous "political machines" so stigmatized by small-town moralists and more recently by rationalistic "experts."

I do not mean to argue that the machine solution to the problem of trust and order was without problems of its own. But the moralist critique of the machines has unfortunately obscured their real nature. Although the machines were often characterized by graft and corruption—particularly in their early phases—at the same time they performed an extremely important social function. Behind the sensational news stories about corruption, the machines were actually complex associations of diverse groups bound together by personal and practical—including gainful—ties. These associations were important in giving the man at the bottom a sense of direct participation in the city's life as well as a feeling of security and trust which inspired his cooperation.[1]

The growing middle-classification and education of the American people has promoted a growing dominance of the moralist and rationalist approaches to urban politics, and the result has been a progressive displacement of both political and cooperative problem-solving, and of the social trust it promoted. The conscious and deliberate subversion of the former cooperative system has resulted in a massive cutting of the ties between individuals and their political leaders, leaving increasing numbers in our larger cities isolated, insecure, and distrustful of both government and each other. Thus the moralist and rationalist approaches have done little to solve social problems and social conflict, but have aggravated both.

The current crisis in public sector labor relations is concentrated in cities of the northeast and midwest, and in Los Angeles and San Francisco. The problem emerges from a very special social context and setting common to all of those cities in a greater or lesser extent. There is no better way to understand the problem and thereby to find its solution than by comparing and contrasting the two dominant styles of public sector labor relations, which we will examine in the machine politics of Chicago Mayor Richard Daley and the reform politics of former Mayor John V. Lindsay in New York.

THE URBAN POLITICAL CYCLE: PAYOFFS, REFORM, AND RATIONALISM

Most analysts agree that pluralistic conflict is the dominant social condition in America's old industrial cities.[2] Almost all of these cities are built on collections of racial, ethnic, religious, economic, and cultural subcultures and groups which are partially independent and even isolated from each other, but which overlap and interact in vastly complex and largely unpredictable ways on concrete issues in specific situations. No single group—or even small coalition of the largest groups— ever achieves dominance for long in most of them.

The immensely complex and changing conflicts produce

what analysts have variously called "immense centrifugal" forces (Mandelbaum 1965), "fragmentation," "polarization," and even (despairingly) a "Byzantine mosaic." At the center of most major difficulties in these cities lies *the core problem of social order*—constructing sufficient order among these disparate groups to deal successfully with their problems.

Various coalition strategies and structural reforms, such as "strong mayor systems" and "city managers," have been used to deal with this atomization. Some are temporarily successful. The best-constructed coalition eventually fragments, and "rational, structural solutions" are found to be largely—not entirely—symbolic illusions which can only temporarily mask and shift the realities of pervasive conflict.

The outcome of this process traditionally has been a "political cycle" which falls roughly into three stages—with no common time or period observable—in which the first stage exists only in the first cycle. For reasons that should become obvious, the first stage does not recur.

The first stage ordinarily is an amalgam—not yet a coalition—of the subcultures, which feels that the city faces a set of major and urgent social problems. Occasionally—but less often—the first stage involves an amalgam beginning to see a set of tempting opportunities to pursue certain urban policies. At some point, of course, these two modes come together and are difficult to distinguish.

The second stage brings a political coalition to deal with the problems. Unless the problems are really intractable, which is rare, these coalitions succeed over long periods of time only by welding the coalition together with some form of public "payoffs" or "spoils." Since it is the problem that initially brings the coalition together and holds it so, the more successful it is either in solving problems or—probably more common—until the social perception of a problem wanes, the more the coalition must resort to payoffs to keep the subcultures working together. Thus "corrupt political machines" are born.[3]

The "machine" never lives up to its image, because the

coalitions never achieve the rationalized coordination and functional interdependency suggested by the image. Some parts of the machine generally envy and distrust the other parts, and these weaknesses tend to be overcome only by personal allegiance up the ladder to the boss. For example, a coalition of Germans and Irish formed a crucial link in the famous Tweed machine in New York City; the Germans resented the greater power and spoils of the Irish, and when they switched their allegiance to Tilden's reformers, Tweed's fate was sealed.

The more successful the machine, the more visible the success of its dominant parts and the greater the envy and distrust of the lesser partners. Machines thus build up their own internal dissension as well as external pressures.

The third stage brings a period of reaction, especially against the payoffs used by the machine to repair the coalition's disintegration. During the "reform stage" other groups in the city attack this system and form a new coalition dedicated to ending "corrupt politics," cutting taxes, and reducing the payoff system. The coalition originally formed to deal with perceived social problems now itself *becomes* the perceived problem, and thus is eliminated by the new coalition.

Having destroyed the old political machine, the reform coalition discovers it has mounting difficulties holding itself together. Furthermore, the tax reductions make it difficult to deal with new social problems. As a result, the reform coalition will either lose to a new machine or begin a new payoff system and create its own machine.

Some reformers—one thinks of John Lindsay—seem to suffer from a political idealism which takes the form of the moralism or rationalism mentioned earlier. The moralists not only oppose the old machine; they often move immediately to destroy some of their own political power base through the "politics of disintegration," in Lowi's (1964) apt phrase.

When such a reformer combines moralism with all the paraphernalia of "scientific rationalism," as Lindsay did, he sweeps away a myriad set of traditional social ties and feelings of allegiance and trust. This makes people prey for any coalition of other groups; it vastly heightens the sense of injustice, and thus encourages demands for more and more.

Faced with almost certain defeat, reform movements become forced to join the coalition of opposing forces and use massive payoffs to hold them together.

CHICAGO'S MACHINE POLITICS AND PUBLIC EMPLOYEE UNIONS

As everyone "knows," Chicago is the only major American city still governed by a traditional political machine. Actually, it has a modified form of the traditional pattern—or at least of the popular conception of it. Because of the moralistic focus of so much news on the "machine corruption" of Chicago, the very name of Mayor Daley has become synonymous to many people with the word "Boss." (This is the obvious basis for the title of Mike Royko's well-known moralistic book on Daley, *Boss* [1971]—as it was for the once-famous work by Denis Tilden Lynch on *"Boss" Tweed* [1927]. Very different tones are found in the less popular works by Gleason [1970] and O'Connor [1975].)

The basic political structure of Chicago has been the same throughout most of this century. As Gosnell (1937) showed in his classic study, the machine is built on the bedrock of ward captains who keep voters in line by rewarding and punishing them with city services and non-services.[5]

The thousands of workers in the machine are rewarded legally by giving them patronage and civil services jobs, generally on a "temporary" status so that they do not have to pass the ordinary exams. Daley's successful use of the temporary status was vital to building his organization:

> As Daley quickly proved, it was relatively easy to circumvent the job security system set up by the Kennelly administration; without disturbing the Civil Service ratings so precious to Kennelly, and so aggravating to the ward bosses, Daley resorted to

making temporary appointments of deserving precinct workers to better paying jobs. So long as those holding the temporary assignments behaved themselves and brought in the vote on election day, they had all the job security they needed. As death and retirement took their toll of ward superintendents and top-flight clerks at City Hall and in other coveted areas of the pay-roll, Daley's supply of positions to be filled on a "temporary" basis increased—his Civil Service Commission exhibiting a remarkable lack of interest in holding examinations to fill the vacancies. (O'Connor 1975:128-29.)

This temporary status is vitally important as well in maintaining machine discipline, because it permits the boss to dismiss party workers without following the almost impossible route of civil service procedures. A worker who steps out of line is let go (punished), whereas civil service status would protect him (Banfield and Wilson 1967:108) and, presumably, allow him to make stronger demands for personal benefits.

There is a major difference between Chicago and the popular conception of the traditional machine model: in Chicago a self-correcting mechanism tends to prevent massive payoffs within the city (Meyerson and Banfield 1961; Banfield and Wilson 1967). Popular conception has major parts of the machine coalition extorting vast payoffs as the price of continued support. For several reasons this has not yet happened in Chicago. One reason may be the personal strategies—Banfield and Wilson (1967:124-25) call it statesmanship—of the men who have been mayors. Another is a peculiar combination of the discipline inherent in the power of the machine leader, the nonpatronage status of most public employees, and the machine's increasing dependence on a coalition with the business and suburban vote.

The suburban-business interests have become necessary parts of Daley's machine because the inner city wards no longer have enough votes to elect him and vote fraud is no longer very practical. The machine mayoralty system thus combines discipline within the machine with a restraint on machine payoffs in order to provide "good government," which primarily means lower taxes and legality. Mayor Daley has summed up the need to provide clean government by remarking, "Good government is good politics." Some observers, such as Royko (1971) claim that the machine is paid off in addition by the willingness of the mayor and the rest of the machine to ignore lucrative ("Mafia") corruption such as gambling and other rackets. If so, it is a form of payoff that does not bankrupt the city.

The result of all this is a machine that does not depend on massive payoffs either to its constituent parts to hold them together or to its top leaders. It is thus a balanced coalition machine that runs a "tight ship." This model was probably common among machines that endured over long periods. (See, for example, Miller's [1968] discussion of the Cox machine in Cincinnati.)

In Chicago the big unions are a vital part of the machine:

> There is no city in the nation where the affinity between labor and government is closer than in Chicago. Daley is labor's man. From his first campaigns in 1955, the unions gave gobs of money to his election funds, the political action sections of both the AFL and CIO whipping up votes for him. In return, Daley has taken care of labor—appointing union chiefs to sensitive positions in his administration. (O'Connor 1975:135; also see Royko 1971:66-67).

A. H. Raskin (1972:123) has noted how Daley manipulates the union heads: "Unionization has not undermined Daley's influence over civil service employees. If anything, his bonds to the union leaders have heightened that influence. Even their battles with the Daley administration are sham battles, quickly settled on terms that bring little unhappiness to City Hall." Anderson (1972:38) has noted that the absence of legalized collective bargaining rights for the unions in Chicago led to informal granting of these powers to those unions strong enough to demand them—police, firemen, and teachers— which probably keeps the general municipal costs down in significant part at the expense of the weaker unions.

The powerful unions have certainly received large benefits, but not as large as those in New York and similar cities. The machine discipline is partially extended to leaders of the powerful unions. In general, the unions' costs are kept down largely by maintaining productivity and preventing the massive proliferation of hiring aimed at cutting work loads.

The overall effect has won the admiration even of liberal Democrats like Mayor Richard Hatcher of Gary, Indiana: "However well or poorly Mayor Daley may use his authority, the actions of America's last great political machine in Chicago demonstrate convincingly that patronage politics provides a way to get things done" (quoted in Raskin 1972:123). He should have noted that only *with discipline* can patronage politics encourage good work both for the machine and the public, and thereby prevent a fiscal hemorrhage such as occurred in New York at the hands of a weak substitute machine which, as we shall see, was forced to use ever greater payoffs to an escalating work force to hold together an alienated and distrustful electorate.

THE LINDSAY EXPERIENCE:
REFORM, RATIONALISM,
AND THE URBAN GÖTTERDÄMMERUNG

In 1965 John Lindsay was elected mayor of New York in the classic role of the reform politician opposing Tammany Hall machine politics. In his campaign it is interesting that he concentrated specifically on denouncing Mayor Wagner's budget deficit of $255 million, financed by selling short-term revenue anticipation bonds. (City comptroller Abraham Beame, himself a Democrat, also denounced Wagner's plan as "fiscally unsound" and an attack on the city's fiscal integrity [Gottehrer 1969].) He most especially denounced the "payoffs" Wagner had given his allies, the public employee unions.

Not having come up through the ranks of city politics, Lindsay lacked a gut understanding of coalitions. Such understanding as he had was based on rationalistic theories prevalent among academics of the day, especially those in schools of industrial relations, and on traditional Anglo-Saxon public morality. Even some academics who knew the politics involved supported his "systemic" approach to solving the city's problems (see Rogers 1971:56). Lindsay took a moralistic, rationalistic, even computerized view of the city's political dilemmas. His own statements about this as late as 1969 show clearly how he continued to look at the feudal conflicts of the city's many agencies as a problem that could be solved by "rational systematization" (see Lindsay 1969:81-87).

Lindsay and his advisers were convinced that the feudalistic structure of the city administration, with all its enfeudated and conflictful authorities, could be "rationalized" and that this would go far to solving its problems. They failed to see that the feudal structure resulted largely from the complex compromises required by the reality of the city's social structure, with its conflictful subcultures and groups. By focusing so much effort on this "rationalization drive," they avoided dealing with the real problems, inflamed the conflictful demands on the city and the struggle for power, and actually undermined political support that could have been vital in dealing with their biggest political problem—the public employee unions and the growing fiscal crisis.

The contrast between Robert Wagner's cautious, cunning, old-political approach to "governing" the city and John Lindsay's impatient, optimistic, swashbuckling, moralistic approach was startling. Knowing the labyrinthine realities from the inside and knowing the cunning jealousy with which every minuscule feudal lord fought to protect the independence of his domain, Wagner saw that without a powerful political coalition the only realistic role for a mayor was to settle disputes among the lords by marginal readjustments of benefits. Except for his move to consolidate negotiations with the labor unions—which was not catastrophic as long as negotiations were carried out with his personal feudal approach—Wagner more or less accepted the popular view that the city is "ungovernable" (Carter 1964), and adopted a "foxhole" strategy of minimizing costs which sought above all else to avoid conflict and preserve social order and social trust. Pursuing this approach, Wagner avoided inflammatory rhetoric and idealistic promises of utopian reforms.

Wagner's approach, like Mayor Daley's, gives at least silent recognition to the essential ingredients of social trust and order in a complex society. In such a society trust and order are a thin "membrane" of civilization stretched over intractable conflicts—a membrane that can easily be broken by a crusading, absolutist morality insensitive to its fragile structure. Moral crusades *within* a high pluralistic society—as opposed to popular crusades directed *outside*—can only result in internal warfare. And internal warfare can only be stopped by force (which no city authority has), or by massive payoffs to reconstruct a governing coalition.

Regardless of how well Wagner understood in the abstract the Burkian conservative strategy for a conflictful, pluralistic society, he acted that way. His motto appears to have been: "When in doubt, don't." Lindsay's implicit motto was the opposite: "Don't doubt, do something rational to produce sweeping changes." Barry Gottehrer (1969) has captured the contrast beautifully.

We noted that in Chicago Mayor Daley has held down city budgets through a cooperative system which paid employees well, but which controlled expansion of the work force. In New York Lindsay's idealistic rationalism exacerbated conflicts, thus creating tremendous demands for ever greater "services" referred to by local politicians as *"essential."*

Increasing services in New York tend to provide large subsidies for the middle class. One reason, as noted, is that new services usually result in large increases in the public work force—with large, commensurate increases in the public payroll. Since "services" are mostly provided by middle class people, increasing services is one way to buy loyalty from both their providers and recipients. The extent of New York City's bloated public work force may be indicated by a comparison with Chicago. Although whatever perceptible quality difference exists between them would seem to favor Chicago, in 1974 that city had only 352 employees per 10,000 population compared to New York's 528 per 10,000. A second form of payoff to the middle class occurs in programs such as the subsidies for the City University, which go either to people who are already middle class or who will be after graduation.

The middle class subsidies inherent in increased ("essential") services operate like a high-priced political payoff system which becomes necessary to replace the old machine. However, as the Lindsay experience demonstrates, the substitute "welfare-state machine" is an enormously expensive way to buy back social peace (for details see Douglas 1975).

Although there are obvious differences between them, Lindsay's experience in New York City reveals some fascinating parallels to that of Boss Tweed a hundred years earlier. It is often forgotten that Tweed, like Lindsay, presented himself as a "reform" politician who put together a powerful coalition of offices and interests in 1869 to overthrow the "corrupt" machine of Fernando Wood (Mandelbaum 1965). To hold together his coalition, Tweed pursued his motto of "something for everyone." A program which combined increased expenditures with reduced taxes soon strained the city budget, and Tweed resorted to funding the resulting deficits by short-term revenue anticipation bonds. The Tweed machine collapsed as the city came close to bankruptcy. Tweed, of course, did not have public unions to contend with—and they turned out to be Lindsay's largest problem.

Lindsay aggravated his problem by uniting the largest power bloc in the city, the public employee unions—by placing them in direct, rationalized negotiation with one agency—and thus deprived himself of any effective counterweight of political maneuvering. He had long recognized that "the plight of the cities is on the bargaining table." What he did not understand when he came into office was that this plight was a direct result of the complex political forces of the public employee unions and of the ancient feudal nature of urban politics. Most important of all, he did not realize how powerful the unions had become through the coalition formed during the Wagner years in order to present a united front to the city's negotiators. Conversely, he failed to realize how limited his own powers were as mayor of such a pluralistic and conflictful society, regardless of the relatively "strong mayor" system on its law books.

These failures of understanding led Lindsay to take actions actually decreasing his own power while simultaneously taking on the unions in direct confrontation. His attacks on Wagner's payoffs and his "Yalie" manner made union leaders personally angry and anxious to put him in his place (see Gotbaum's comments on "nobless oblige" [1972]). His crushing defeat in the transit strike two weeks after he took office apparently taught him that something had to be done about the public employee unions—whom he moralistically denounced as "power brokers."

In trying to contain the public unions, Lindsay could have tried to build a power base with the other major groups. But instead of following Wagner's path of trying to outwit the unions with political shrewdness and to use every device available to reduce their power and increase his own, he chose a fundamentally different course.

Ignoring the basic urban social problem, Lindsay "rationalized" the gamut of city and union relations by introducing whole new "structures" and "professionalized negotiation procedures." Toward this end he created the Office of Collective Bargaining, established the tripartite negotiation procedures, and hired a corps of professional negotiators. Once again he failed to see that rationalizing the process thereby introduced an adversary element into a process whose ultimate objective—in a setting of social conflict—was social trust and order. Lindsay merely shifted the business of coalition politics to the bargaining table—and wound up giving the unions even more power over the outcomes.

In his determination to rationalize official-union conflicts, Lindsay had Ida Klaus do the most thorough study ever done of public employee and official relations. She produced a clas-

sic statement of "employee democracy" which urged the city
to share power more rationally with the unions in order to get
better services: "Human nature is such that paternalism, no
matter how bounteous its gifts, may be of less real satisfaction
and advantage to both sides than the process of reasoning together around the family table, no matter how meager the
fare" (Raskin 1972:125). No one could deny the idealism of
this sentiment, but as Raymond Horton shows in Chapter XI,
no one can deny either that the settlements that came out of the
sentiment and its structural embodiments were a disaster.

The general analysis of what happened is simple enough.
The Lindsay administration sincerely pursued its policy of
rationalizing relations with the public employee unions, but
Horton (Chapter XI) notes that as the mayor's 1969 reelection
campaign approached, city-union relations became uncom-
monly friendly.

The union leaders looked at the bargaining table as *the pursuit of politics by other means*. They made certain that they
would not accept any rationalized structure of collective bargaining power which could not easily be worked to their benefit. In general, they did this by using their potential power to
get a collective bargaining system under which they retained
all the legal and extra-legal powers they started with and were
ceded new powers; then they continued the political struggle
within the new system while the Lindsay administration with-
drew its political forces from the battle scene.

Ironically, Lindsay's system for rationalizing relations with
the unions deprived him of one of the most potent weapons a
weak political administrator can have in dealing with powerful
employees—the weapon of stall and confusion. If the political
administrator is actually weak, his only effective strategy may
be to stall and confuse the demander by bogging him down in
labyrinthine and conflicting bureaucracies, making it hard for
opponents even to know who has the authority to pay them off.
At the extreme, such overlapping and confusing authority
even makes it possible to repudiate an earlier agreement if it
proves disastrous, on the grounds that the employer making it

lacked authority to do so.

Instead, Lindsay swept away all of the hedgerows behind which he could have hidden.

> In the field of labor relations there was no policy; labor relations were handled by the Budget Bureau on an ad hoc basis and there was no overall record of the more than two hundred separate contracts between the city and its public employees. Only with the establishment of our Office of Collective Bargaining did a systematic program begin to emerge. (Lindsay 1969:84.)

Lindsay thus made the process of demanding more from the city more efficient, speedy, and effective. This "rationalized" procedure vastly speeded up the payouts to the demanders, but as Lindsay's own budget director pointed out, it did so on the basis of pseudo-rational premises and data:

> Actuarial pension plans have typically [in the past] been set up and modified only after a careful and detailed examination of costs, benefits, actuarial and investment assumptions. On the other hand, pension provisions in the collective bargaining process have sometimes been resolved within a week or even a day. It is necessary to work with rough cost figures. The meaning of various provisions is often not totally clear to all parties. It was my experience as director of the budget that most such provisions have ultimately cost New York City more than the estimates at the time of bargaining. (Hayes 1972:95.)

Lindsay evidently did not realize that most official information being used was problematic (often *necessarily*) and even corruptible (see Douglas 1971: chapters 4 and 5). As a result, the new efficient administration wound up making hasty decisions that were mistakes. It is actually more rational to take three years to make a mistake than to do it in a few days, especially when the mistake leads to immediately increased spending in a city that is going bankrupt.

The unions responded to the mayor's "rational" process in predictable fashion. They turned the situation to their own advantage and won both the battle and the war. The major pension benefits, which have left the city with accrued deficits exceeding $6 billion in its pension funds and threaten its entire future (see Douglas 1975), were professionally, speedily negotiated through this "rationalized" structure.

CONCLUSION

Almost all of America's old industrial cities face a situation similar to the situation in New York. As a result, most have rapidly increased their tax rates to cope with a familiar pattern of deteriorating circumstances: eroding tax bases resulting from a declining middle class population, declining private sector employment, increasing welfare loads, and mounting financial obligations.

City officials facing this situation are often in an extremely weak position. They almost always are elected by shifting coalitions to an office often constrained by charter or constitution; they are limited in dealing with the bureaucracy by civil service rules that frequently gave the bureaucracies an effective veto power over most official policies long before powerful unions existed (Lowi 1967). They have also been weakened by the spread of nonpartisanship in urban government—including the shift to managerial "rationalized" systems—which largely deprives them of the power that comes from the party faithful; they face a public that has been increasingly alienated and distrustful of government politicians at all levels; and they are lucky to last a second term.

The mayor's own general powers have been steadily eroded, and the public employee unions have increased their monopolistic powers at an astonishing pace since the early 1960s. City officials themselves granted them group monopoly powers by legally preventing competition for public employees, in the totally mistaken belief that "economies of scale" realized by monopolies would produce better and cheaper service. Individual members received legal "entitlements" to their jobs by civil service regulations, so the officials could not discipline them. The unions benefited from the residue of public sympathy to unions and, above all, from the legal monopolistic powers already granted to private sector unions. The public unions found in the 1960s that officials were powerless to enforce laws against strikes, and they were able to reach an *entente cordiale* among themselves to prevent inter-union competition and to amplify the power of all by coordinating efforts. Through these means, public employee unions found they could manipulate and dominate collective bargaining and thereby greatly increase their power.

City leaders faced with this situation have two basic options open to them. The older method, mastered by Mayor Daley and the City of Chicago, involves a system of close cooperation between the unions and City Hall. If there is no collective bargaining in Chicago, it is because to a very real extent the unions are *participants* in city government, and wage decisions are made in consultation with union leaders, not by "bargaining" with them in the adversary setting that the arm's-length connotation of the word involves. I do not mean to argue that this system is without its faults. But it does preserve labor peace, it does maintain a high degree of social trust and order, and it does ensure high-quality city services at a price the city can afford.

The other option open to city officials is symbolized by John Lindsay's tenure in New York. The results of the "reform model" are rather clear from New York City's experience. When a weak mayor—that is, one without great formal power and authority—in a highly pluralistic and conflictful city purposefully pursues the "politics of disintegration" (Lowi 1964:224), or decentralizes and "rationalizes" his few powers by vesting them in partially independent boards and committees and by insisting on treating political issues "idealistically" and rationalistically, he tends to destroy the fine fabric of trust among the conflicting groups.

The inevitable result of the second approach is to guarantee the necessity of a massive payoff system to maintain some semblance of order. The present state of New York City, courting financial ruin, stands as a monument to the effects of moralism and rationalism in urban politics. Unfortunately, the indications are that both moralizing and rationalizing are, if anything, increasing their hold on public sector labor relations.

VII

EQUITY AND EQUALITY IN PUBLIC WAGE POLICY

SEYMOUR MARTIN LIPSET
Professor of Political Science and Sociology, Stanford University
Senior Fellow, Hoover Institution on War, Revolution and Peace

Equality and achievement in public wage policy. The communist countries. Soviet Union. Admission to higher education. Income levels and attitudes toward equality. Mainland China. Western welfare-planning states: Sweden and Israel. Trade union policy and government employment in the U.S. The vulnerability of governments. Units of equity. Equality and equity in higher education. Conclusions.

Rising government ownership and planning of economic activity, often involving the setting of wages, have made the general issue of equality and equity a matter of public debate and democratic policy. The very expansion in public ownership and control, which is maximized in Communist countries, reflects the increasing influence of equality as a social end. In Communist countries it is the ultimate ideal.

The goal of equality as a public objective did not, however, originate with Karl Marx or with the socialists of modern industrial society, but was first discussed by the ancient Greeks, particularly Plato and Aristotle. Approaching modern times

Alexis de Tocqueville, the great student of American democracy and of equality in general, contended that once the idea of equality came into the world, it would be irresistible; that the great majority of the population, who were less privileged, would impose their commitment to equality on the social order.

For most Americans through much of U. S. history the concept of equality meant equality of opportunity—that everyone should have an equal chance to earn an unequal reward. However, the logic sustaining equal opportunity has led many people back to equal results; for as long as children are raised in unequal conditions, they will begin and end unequally.

The increasing commitment to equality of condition in most Western countries conflicts with the achievement emphases traditionally associated with a free market system. The latter are premised on the need for unequal rewards to motivate people to perform adequately in the different roles required by a highly differentiated society.

The tension between these two values—equality and achievement—is implicit in the title of a recent book by the Brookings economist Arthur Okun (1975)—*Equality and Efficiency: The Big Tradeoff* (See also Lipset 1963.) Okun, like most economists concerned with the issue of inequality, assumes that a certain degree of inequality is necessary to motivate people. The same argument is made by the functionalist school of sociology (Lipset 1968, 1976).[1] Functionalists and most economists assume that the variety of positions to be filled in societies differ greatly in their requirements for skill, education, intelligence, commitment to work, willingness to exercise power resources, and the like. These theories assume that differential rewards for varying jobs is society's mechanism for encouraging the most able people to perform the most demanding roles so that society can operate efficiently.

Although Okun recognizes that efficiency requires some inequality, he and a variety of sociologists such as Melvin Tumin (1966) argue that the present distribution of reward in

American society and the West generally is much more unequal than is necessary to motivate people.

The issues of equity and equality—especially of the tension
between increasing demands for equality and the competing
importance to both equity and social efficiency of differential
rewards—are evident in the rising conflict in public sector
labor relations. The pressure for equality from public employee unions is evident enough, but as Theodore Kheel notes
in his discussion of the 1966 New York City transit strike
(Chapter I), the problems of equity and appropriate differentials also frequently appear as important themes in public labor
disputes.

The conflict between equity and equality appears in surprisingly different economic, political and cultural settings. To
understand these issues as they underlie current public sector
labor unrest, as well as how they may influence the future
course of public wage policy, we would do well to examine
how the conflict between these two values has been resolved in
different contexts both in the United States and abroad.

COMMUNIST SOCIETIES

Given the absence of free politics and free markets in Communist countries it is impossible to know to what extent a
struggle to secure greater equality goes on in these countries.
Although comparisons are difficult, efforts to gauge the variations in income and prestige of different occupations suggest
that the range among them is quite similar to that in some
Western countries, including the United States.[2]

It is interesting to note that Soviet social scientists have
come up with interpretations explaining widespread differences in salaries in the Soviet Union that are almost identical
to those of Western social scientists. Thus the Soviet analyst,
G. V. Maltzev (1974) contends that in a socialist society "the
idea of equality has never meant an endeavor to make everyone alike. The artificial equalization of incomes and other
measures aimed at leveling the social and legal status of indi-

viduals have nothing in common with such a society." Maltzev goes on to argue that anti-Communists libel the Soviet
system when they argue that it seeks to negate "all personal
initiative, therefore depriving man of the right to become
rich." He points out that "the distributive practice of socialism
is based on the continuous growth of personal income and social wealth. Socialism encourages high incomes and does not
deny the right to show personal initiative."

Another Soviet scholar, L. F. Liss (1973), notes that the
variation in prestige and other rewards given to elite occupations is determined by "societal needs." He argues, in language reminiscent of Western functional sociologists, the
necessity for a system "of competitive selection of the most
deserving, prepared and capable individuals" who are differentially rewarded.

In effect, Soviet scholars explain inequality in terms almost
identical to those of Western scholars. Both argue that inequality of reward is necessary for an efficient economic system and
social order. The Communist writers presumably believe this
will be true only until the era of abundance is reached which
Marx foresaw as a precondition for Communism.

Admission to Higher Education

Perhaps the most interesting evidence concerning the pressures for inequality and in a reverse sense for equality in the
Communist countries pertains to the consequences of different
policies for admission to higher education. The great desire to
get into a university reflects the importance of educational at-
tainment to upward mobility (or simply job placement) in a
state in which all industry and occupations are governmental
and there is little room for independent entrepreneurship.

To one extent or another, arguments over admission
policies have occurred in almost all Communist countries,
from the Soviet Union to Yugoslavia. Basically, the available
data indicate that, as in the West, the children of the better
educated and the privileged have a considerable advantage in

winning admission to higher education. Detailed studies by
social scientists in the European Communist countries show
high correlations between family social background—parental
education, income, number of rooms—and grades achieved.
In many Communist countries, particularly the Soviet Union,
many more students seek admission to higher education than
there are places for them. The reason is that young people are
allowed to continue through high school if they have the desire
and presumably some aptitude. The Communists, however,
have not expanded higher education to keep up with demands
for entrance and as a result, in a number of countries, the ratio
of high school graduates to available places in higher education increases from year to year.

The increasing competition and pressure on young people to
get into a university has had the effect of encouraging a variety
of legal and illegal methods to facilitate admission. Private
coaching schools charging stiff fees prepare students for university entrance examinations. Soviet authorities repeatedly
discover successful organized rings which collect bribes from
applicants or their families to get them into the university. For
these and other reasons, in an open competitive system in
which people are admitted according to the grades they receive
in high school or achievement test scores, the proportion coming from privileged background steadily grows.

During the Khrushchev era an attempt was made to modify
this situation in the Soviet Union by setting up quotas for students from worker and peasant backgrounds or who had
worked in manual jobs for two years before applying. This
policy was opposed and dropped after Khrushchev was de-
posed (Lipset and Dobson 1973:164-69). Issues arising from
similar phenomena have been discussed in Yugoslavia and
China (Wachtel 1973:75; Goodstat 1973:192-99; Wheelwright
and McFarlane 1970:108-11, 173-77).

Income Levels and Attitudes toward Equality

Other evidence of attitudes toward equality in Communist
countries is indicated from public opinion surveys taken some

years ago in Poland, which revealed that the less privileged people were, the more likely they were to feel that the income differences should be narrow. Conversely, however, the more privileged individuals, those with university educations who were working in professional positions, felt that the income range was too narrow. Polish sociologist Andrzej Malewski reported (Labedz 1959:10) that, at the extremes, 54 percent of the Polish workers interviewed favored "relatively equal incomes," as contrasted with 20 percent of the executives. Fifty-five percent of the latter were strongly against sharply narrowing the income gap, as compared with only 8 percent of the manual workers (Labedz 1959:10; Wesolowski and Slomozynski 1969:206-8).

Further evidence of the strong correlation between income and attitude toward income differentials has been reported from Czechoslovakia, where a group of social scientists openly advocated increases in inequality to encourage economic growth (Richta et al. 1968). The same tendencies are also evident in Yugoslavia, the freest of the Communist countries (Wachtel 1973:107-11; on wage differentials increasing in Yugoslavia and Czechoslavv-vvavakia following liberal reforms, see Parkin 1972:173, 178).[3]

Equality and Inequality in China

Much of the turmoil in China revolves around issues of equality and inequality. Seemingly Chairman Mao and others defined as left-wingers in the Communist party are concerned with fostering equality, with preventing the growth of a dominant bureaucratic upper stratum such as exists in the European Communist countries. Mao's great fear, however, appears to be that once he is gone, the tendencies of those in privileged positions will be to institutionalize these privileges, to secure economic rewards, to make higher education more accessible to those coming from the best educated families, and to extend these privileges much as they have been in the Soviet Union.

Before the Cultural Revolution of the second half of the

1960s revived the emphasis on egalitarianism, Mao frequently agreed with the need for a differentiated wage policy. In order to "stimulate production," he advocated "a system of individual bonuses, graded according to the quality of the work." He defended the differences in income between the country and the city on the grounds that "the productivity of the workers is much higher than that of the peasants" (Goodstadt 1973:88-89). In 1961 *The People's Daily,* the organ of the Chinese Communist Party, editorialized: "The more precisely a man's output is reflected in his wages, the more material interest will persuade him to take greater interest in what he produces, and in his own productivity and efficiency" (Goodstadt 1973:132). An article in the paper the same year defended inequality by reiterating Marx's analysis that communism and equality of condition could only occur under conditions of abundance, and that inequality necessarily followed from economic scarcity. The author argued that "China must remain a 'pre-communist' society as long as material shortages prevailed" (Goodstadt 1973:135).

With the advent of the Cultural Revolution, the Maoist line has reemphasized egalitarianism in wage policy and the abolition of income differences between country and city. The head of the state, Liu Shao-chi, was the villain of the Cultural Revolution; he was denounced repeatedly for emphasizing "material incentives" and differentiated wages (Goodstadt 1973:153). Moral incentives are to replace material ones (Wheelwright and McFarlane 1970:141).

But in spite of much propaganda to the contrary, ideological rejection of inequality has not been followed by anything close to wage equality. A comprehensive study of the Chinese industrial wage system notes that continuity in effective policy, rather than major changes in tandem with ideological shifts, has characterized the wage system from 1952 to the present. From the start of their regime, the Chinese Communists have stratified urban occupations in wage grades, eight within industry and many more in government and professional employment. This pattern has continued since the Cultural Revolution. "In particular, most [recent foreign] visitors found eight grades systems for production workers which were very similar to or identical with those described by earlier sources" (Schran 1974:1029). Peter Schran concludes (p. 1031): "In summary, it appears that the wages system in the state operated sector of industry in China has changed very little from its inception during the 1950s until present times— in spite of recurring efforts to promote a more rapid transition to communism."

Following his 1973 visit to China, Doak Barnett pointed out the extent of current variations, when he noted the existence of "surprising and significant income differentials, despite the extraordinary stress that the regime has placed upon egalitarianism. Incomes at the top are as much as fifteen to twenty times those at the bottom" (Barnett 1973:103-4; Watson 1972:149; Teiwes 1974:337-38; Prybyla 1975:266-78).

Similar policies appear to exist for the rural economy as well. There,

> piecework rates are used. Work points, as before the Cultural Revolution, are determined according to the amount of work done. . . . Finally, while bonuses do not exist in the countryside, in a sense continued cultivation of private plots at pre-Cultural Revolution levels (roughly 7 to 8 percent of a commune's sown area) provides a functional equivalent. Here the peasant can gain material rewards in return for additional labour and ingenuity. Overall, changes in the remuneration system in the countryside since 1965 appear marginal. (Teiwes 1974:338.)

WESTERN WELFARE PLANNING STATES

Socialist and other egalitarian doctrines have made considerable headway in all Western countries. One result is that the incomes of a large sector of the population are now determined by state policy either through legislation or through collective bargaining for state employees. Thus, general issues of equity with respect to the rewards for different occupations have become a matter of public policy and debate in the West as well as the East. Because Western countries are democratic and have competition of parties and free trade unions with the right to strike, arguments about equity and equality form a key part of their political and economic conflicts.

In most countries class-linked conflict reflects the different views about income equity comparable to those in the Polish public opinion surveys discussed earlier. The unions and the parties supported by manual workers favor narrowing the income gap between the more-lowly, less-skilled occupations and the more highly skilled, well-educated professional ones. Unions generally are opposed to merit increases, not only for egalitarian reasons, but also because they give employers and supervisors power to discriminate among workers. Income equality policies, on the other hand, offend the sense of equity of the highly educated strata. These tendencies can be seen most strikingly in countries like Sweden and Israel where Social Democratic parties have ruled for many decades and where powerful socialist trade unions and cooperatives play an important role in the economy.

The Swedish Situation

In many ways the situation in Sweden presents a prototype of the problems of dealing with wages and equality in a Western social democratic society. Sweden has had a socialist or social democratic government since the early 1930s. Although the proportion of industry owned by the government is relatively small—6 percent, with another 4 percent in the hands of cooperatives—the government follows a policy of "functional socialism." This includes intervention in the economy, as well as commitment to a broad welfare state program. The labor force is highly organized, with approximately 90 percent belonging to unions, as compared to some 28 percent in the United States (Adler-Karlsson 1970:9-28).

The big issue in Sweden concerns wage equalization. The LO unions—representing manual workers—seek to narrow

the differences in income received between skilled and unskilled workers, and also to reduce differences among manual
workers, white-collar employees, and professionals (Johnston
1962:33-34, 267-78; Wheeler 1975:35).

During the 1940s there was "a general compression of the
earnings structure," with the least paid improving most, while
wages paid to public service employees and salaried employees generally declined. In the 1950s the white-collar and
professional confederations (TCO and SACO) grew considerably, and resisted these tendencies while seeking to maintain
or restore "traditional differentials over manual workers."
SACO has sought to justify differentials by emphasizing "the
importance of reimbursement to university-educated persons
for the cost of the training they undergo" (Johnston 1962:
304-5, 278). The TCO has made similar arguments (Wheeler
1975:35).

The LO and the Social Democratic movement generally
remain committed to narrowing wage and income differentials. In practice, however, the LO has increasingly accepted
the continuation of wage differentials. Its main concern since
the 1950s has been "with making the wage structure more
equitable in the sense that it is more *rational,* the criteria for
this being derived from job requirements." It also favors
across-the-board raises of the same amount to all, rather than
percentage increases.

Swedish tax policies are also designed to equalize incomes.
Most of the members of the professionals' federation, for example, are in an 80-90 percent tax bracket, which means that
they require a 10 percent gross increase in income to achieve a
1.5-2.0 percent net. SACO has insisted without success that
the raises negotiated for high-salaried professionals should be
designed to maintain their relative income position as national
productivity, the supposed basis for wage increases, rises
(Wheeler 1975:36).

The SACO unions and the Federation of Government Employees (SR) have occasionally gone on strike "in opposition
to Socialist efforts to promote egalitarian policies" (Hancock

1972:276). Perhaps more important, some well-educated professionals have emigrated, and many more refuse to work full time, as they find it would cost them more in taxes than they can earn. The resistance to income equalization also takes illegal forms. Thus the Swedish government estimates that it "loses $3 billion annually from . . . tax cheating—a sizable dent out of the state's annual budget of $22 billion."[4]

There is considerable evidence from public opinion polls and other sources that many professional people are quite unhappy about their situation in Sweden. A study of the opinions of university faculty shows that the large majority of the members support the non-socialist parties (Gras 1972:68-71). The Conservatives, in fact, are quite strong among academics. Such support for "bourgeois" parties is hardly typical among professors in most Western countries and Japan.

Israeli Socialism

Unlike Sweden, in Israel many professional employees belong to unions which are affiliated to the dominant manual labor federation, the Histadruth, although professors, lawyers, and a number of others do not. Almost all employed persons are members of unions, together with some self-employed. Sixty percent of the *entire population* belong to the Histadruth (Lowenberg 1973:249-56; Zweig 1970:162-84). By comparative world standards, Israel ranks among the most equalitarian of nations (Pack 1973:175-99; Kravis 1973:61-80).

In their efforts to maintain "the slight income differential which separates them from the bulk of white-collar workers," the professional unions, whether affiliated to the Histadruth or not, formed a committee for united action soon after the creation of the state. The committee resists government "attempts to create a unified wages and salaries policy." It supports "formal status differences within the various professions according to the level of training and specialization (Ben David 1970:213-14).

Israeli academics, like their Swedish counterparts, oppose

the dominant Labor parties. A survey of the faculty of Tel
Aviv University in 1970 indicates that only 19 percent of its
members supported left or socialist groups. The overwhelming
majority, 74 percent, were for liberal, anti-statist parties,
rather than the more populist nationalist right. As Eli Ben
Rafael notes (1976:263-65), Israeli academe is characterized
by "political liberalism [in the European sense] and professional elitism." No wonder, therefore, that the faculty unions
which are highly supported by their rank and file are not affiliated with the general federation of labor.

Professional employees working for the government and
even for private industry have shown their resentment toward
egalitarian policies by repeatedly going on strike. In many
ways the Israeli professionals are more militant than the manual workers. In recent years there have been strikes by professors, television staff, airline pilots, and physicians. Through
these strikes, professionals have tried to widen the income
gap, to break away from policies which have linked their
salaries to patterns set by manual workers.

The upper middle class occupations which have been most
militant in Israel are those which are more likely to have an
international frame of reference. Israeli professors, for example, are in steady contact with academics in other countries.
The same is true of physicians, airline pilots, and the highly
educated middle class in general. The Israeli upper middle
class, particularly the educated professionals, are torn between
accepting the need for egalitarianism in a Spartan besieged
state, and resenting their low standard of living as compared to
the way of life for people in their situation abroad. An international frame of reference has the effect of leading some,
perhaps many, to move to other countries for short or longer
periods of time. Hundreds of thousands of Israelis now live in
the U.S. and Canada.

The Israeli Laborite political establishment is consequently
pressed to do something about widening the income gap. One
solution has been the creation of "dirty" forms of tax avoidance. With the official connivance of the government and tax

authorities, special tax deals are arranged in negotiations with the government which provide for nontaxable forms of income, defined as payments for professional expenses. The academic community, for example, is allowed a variety of such benefits, including substantial allowance for books, for use of telephone at home, for automobile travel within the country, for travel abroad, a thirteenth month's pay for marking exams, and others. Engineers, in shorter supply than academics, have been given even more liberal tax advantages or extra benefits. Such forms of "dirty" pay are not limited to the middle class. Manual workers with strong unions such as longshoremen also receive extensive nontaxable benefits.

Progressive income tax rates permit governments to appear to support greater equality of result, and so curry favor with the more egalitarian segments of the electorate. But by permitting tax avoidance, they enable some who are hit hardest by the taxes to recoup their position to some degree. Those who are self-employed are, of course, in the best position to avoid high taxes and even to evade them illegally.

TRADE UNION WAGE POLICY AND GOVERNMENT EMPLOYMENT IN THE UNITED STATES

The Vulnerability of Governments

In mixed Western economies, concepts of equality and equity affect the demands of unions. Economists now recognize that the prevailing sense of equity often overrides market forces in determining what labor organizations will accept. Arthur Ross (1948:49-50) pointed out some time ago that "comparisons play a large and often dominant role as a standard of equity in the determination of wages under collective bargaining" (Ross 1948:26). Bok and Dunlop (1970:109, 224-25) also emphasize the political pressures operating within the unions which press for a common standard:

> As union members become aware of conditions in other plants, they are likely to protest if they receive lower wages and benefits than members doing similar work elsewhere. As a political institution, the union is sensitive to pressures of this kind. Hence, the desire for "equity" often reinforces competition as a force for standardizing wages and benefits. In fact, the demand for equity may even lead to uniform wages and conditions among firms that are not actually competing with one another.

Several factors have encouraged the labor movement to use government salaries and wage policies as a pacesetter. One factor is the increase in government employment in widely disparate fields. Second, for a number of reasons elaborated by Wellington and Winter in Chapter IV, the government as employer is more vulnerable to union pressure than is private enterprise. To comprehend the reasons for this vulnerability, it is important to understand a basic difference between private and public bargaining. Strikes against private firms apply economic pressure, while labor stoppages in public institutions are directed not at the employer's income, but at his political support. Politicians who set policy must seek the votes both of workers and of the consumers of public goods and services.[5] Because there tend to be few practical substitutes for them, demand for public goods and services often tends to be inelastic, and the public's resulting reluctance to endure prolonged public employee strikes weakens the bargaining power of governmental units. These and other factors almost invariably result in a steady upward pressure on wages and other benefits.

The past willingness of governments to agree to higher wages and improved working conditions, presumably because of politically relevant factors and values, appears to have resulted in higher standards in nonunionized as well as unionized sectors of public employment. Perloff, in a comparison of nine occupations in eleven American cities, found that in nine of the cities those employed in the public sector generally received more than those in the private sector. The occupations surveyed included nonunion jobs such as accounting clerks, computer programmers, keypunch operators, payroll clerks, and stenographers, and unionized crafts such as carpenters, electricians, printers, and plumbers (Perloff 1971:46-50).

Wages for public employees should vary with the political climate of the community, the relative strength of the incumbent administration, and the overall lobbying-pressure group power of the labor movement as a whole. Since union political influence is maximized in central cities and in industrial states, such units should be relatively liberal in their wage policies.

Units of Equity

Unions seek to capitalize on equity sentiments. To do so requires finding appropriate units of comparison, to create a "sense of pertinent similarity," so that the comparisons will engender sentiments supporting a union's demands. In general, the size and scope of an employment structure influence wage rates by directing the attention of its participants towards making certain comparisons. The common ownership of multiple employing units creates for union members and leaders units of comparison, or frames of reference, quite different from those which operate under conditions of widespread variation of ownership. In an earlier work discussing determinants of trade union wage policy, Martin Trow and I (1957:396) suggested three relevant propositions.

> (1) Individuals or groups who are subordinate to the *same* authority are more likely to use each other as reference groups, than if the reverse were true.
>
> (2) Workers in a large "membership" structure are likely to use abstract status reference groups, such as class and steel workers. Workers in smaller membership structures are more likely to use face to face relationships such as bench-mates and neighbors as their reference groups.
>
> (3) Workers who see *structural elements as general status categories* are likely to use these categories as reference groups.

> For example, workers are more likely to become incensed over
> wage differentials between the plants of one company than they
> are over the same differentials between different companies.

Government is clearly the largest single employer in modern society, dwarfing all private firms. Those employed in the public sector, therefore, are likely to see comparisons with the rewards of other government employees as legitimate. Such comparisons for wage policy are enhanced by a presumably widely held and diffusely defined norm or value prescribing "impartiality of treatment by government" (Ross 1948:57). A number of governmental units have formally been obligated by law to pay the "prevailing wage" for a given job, or wages comparable to the highest paid in other supposedly similar governmental jurisdictions.

Public service unions will look for optimum comparisons within the government sector, either in their own political unit, or in other states and cities, or in the private sector with similar jobs. Obviously, there is no objective way to determine what is comparable work. For example, is there cause for parity between firefighters and policemen? Are they subject to the same insecurities, dangers, hours, or skill training requirements? Examination of union literature reveals a steady hunt for favorable units of comparison. When conveyed to their members, the pay scales become new standards of equity for their jobs. Some of these points may be illustrated by reference to developments in higher education, a field which has moved from almost no union representation in 1968 to the point where the faculties at over four hundred campuses are represented by collective bargaining agents, more than 90 percent of whom are in publicly supported schools.

Equality and Equity in Higher Education

The pressures for upgrading the bottom are maximized where the employer and the union are the same. Thus the recent wave of unionism in public sector universities has brought about efforts to pay comparable wages to faculty in different units of multi-campus state universities. One faculty leader of the American Federation of Teachers has proposed a general policy to be applied in all schools of a "professional salary schedule ranging from $10,000 to $30,000 to be attained in a reasonable number of steps by all faculty members in annual increments with a change in title upon reaching the maximum rank" (Kugler 1969:184). In the first unionized major institution, the City University of New York (CUNY), the initial contract resulted in parity between faculty at the two-year community colleges and the five-year schools, with the junior-college full professors jumping from the previous high of $21,950 to the new high of $31,275 (Margolin 1969). The increase in the maxima for junior college professors was more than twice that secured by those in the senior institutions. As a result, two of the CUNY two-year schools are now among the top twenty institutions in the United States, as judged by the average compensation received by their faculty according to the AAUP reports. Comparable developments occurred in the State University of New York following unionization. In the first comprehensive contract in 1972, the lower-paid and less-statused nonteaching professionals, who are included in the faculty union, received a higher general increase than the teaching faculty (Garbarino 1973; Kemerer and Baldridge 1975:73-77).

The opposition of labor groups to both individual bargaining and merit increases for superior work or skills illustrates the emphasis on equal treatment inherent in unionism. Justice Robert Jackson emphasized this aspect almost three decades ago:

> The practice and philosophy of collective bargaining looks with suspicion on . . . individual bargaining. . . . The workman is free, if he values his own bargaining position more than that of the group, to vote against representation; but the majority rules, and if it collectivizes the employment bargain, individual advantages or favors will generally in practice go in as a contribution to the collective result. (Cited in Wollett 1971:18-19.)

This principle not only has been emphasized in contracts covering manual workers; it has also been applied to professionals such as college professors. A review of the situation in unionized universities concludes:

> bargaining agreements tend to substitute the "objective" standards of seniority and time in rank for the principle of merit. . . . The argument is that faculty members of equal rank and longevity are entitled to equal pay. While a few clauses are found which allow for merit raises above and beyond the minimum salaries provided for by the contract, pressure upon the administration to abide by the scale may inhibit the free distribution of merit increments. (Mortimer and Lozier 1972:27; see also Kemerer and Baldridge 1975:128-29.)

An example of this opposition took place in the California University and State College system, the largest single multicampus university outside of New York. In 1972 the Board of Trustees announced that it had a limited amount of uncommitted salary funds and wished to allocate them through merit raises. The two largest national faculty unions, the NEA and the AFT, opposed distributing the money on the basis of merit, and successfully convinced the state Department of Finance (the deciding body) to require the same general percentage increase for all faculty. The United Professors of California, the AFT unit in the system, asserted that the trustees had four methods of allocating the money—either differentially, by merit or by lot, by seniority or by an across-the-board raise. In their brief to the trustees, the UPC noted that there was not enough money to fund their preference, which was a significant across-the-board raise, so while they preferred seniority, they were willing to distribute the money by lot. The UPC stated its complete opposition to any form of merit raises and presented its case in the following terms:

> UPC's plan . . . rejects merit evaluation as a condition of advancement from one step within a rank to the next higher step. If a faculty member is adjudged good enough to be retained, he

is good enough to merit a 5% salary increase. . . . We see no reason why some step 5 Assistant Professors are denied a step increase. . . .

Similarly, UPC rejects merit in moving Associate Professors 5's to step 6. If they are good enough to keep, they are good enough to be rewarded for their additional experience with more pay. Since there is not enough money for all step 5 Associate Professors to receive a step increase, *the choice should be on some non-invidious basis, either seniority or by lot. Of the two possibilities, seniority seems preferable.*[6] [Emphasis added]

A primary characteristic of professions has been their view of the so-called "replaceability factor." Doctors, lawyers, actors, artists, or scholars are not viewed as readily interchangeable by anyone else with the same basic training and adequate performance record. The range of quality which affects the hiring, pay, and retention of professionals is assumed to be quite different from that existing among manual workers or semi-professionals such as nurses or public school teachers.

The egalitarian norms of unionism, which imply that every qualified worker in comparable occupations should be treated like every other one, clash with these meritocratic emphases. As we have seen in the case of faculty union opposition to merit increases, professional unions try to reduce or eliminate the power of management to differentially reward employees. This emphasis appears also with respect to the issue of job security, or as it is termed in professional fields, tenure. Unions seek to have new appointments defined as "probationary," which implies a claim to permanency for anyone who demonstrates that he or she meets a minimum performance standard. In the case of academe, this means rejecting the assumption which has existed among the research oriented institutions, that scholars not be awarded lifetime tenure until after a period of some years, during which they have demonstrated their competence to be significant contributors to the world of scholarship or art on the basis of competitive evaluation.

Professorial unions, largely based on the two- or four-year undergraduate teaching colleges, reject the competitive basis of evaluation of scholars with others not at the institution who might replace the candidate. As in industry, they insist that once appointed, a person should have a superior claim to a permanent position, even if a more able person should subsequently appear. In academe, faculty unions object to efforts by universities to maintain tenure quotas, that is, to limit the proportion who may gain tenure, in order to keep institutions open to new talent (Kemerer and Baldridge 1975:125-33).[7]

In response to these emphases, David Riesman reports "the impression that procedures for assessment of faculty for tenure, and for the handling of grievances make it extremely difficult, at times, nearly impossible, to raise the level of faculty quality" (Riesman 1975).

As indicated earlier, faculty unionism is largely a phenomenon of the public sector. Some students of unionization in higher education have suggested that the creation of two sectors, a public unionized one and a private unorganized one, will lead to a situation in which "private colleges and universities might be able to far outstrip their distinguished public competitors, once unionization has embraced the latter" (Reisman 1975:427).

The current period of increased budget difficulties for universities which has occurred during the 1970s will be followed in the 1980s by a reduced college age cohort as a result of the sharp decline in the birthrate in the 1960s. This fact has led many of the leading private universities to place an even greater emphasis than before on scholarly excellence, evaluated in a highly competitive context, as a requirement for tenure. From Stanford to Yale, administrators of such institutions have announced that the percentage of junior faculty who may expect to be promoted to a tenure position has been reduced sharply. In the absence of any faculty union, such proposals have met with little or no faculty opposition. Conversely, administrative proposals to tighten tenure granting procedures, to increase emphasis on merit in promotions, or to reduce the proportions gaining tenure, have been met with strong and sometimes successful resistance from faculty unions at schools such as the City University of New York, the California State University and Colleges System, and the University of California (Ladd and Lipset 1973:72-81).

Although the story of collective bargaining in higher education has hardly begun, perhaps the most interesting and significant part of it thus far is the fact that the egalitarian principles developed over many generations in "blue-collar" unionism have been successfully transferred to parts of academe, in spite of the enormous difference in structure and role.

CONCLUSIONS

Over time it seems likely we will see continuing struggles among people who work for wages or salaries over issues of equity and equality. Those with an historic claim to higher status and income, including the better trained, will defend or extend the arguments for meritocracy, while the less skilled will emphasize equality. Unions seem likely to continue pressing to narrow existing gaps in wages and working conditions. The American tradition has favored meritocracy and has stressed opportunity for those who are more able; but it is clear that this emphasis is changing.

While the emphasis on equality is increasing, our discussion may help indicate the effective boundaries of any public policies aimed at securing equality of condition. For it is clear in societies as different as the USSR and the United States that inequality and stratification persist. In societies of all political and economic systems there is a correlation between family socioeconomic background—the place in which individuals begin the race for success—and their ultimate position. Even in societies dedicated to ultimate equality of result, such as the Soviet Union and China, it is evident that substantial inequality continues to dominate public wage policy.

The principal argument against equality with respect to university admission policies and to societal rewards is that of social efficiency. This emphasis is particularly strong, as we have noted, in the Communist countries, including China (Wachtel 1973:185-86).[8] The argument is not likely to have much political weight among leftists in Western societies, however, since the notion that individual rights should be sacrificed for collective benefits is not accepted in these countries.

A second, evasive pattern seems to emerge in societies emphasizing greater equality of result, one which is likely to appear with increasing frequency in Western countries as such pressures advance. Because overt resistance to egalitarian changes is difficult, supporters of inequality will probably continue to wage what is in essence a behind-the-scenes battle using what the Israelis correctly describe as "dirty" methods. The situation presses people to evade the rules in order to secure those advantages that their situation in society and their sense of equity dictates they should get. We must expect, therefore, to see a great deal of evasion and avoidance of official regulations with respect to income and rewards, as well as with access to those institutions which place people on the road to "success." The Communist societies, which are characterized by high levels of illegal or "gray" methods of achievement in state institutions, may point the way to future comparable trends in Western societies.

The tension between equity and equality dominates public wage policy in every sphere of public sector labor relations; and perhaps the major challenge to policymakers dealing with public employee unions and mounting public sector labor unrest will be to maintain an uneasy accommodation between these two values.

VIII

PUBLIC EMPLOYEE COMPENSATION LEVELS

DANIEL ORR
Professor of Economics, University of California, San Diego

Past compensation levels. Private sector collective bargaining: effect on earnings. Potential consequences of public sector bargaining. Measured effects 1950-1974. Public-private wage differentials. Why public employees make more.

LOOKING BACK

In the job market of the 1950s government or civil service employment was portrayed as a career for somebody content to do routine work and careful to avoid mistakes. The appeal of the calling lay in the elements of predictability, security, and fair if unspectacular compensation. Salaries in the U.S. civil service were somewhat lower than one could earn in a private corporation, but benefit plans—especially retirement and vacations—were much more attractive. And the element of security was indeed present. Through the Eisenhower administrations the federal government had not yet grown used to the giddy pleasures of peacetime deficit finance; and as a

131

consequence an occasional "rif" (reduction in force) was not unknown in some bureaus or agencies. But the civil servant who had been laid off had priority on job openings in other bureaus; and in a job market where many had memories of the 1930s, the civil service exemplified a high degree of freedom from risk.

Federal employment, while appealing to those among the most talented and highly trained, typified the character of government employment relative to the private alternative. There are, of course, very different kinds of jobs in government, such as police and fire fighting, which embody risk or adventure. But the characteristics of unspectacular compensation with a high degree of security dominated in state and local work as well.

About 1966 the average value of government worker compensation began a steady rise relative to compensation in private employment. Legislation was passed in many states authorizing collective bargaining for government workers; a decade earlier, unions had been formed for federal employees. Increasingly, public employees—including such sensitive job classes as teachers, sanitation workers, firefighters, hospital workers, and police—resorted to the strike. The trend has been an acceleration in the growth of public employee unions and the extension of bargaining rights, with *de facto* threat of strike, into many new locales and many new catagories of government service.

Recent years have seen numerous apparently spectacular wage advances on the part of public employees: street sweepers in San Francisco are earning a comfortably middle-class wage (about $17,000 per annum); gardeners in the same city went on strike, demanding a scale of up to $21,000; professors in New York's City University scored spectacular gains in 1969 when their school temporarily became the salary lodestar of American academe via the bargaining table; and so forth. In Chapter XI Raymond Horton tells the particularly spectacular story of New York City, in which public employee wage and benefit increases from 1966 to 1974 contributed to the city's *de facto* bankruptcy.

The purpose of this chapter is twofold. First, we shall examine government compensation levels and assess, to the extent possible, the potential impact of unionization and collective bargaining. And second, we shall consider some elementary ideas from bargaining theory, to understand how we have gotten where we are and to assist in predicting the likely future consequences of growing unionization and collective bargaining.

PRIVATE SECTOR COLLECTIVE BARGAINING

Unionization and collective bargaining are formally similar to a monopoly or cartel. In the latter, a group of firms collude to restrict output and thereby obtain a higher price for the goods they produce. A union similarly restricts the supply of labor to an employer and thereby achieves a higher wage. In both applications, success in achieving a higher price depends on the response of demand to a change in price for the monopolized good—or, in economist's terms, on the elasticity of demand for that good. If demand is highly inelastic at the prevailing price or wage, a small cut in supply will cause a large price increase.

The elasticity of demand for labor by the producer of a particular good or service depends on:

(1) The elasticity of demand for the output that labor produces. (Other things being equal, the larger the percentage price rise when output is cut by 1 percent, the greater the prospective wage gain that will result when the producer's labor supply is monopolized by union action.)

(2) The ability of management to substitute other inputs, especially capital. (Other things being equal, the more easily a producer can obtain extra capital without large increases in the cost of doing so, and the more readily that capital can be used to replace labor,[1] the less willing the producer will be

to absorb large wage increases; he will substitute capital for labor.)

These conditions tell us very little about the bargaining process itself. They simply indicate conditions under which bargaining *may be* successful from labor's point of view: conditions under which higher wages will not cause sharp reductions in employment.

In private industry applications where it has proven successful, collective bargaining has produced estimated wage increases up to 20 percent above levels without bargaining.[2] Union leaders normally claim that such gains are paid for out of profits; what the workers get, the fat cats—the bosses and owners—give up. However, there are other possible origins of such gains. First, it is possible that unionization leads to greater overall productive efficiency and hence to increased output. Second, it is possible that wage gains for some unionized workers cause worker displacement, thereby increasing the numbers of nonunionized workers as well as of workers in other unionized occupations—especially occupations with weaker control over entry by new workers. The result will be reduced wages among the latter groups.

The three possible sources, then, of higher wages for unionized workers are (1) an increase in "labor's share" compared to the share going into profits, (2) greater overall output, and (3) an increase in the wages of unionized labor at the expense of some wage reductions among other (both union and nonunion) workers.

From the standpoint of economic theory, the fact that collective bargaining begins by reducing the supply of labor makes the first possibility—greater overall output in unionized trades and industries—extremely remote. Restricting labor supply is a way to reduce output, not increase it; if unionization has significant effects upon productive efficiency, the effects are likely to be negative, not positive.

The second possibility—that bargaining produces for labor an increased piece of the profit "pie" and for ownership a reduced piece—seems inconsistent with the behavior of "labor's share," which is the measured ratio of wages and salaries, through time, to the total value of output in the economy. Since the turn of the century, labor's share has remained around 70 percent of national income, give or take 4 percentage points. There is no discernible increase in labor's share during periods when union membership is growing, and no discernible tendency for it to drop when union membership declines. Hence it appears unlikely that union gains result from ownership losses.

The third possibility—that collective bargaining has displaced workers and thereby reduced wages for lower-paid workers—appears most likely. The mechanism for this is particularly simple: unions restrict the entry of labor into unionized trades and industries. The excluded labor seeks employment elsewhere: consequently the labor supply is greater and the wage rate lower in less desirable and therefore lower-paid trades and applications.[3]

In summary, then, industrial collective bargaining has probably caused some overall reduction in the total value of society's output (real national income) and has increased the compensation of better-paid unionized workers and thereby reduced that of lower-paid workers, both union and nonunion. The losses in output are due to the costs of the bargaining process—lockouts, strikes, work slowdowns, "work to rules," etc.—as well as to the reallocation of labor to less productive and valuable uses.

THE POTENTIAL CONSEQUENCES OF BARGAINING IN THE PUBLIC SECTOR

Is the pattern of consequences that is observed in the private sector likely to hold in the public sector? Or is the bargaining process involving public employees likely to embody crucially different features, and hence to create crucially different outcomes? To get a clearer view on these questions, it is helpful to consider what is involved in the bargaining process itself.

A theory of bargaining was formalized by mathematicians, beginning in the 1940s, as a product of work on the games theory.[4] It is far from sufficient to convey all the many rich and subtle aspects of real life bargaining situations; however, it is sufficiently well developed to yield provocative predictions about the consequences of unionization in government employment.

Formal bargaining theory views the process as involving two parties whose interests are in varying degrees both mutual and opposed. The mutuality of interest stems from the assumption that both bargainers stand to gain if an agreement can be reached. The opposition results from the condition that the total potential gain is not unlimited, and that to some degree increases in gain for party A must reduce gains for party B.

If bargaining fails to arrive at a mutually acceptable outcome, the two parties each go their separate ways, neither enjoying the gains that could have been theirs had the process worked out; alternatively, if bargaining fails, one or both bargainers may feel it necessary to carry out threats made during the process. Either way—acceptance of status quo or enactment of threat—the result of failure to achieve a successful bargain is known to both parties. And their willingness to make concessions during the bargaining process will depend on the relative degree of distastefulness to each of a failure to agree.

Thus the gains attainable through bargaining are finite; the cost of failure to arrive at a bargain falls in some degree on both parties, and the benefits of various possible outcomes are known to both parties. The bargaining process itself—including any threats that may be made during the process—has no bearing on the range of possible outcomes.

Such a formal model may serve tolerably as an analytical framework for industrial bargaining. Unions weigh the likelihood of achieving different possible compensation levels against the costs they may have to incur via industrial action to achieve those levels. Management weighs the benefits of strike or slowdown avoidance against the cost of higher compensation, while considering the possibility of substituting other inputs for labor. There are significant and clearly defined limits on the ranges of action that are open to bargainers who behave intelligently: management does not seek to precipitate a strike by intransigence, nor does labor seek wage rates that would ultimately lead to shutdown.

There is, of course, an impact on "the public interest" in industrial bargains. Excessive settlements by weak management lead to excessive prices. But most goods have substitutes; and management must fear the long-run loss of markets if settlements are excessive.

Government employment bargaining, however, is relatively more complex and subtle. Elected public officials are either directly or ultimately involved in determining the outcome. Whereas the public response to an industrial bargain is impersonal, and transmitted through the market prices that eventuate from the bargain, most public employment involves a monopoly in the provision of some service. Private schools and private scavengers are alternatives to the Board of Education and the Department of Sanitation; but those alternatives would be more attractive and meaningful if the taxpayer could opt out of schooling or garbage collection with a rebate of tax. Having paid for municipal services, one is less prone to turn to a private alternative.

While customers can simply transfer their business away from a private manager who tries to pass along the consequences of a bargaining disaster in the form of unreasonably high prices, that recourse is much stickier in the domain of publicly provided services. True, taxpayers can vent their displeasure at the polls by turning down bond issues or voting out spendthrift officials. Offsetting that possibility, however, is the prospect that public employees themselves as voters will work on behalf of sympathetic and generous politicians; and also the prospect that if the politician is too jealous of the public purse he may trigger a strike that can have even more severe consequences for reelection than can a generous wage settlement. Hence we have a model of political payoff in collective bargaining in which the interests of the bargaining agents are reciprocal to a degree unknown in the private setting. A generous settlement may advantage not disadvantage the "management" bargaining agent.

The result is a complex array of incentives for the public manager:

(1) Favorable wage settlements, rather than leading to reductions in employment through the substitution of capital for labor, may have just the opposite effect: first, higher wages may lead to larger operating budgets and smaller capital budgets, or they may crimp the capital budget by creating voter resistance to bond issues; second, the political clientele group is reduced if higher wages are accompanied by layoffs, and so in order to capitalize on the satisfaction of the benefited voter bloc, employment may be increased rather than reduced when wages go up. This, of course, contrasts with the usual view that when an increase in price is accompanied by an increase in quantity sold, the causal factor is increased demand. In the case of public employment, a price increase may be accompanied by increases in the work force for political reasons, not because of voter demand for more services. Such employment increases can be either direct or hidden; earlier retirement with high benefits, or longer vacations and shorter workweeks are respectively hidden and direct forms of employment increases.

(2) A strong incentive exists to defer or postpone higher compensation. A politician with higher aspirations may be tempted into fiduciary extravagances that his successors will have to pay for; he himself will have moved on to bigger and better things. Pensions seem to be a favorite device for deferring payment and creating future obligations.

Whereas "the public interest"—the interests of those not directly involved in bargaining—are protected by market processes in the private sector, no comparable mechanism of protection exists in public sector bargaining. Unless the bargaining process is revised, or unless voters grow markedly in sophistication relative to the bargainers themselves, the continuing result of this process is almost sure to be a collusion of management and employee interests against the voter/taxpayer/citizen interest.

MEASURED EFFECTS

The qualitative impact of growing government employment, with increasingly strong commitment to collective bargaining (as discussed in the previous section), seems quite clear and unambiguous. Collective bargaining creates incentives and power relationships within the processes of government resource allocation that will likely create important consequences for the size of the governmental labor force, the average workload of government workers (their productivity), and the compensation of government workers relative to private civilian employees.

The modern spirit, however, is to discount or ignore such qualitative analyses unless the indicated effects are significant. Thus, data are processed (usually by linear regression analysis) and judgments rendered on the statistical significance of the relationship or effect in question. The prior questions—How good are the data? How appropriate are the tests to which the data are subjected?—are seldom given thorough attention.

No high-quality data exist to study relative compensation levels in government compared to private employment. The U.S. Department of Commerce, however, does generate data on employment, wages, and compensation in various sectors and industries of the economy, and it is possible from these to make crude comparisons between compensation rates for workers in different industrial sectors and in government.[5]

From Table 1, which presents a biennial summary of the data, we observe the steady growth in state and local employment since 1950, as well as the sharp increase in membership of two important public employee unions, beginning in the late

TABLE 1

	Government Employment		Average Compensation per Full-Time Equivalent Worker			
Year	Federal	State/ Local	Government	Private	Ratio G/P	Union Membership*
1950	4,117	4,285	3,181	3,145	1.011	N.A.
1952	2,583	4,522	3,437	3,626	.948	N.A.
1954	2,373	4,859	3,654	3,932	.929	N.A.
1956	2,410	5,275	4,137	4,452	.929	N.A.
1958	2,405	5,892	4,661	4,709	.990	N.A.
1960	2,421	6,387	5,077	5,170	.982	280
1962	2,539	6,849	5,416	5,564	.973	326
1964	2,528	7,536	5,960	6,043	.936	374
1966	2,861	3,618	6,474	6,615	.979	481
1968	2,984	9,358	7,352	7,373	.997	659
1970	2,881	8,528	8,782	8,348	1.052	769
1972	2,795	9,237	10,502	9,519	1.103	822
1973	2,874 (1974)	11,784 (1974)	11,164	10,153	1.099	N.A.

*Combined American Federation of State, County and Municipal Employees, and American Federation of Government Employees (in thousands).
Sources: *Union Membership and Government Employment: Statistical Abstract of the United States* (various editions); compensation data: U.S. Department of Commerce, Office of Business Economics, *National Income and Product Accounts of the U.S., 1923-65; Survey of Current Business,* July issues 1967-1974.

1950s. From 1952 to 1966, an average full-time government worker's compensation stayed roughly at parity with private wages for equivalent work; during this period government wages occasionally fell as much as 8 percent below the private wage rate, but for most of the period hovered within 3 percentage points of private wages. In the years since 1966 compensation in government employment has risen steadily relative to the private sector until 1973, when the gap had widened to favor government workers by about 10 percent. There is no reason to assume that the 1966-1973 trend has been reversed since that time.

It is important to note certain factual information that Table 1 does not provide. For example, one might argue that government employees on average are better educated or more experienced than their private counterparts, and therefore should expect to earn more. If this is true, compensation differences would be accounted for by federal pay policy, which is committed to pay employees comparably to the private sector—taking training, experience, and skill into account as much as possible. A number of states also try to maintain comparable pay scales.

No good evidence exists on nationwide differences between compensation in private employment and compensation in all categories of government employment—federal, state, and local. We do, however, have an extremely competent and interesting study of pay differences between *federal* government and private employees in an area including the District of Columbia, Maryland, Delaware, and Virginia.

Princeton economist Sharon Smith (1976) analyzed employment-and-wages information on individual households from the censuses of 1960 and 1970. She compared average wages and average earnings (not including fringe benefits) of

TABLE 2

	1960	1970	% Change
Federal average earnings	5,172	7,848	51.74
Private average earnings	3,150	4,656	47.81
Ratio F/P	1.6419	1.6856	
Federal average wages	2.69	4.23	57.25
Private average wages	1.93	2.88	49.22
Ratio F/P	1.3938	1.4688	
Unaccountable earnings difference	65%	65%	
Unaccountable wage difference	55%	52%	

federal government employees and private employees. Her results are summarized in Table 2.

In 1960 federal earnings were 64.19 percent higher than
private; only 35 percent of that difference is accountable by
education, experience, family status, race, or other "explana-
tory variables." The *unaccountable* earnings difference thus is
65 percent of 64.19 percent, or about 41 percent. A larger
unaccountable difference—about 44 percent—was found for
1970; federal earnings rose more rapidly than private earnings
in the intervening decade.

Other analysts have discovered earnings differences between government and private employment. Typically, earnings differentials for state and local employment show up as
smaller than for federal employment, and differentials vary
from region to region; but the pattern of higher earnings for
government workers is clear.[6]

How can the Smith findings reported in Table 2 be recon-
ciled with the aggregate data in Table 1? First, and most obviously, federal employment is more highly paid than employment at other levels of government. Second, private earnings
per worker in the Middle Atlantic labor market average in
part-time people on a one-for-one basis, while private earnings
per full-time equivalent worker nationwide (in the Department
of Commerce study) add part-timers together to get full-time
equivalents. Earnings comparisons per person that include
part-time people will increase estimated wage differentials between public and private employment because of a higher incidence of part-time employment in the private sector than in
government.

Whatever the reasons for the indicated differences, the
Smith study suggests that a very substantial and quite possibly
growing premium is collected by individuals who are fortunate
enough to be federal government employees.

The *qualitative* analysis of this chapter (and of several other
chapters in this volume) suggests that collective bargaining
will lead to growth in government employment, as well as to
growth in compensation levels of government employees.

There have been no competent large-scale statistical analyses of that suggestion, primarily because no adequate data base seems to exist for such an undertaking. Thus, a study of total compensation differentials between public and private employment, using individual household data, will not be immediately forthcoming. If it is true in fact that local politicians are fond of paying off with promises of future benefit, *total* compensation differentials should be even greater than earnings differentials or wages.[7]

CONCLUSION

Based on various studies to date and on examination of the aggregate data in Table 1, it seems safe to offer the following conclusions:

1. Since the middle 1960s, government employee earnings have grown steadily relative to private employee earnings.

2. These differences are in large part unaccountable in terms of qualifying worker attributes.

3. The growth in these wage differences has been accompanied by an increase in public employee union membership.

Two distinct issues emerge from such data on government vs. private wage differentials. First, there is the issue highlighted in Table 2; do government employees systematically receive greater compensation than they could expect to get in private employment? Sharon Smith's work on this question, and the findings of other analysts, clearly suggest that the answer is yes.

The second question is simultaneously more difficult to answer and more vital. To what extent do the growth of government employee unions and the increasing recourse to collective bargaining forebode that these favorable differentials for government employment will persist or grow? The recent surge in government wages compared to private may mean that the buying of votes through collective bargaining settlements is well underway; or it may mean that "society" wants more government service and is having to pay higher wages to get it; or it may mean that government employment is simply more recession-proof than private employment.

Seldom in the past, however, have economists based their prescriptions solely or even principally on the kind of data and analysis that are available to illuminate these questions. The benchmark questions of good analysis always have been: What are the incentives created by a particular institutional arrangement? What redistributions of power does an arrangement convey, and how is power likely to be used? Examined in light of those questions, the institution of industrial-style collective bargaining in the public sector is a threatening one.

A constitutional scholar once explained to me that residents of the District of Columbia originally were constitutionally denied the vote in federal elections, because the founders feared the symbiotic potential in the interaction between government employees and politicians. The founders, in their appraisal of power and incentives, may have seen things clearly, and perhaps their view generalizes to all levels of government. Devices like the Hatch Act thus may be inadequate as safeguards against the exploitation of government growth.

IX

COLLECTIVE BARGAINING AND THE RIGHT TO STRIKE

DAVID LEWIN
Professor of Business, Columbia Business School

Government labor policies. Strike incidence 1966-1974. Collective bargaining model. Voter support of public sector unions. Labor-management relations. Nonunion employees. Union security. Market forces and public sector unions.

Few issues in public sector labor relations are as widely or heatedly debated as the strike. Understandably, most unionists argue for the unlimited right of public employees to strike—against the equally understandable opposition of most government officials and managers. Academic observers of the public labor scene, who also display diverse views of public employee work stoppages, tend more than others to focus on substitutes for the strike. Public policy, as fashioned by legislation and judicial decisions, has been largely antagonistic toward public employee strikes but not very successful in preventing them.

The public's view toward public employee strikes seems to be in flux. Until only recently the public supported a variety of anti-strike measures in the governmental sector, but lately they

145

have shown an increased willingness to take at least some strikes. Indeed, this paper will argue that a critical reassessment of public employee strikes is occurring in American society to weigh the costs and benefits of attempts to prohibit strikes. This assessment is related to the increasingly constrained economic environment of government, and out of it a reappraisal of public policy toward government work stoppages is emerging that will lead to broadened public employee strike rights and diminished reliance on contract arbitration.

THE EVOLUTION OF PUBLIC SECTOR LABOR RELATIONS AND STRIKE POLICY

The rapid growth of public employee unionism in the United States from 1960 to 1975 spurred state and local governments to reformulate their labor policies. Many—not all—adopted collective bargaining in one form or another. This was particularly true in the industrial northeast, where private sector workers are well organized.

To some—especially critics—the introduction of formal collective bargaining into government represented an attempt to extend the private sector bargaining model to public employment. And on the surface this seemed to be the case. After all, several key public sector labor statutes—among them New York State's Taylor Law and the Presidential Executive Order #10988, which originally established the framework for federal sector labor relations—were largely the handiwork of people strongly committed to the American industrial relations system, particularly collective bargaining, and to the notion of joint employee-management decisionmaking over terms and conditions of public employment.[1]

In addition, the new governmental labor relations statutes and policies apparently incorporated many characteristics of private sector collective bargaining. These included the principles of exclusive jurisdiction and representation, criteria for determining bargaining units, procedures for union elections, certification and recognition, grievance arbitration, and development of administrative agencies to regulate governmental labor relations and enforce public policy.

Nevertheless, state and local governments did not simply ape the private sector in formulating their labor relations policies, but departed in several ways from private practice, notably in their treatment of the right to strike. Thus public employees are prohibited from striking either expressly by legislation or, if a statute was silent on the issue, by judicial decision.

Denials of strike rights for public employees are predicated on the view that government is not simply another industry and therefore that public and private sector collective bargaining are not closely analogous, as they seemed at first glance. This view, in turn, reflects several underlying assumptions: first, that the government is a sovereign, duly elected by citizens, and that its employees have no right to strike; second, that the services provided by government are essential, and that their suspension because of work stoppages would impose severe hardships on the public that must pay for them; and third—related to the second—that public employee unions are in an especially strong position negotiating with a monopolist, i.e. government, and operating, therefore, independent of market constraints. Permitting them to strike would enhance their bargaining power and, again, allow them to impose substantial costs on the taxpaying public.

If these rationale supported the rejection of strike rights for public employees, then equity—or simply practicality—required development of substitute procedures for dealing with bargaining impasses in government. Thus in the late 1960s and early 1970s state and local governments increasingly sought mediation, fact-finding, and eventually arbitration—as well as various combinations of all three—in attempting to resolve public sector labor disputes.

In using arbitration—i.e. "interest" arbitration—government once more markedly departs from private industry, where the practice is virtually unknown even in disputes declared by the President to be national emergencies.[2] More-

over, in legislating against the right of public employees
to strike and authorizing arbitrated settlements, policymakers
seem to have been exclusively guided by the criterion of labor
peace. That is, by and large they have formulated labor policy,
assuming that the costs of public employee strikes always exceed the costs even of involuntary settlements, and therefore
that government work stoppages must not be permitted under
any circumstances.

It is doubtful whether this view remains a useful guide to
policy in light of the present financial crisis afflicting many
state and local governments and of the resulting problematic
future growth of the public sector. As background to further
consideration of the issue, however, let us examine the incidence of public employee strikes in American government,
and their relationship to collective bargaining and anti-strike
legislation.

THE STRIKE RECORD AND THE ROLE OF POLICY

Beginning in the 1960s the volume of public employee strikes
increased sharply in the United States (Table 1).[3] Before 1966
work stoppages were limited to an average of about 29 per
year. However, the number rose to approximately 319 between 1966 and 1974. Between 1958 and 1965 the number of
workers involved in these strikes averaged less than 3,900 per
year, in contrast to almost 176,000 over the 1966-1974 period.

The data concerning man-days of idleness lost during the
year because of governmental strike activity are similarly re-
vealing. Prior to 1958 such idleness averaged 26,000 man-
days a year; the number rose to 50,000 between 1958 and
1965, and to 1,431,767 between 1966 and 1974. Both the
number of government work stoppages—which fluctuates less
than other measures of strike activity—and the number of
workers involved in strikes reached a peak in 1970, while the
most man-days of idleness during the year were recorded in
1968.

Public employee strikes are by no means uniformly distrib-

TABLE 1. Public Employee Work Stoppages by Level of Government, United States, 1942-1974

Year	Total[1]			Federal Government			State Government			Local Government		
	Number of stoppages	Workers involved	Days idle during year	Number of stoppages	Workers involved	Days idle during year	Number of stoppages	Workers involved	Days idle during year	Number of stoppages	Workers involved	Days idle during year
1942										39	6.0	23.7
1943										51	10.2	48.5
1944							2	0.4	8.0	34	5.3	57.7
1945										32	3.4	20.0
1946										61	9.6	51.0
1947							1	(2)	(2)	14	1.1	7.3
1948										25	1.4	8.8
1949										7	2.9	10.3
1950										28	4.0	32.7
1951										36	4.9	28.8
1952										49	8.1	33.4
1953										30	6.3	53.4
1954							1	(2)	.8	9	1.8	9.6
1955							1	.2	.5	16	1.3	6.7
1956										27	3.5	11.1
1957										12	.8	4.4
1958	15	1.7	7.5	—	—	—	1	(2)	(2)	14	1.7	7.4
1959	25	2.0	10.5	—	—	—	4	.4	1.6	21	1.6	57.2
1960	36	28.6	58.4	—	—	—	3	1.0	1.2	33	27.6	67.7
1961	28	6.6	15.3	—	—	—			—	28	6.6	15.3
1962	28	31.1	79.1	5	4.2	33.8	2	1.7	2.3	21	25.3	43.1
1963	29	4.8	15.4	—	—	—	2	.3	2.2	27	4.6	67.7
1964	41	22.7	70.8	—	—	—	4	.3	3.2	37	22.5	57.7
1965	42	11.9	146.0	—	—	—			1.3[3]	42	11.9	145.0
1966	142	105.0	455.0	—	—	—	9	3.1	6.0	133	102.0	449.0
1967	181	132.0	1,250.0	—	—	—	12	4.7	16.3	169	127.0	1,203.0
1968	254	201.8	2,545.2	3	1.7	9.6	16	9.3	42.8	235	190.9	2,492.8
1969	411	160.0	745.7	2	.6	1.1	37	20.5	152.4	372	139.0	592.2
1970	412	333.5	2,023.2	3	155.8	648.3	23	8.8	44.6	386	168.9	1,330.5
1971	329	152.6	901.4	2	1.0	8.1	23	14.5	81.8	304	137.1	811.6
1972	375	142.1	1,257.3				40	27.4	273.7	335	114.7	983.5
1973	387	196.4	2,303.9	1	.5	4.6	29	12.3	133.0	357	183.7	2,166.3
1974	384	160.7	1,404.2	2	.5	1.4	34	24.7	86.4	348	135.4	1,316.3

[1]The Bureau of Labor Statistics has published data on strikes in government in its annual reports since 1942. Before that year, they had been included in a miscellaneous category—other nonmanufacturing industries. From 1942 through 1957, data refer only to strikes in administrative, protective, and sanitary services of government. Stoppages in establishments owned by governments were classified in their appropriate industry; for example, public schools and libraries were included in education services, not in government. Beginning in 1958, stoppages in such establishments were included under the government classification. Stoppages in publicly owned utilities, transportation, and schools were reclassified back to 1947 but a complete reclassification was not attempted. After 1957, dashes denote zeros.

²Fewer than 100.

³Idleness in 1965 resulted from 2 stoppages that began in 1964.

NOTE: Because of rounding, sums of individual items may not equal totals.

Source: U.S. Department of Labor, Bureau of Labor Statistics, Work Stoppages in Government, 1974, Report No. 453 (Washington, D.C.: Government Printing Office, 1976), p. 5.

uted among services, occupations, or levels of government. In 1974, the last year for which data are available, more than 90 percent of them took place in local government; over half occurred in public education (where about 50 percent of state and local government workers were employed);[4] and fully two-thirds involved professional, technical, and teaching employees. In the same year, educational work stoppages accounted for 52 percent of all workers involved in government employee strikes and 54 percent of strike-related man-days of idleness. Wages have been far and away the dominant issue in recent public employee labor disputes, with union organization and security, plant administration, and job protection the next most contentious issues, in that order. Moreover, in 1974 more than 60 percent of all public employee work stoppages occurred in governments located in five large industrial states (Pennsylvania, Michigan, Ohio, California and Illinois), with another three states (New York, Washington and New Jersey) accounting for an additional 11 percent of such strikes.

Despite the recent upsurge, strikes in government occur far less often than in industry. In 1974, for example, when according to all measures the volume of government work stoppages was the fourth largest ever recorded, strike-related man-days of idleness as a percent of all working time and the number of workers involved as a proportion of total employment were one-sixth and one-third as large, respectively, in the public as in the private sector of the economy (Table 2). On average, government work stoppages involved 8.5 percent fewer workers and less than one-half the amount of idleness per worker than labor disputes in industry.

With one exception, these differences are not quite as large when only local government work stoppages—rather than all public sector strikes—are used as a basis of comparison. Nevertheless, in considering the issue of public employee strikes and in attempting to regulate them, we should keep in perspective the true magnitude of the problem, and neither overstate nor understate it.

How have collective bargaining and prohibitions on the

TABLE 2
Selected Work Stoppage Measure,
All Industries and Government, 1974

Measure	All Stoppages	Government Stoppages		
		Total	State	Local
Days of idleness as a percent of estimated working time	0.24	0.04	0.01	0.06
Workers involved as percent of total employment	3.4	1.1	0.8	1.6
Average number of workers involved per stoppage	457	418	726	389
Average days of idleness per worker	17.3	8.7	3.5	9.7

Source: U.S. Department of Labor, Bureau of Labor Statistics, *Work Stoppages in Government, 1974*, Report No. 453 (Washington, D.C.: G.P.O., 1976), p. 5.

strike affected the volume of public sector work stoppages? Owing to data limitations, methodological constraints, and measurement problems, little factual evidence exists to support an answer to this question. As the authors of a recent study of public employee strikes conclude, "the most compelling evidence of our work is that . . . policy makers have almost no evidence on which to base assertions about the impact of public policy on [government employee] strike activity" (Burton and Krider 1975:172).[5]

Nonetheless, popular opinion is that public sector strike bars are largely ineffective. To the extent that strikes occur in the presence of statutes prohibiting them, the view that the statutes are ineffective seems justified. But the issue is more complex, for anti-strike legislation may reduce the incidence of strikes below the level that would have occurred without the ban. Thus, to study the statute's effectiveness would require studying, at least in part, what *did not* occur. Furthermore, the effectiveness of a specific bargaining law may best be gauged in relation to other statutes, rather than in isolation.

A recent study followed such a comparative approach in analyzing non-educational public employee strikes that occurred in the United States between 1968 and 1971. The conclusions are instructive:

> those elements that can be controlled by public policy seem to have little impact on strikes. For example, the statutory prohibition on strikes has little apparent impact on the incidence of strikes, nor does the enactment of a law either prohibiting or encouraging collective bargaining by public employees appear to affect materially the number of local government strikes. (Burton and Krider 1975:171.)

While these findings apparently indicate the ineffectiveness of public sector strike bars, alternatively they may suggest that governments accepting collective bargaining for their employees do not thereby encourage strikes to any significant degree. As Burton and Krider note (1975:171), "our findings may encourage the enactment of statutes supporting bargaining rights for public employees."

In summary, beginning in 1966 government employee strike activity increased dramatically in the United States but is still considerably below the volume of work stoppages in private industry. Public sector bargaining laws and anti-strike provisions apparently have little if any impact on the incidence of government employee strikes, which are more closely related to environmental variables than to public policy. However, empirical evidence on the issue is so scanty that it provides virtually no guide for policy.

PUBLIC SECTOR LABOR PEACE AND THE PRIVATE SECTOR BARGAINING MODEL

As noted, the concern for labor peace has dominated public sector labor policy. For some governments, this has meant avoiding collective bargaining, but at a relatively high cost. Perhaps principle among these—though atypical in many ways—is Chicago's municipal government under Mayor Daley, which trades off very generous wages, patronage employment, and even selected use of the closed shop, for a broad scope of managerial prerogatives and an industrial relations system featuring the absence of union representation, unit determination, and formal bargaining.[6] More common, of course, is collective bargaining, accompanied by anti-strike legislation combined with impasse resolution procedures. Initially, statutes authorized mediation followed by fact-finding with recommendations, but more recently they have been amended to provide for some form of compulsory arbitration, especially in police and firefighter disputes. At every point, avoiding overt labor conflict is the principal objective of these legislative schema.

The bargaining model reflected in these laws deviates from the industry model rather than parallels it. It assumes that a strike is more costly than any other form of settlement, including compulsory arbitration. Yet one wonders. The arbitrator or impasse panel empowered to decide a settlement is concerned principally with the relationship between the two parties to the dispute and is not directly accountable to the public. Thus the arbitrator searches for a mutually acceptable "solution" that preserves the continuity of services. The cost of settlement is a subordinate objective, particularly in the absence of incentives for labor and management to agree among themselves.[7] So-called "final-offer arbitration" tends to provide those incentives, but relatively few American governments use it (see Feuille 1975).

While a public employee strike clearly disrupts—though does not necessarily eliminate—government services, it does not interrupt the flow of revenues to government; citizens continue to be taxed for the services, and they do not have the option of withholding payment for them. Thus, the common assertion that government cannot go out of business cuts both ways in public sector labor relations. Striking public employees may not fear losing their jobs—though they are more fearful now than before—but the government that employs them does not forgo "sales" (and sales revenues) even as it temporarily reduces personnel expenditures. From this perspective, a strike may not be the most costly alternative.

More fundamentally, voter attitudes heavily influence government officials in assessing the relative costs of labor peace and labor disputes in the public sector.[8] Until recently there was strong public support for public sector bargaining legislation, strike prohibitions, and impasse resolution procedures. This support had largely developed during a period of sustained public sector growth, as employment grew more rapidly there than in any other portion of the American economy. However, cyclical downturns in the early and especially mid-1970s brought an increasing citizen concern about the costs of government, the levels of public employee wages and benefits, and the role of unions in the fiscal dilemmas of governments, particularly governments of northeastern cities that are losing jobs and residents to both neighboring suburbs and the rapidly growing "sun belt" states. Elected officials, including many who traditionally have received strong labor support, have responded to these concerns by reexamining their commitment to public sector collective bargaining, reappraising the costs of labor peace in terms of mandated settlements, and supporting more permissive policies toward public employee strikes.[9]

Several state governments already have enacted various laws authorizing public employee strikes under certain conditions (Table 3). Some pertain to all public employees; others to narrower groups. Several link strike authorizations to the citizenry's health, safety, and welfare. A few assign a key decisionmaking role to the judiciary; and all but one apply to employees of state and local governments. None of these states permits a public employee strike to occur without one or another procedure—advance notice, mediation, arbitration, injunctive relief—intervening between a bargaining impasse and

TABLE 3
Summary of State Bargaining Laws that
Permit Public Employee Strikes

State	Strike Policy
Alaska	Strike prohibited for essential employees; permitted for semi-essential employees (utilities, schools, snow removal, sanitation) but may be enjoined if there is threat to public health, safety or welfare; strike permitted for non-essential employees if approved by majority of unit in secret ballot election; no direct provision governing teachers.
Hawaii	Pertains to state and local government employees, police, firefighters and teachers; strike prohibited for 60 days after factfinding report; 10 day notice required; strike not permitted where public health or safety is endangered; can be enjoined by circuit court.
Minnesota	Pertains to state and local government employees, transit workers, police, firefighters and teachers; strike prohibited except where employer refuses to comply with arbitration award or refuses request for binding arbitration.
Montana	Pertains to state and local government employees, transit workers, police and firefighters; strike permitted; also pertains to nurses, but stoppage prohibited if simultaneous strike occurs within 150 miles; labor organization must give written notice and specify strike date.
Oregon	Pertains to state and local government employees, police, firefighters and teachers; limited right to strike for employees included in appropriate bargaining unit certified by PERB for which final and binding arbitration is not provided; mediation and factfinding and other statutory procedures must have been exhausted; injunctive relief can be granted if the strike is a threat to public health, safety and welfare; strike is prohibited for police and firefighters, but the dispute must be submitted to binding arbitration if unresolved after mediation and factfinding.
Pennsylvania	Pertains to state and local government employees, and teachers (court employees excluded); limited right to strike after exhaustion of impasse procedures unless strike creates clear and present danger to public health, safety and welfare; injunction may not be issued prior to strike.

Rhode Island	Strike prohibited with qualification that courts may not enjoin the stoppage unless it causes irreparable injury.
Vermont	Pertains to local government employees, police, firefighters and teachers; limited right to strike; stoppage is prohibited and enjoinable if it occurs 30 days after a factfinder's report, after parties have submitted dispute to arbitration, or if it is shown that the strike will endanger public health and safety; for teachers, a strike may be disallowed if it is ruled a clear and present danger to a sound program of education by a court of competent jurisdiction.

Source: Bureau of National Affairs, *Government Employee Relations Reports*, (Washington D.C.: BNA, December 1974), 51:501; and Deborah T. Bond, "State Labor Legislation Enacted in 1975," *Monthly Labor Review*, 99 (January 1976), 17-29.

a work stoppage. Thus the statutes support a limited rather than unqualified right to strike.

The legislation also attempts to distinguish more clearly different degrees of essentiality among public services. This has departed from the previously noted tendency in the initial phase of public sector bargaining to view all services—and therefore all employees—as equally essential. The more recent position, supported by researchers, is that these services vary considerably in essentiality, with police and firefighters —perhaps the order should be reversed—typically regarded as the most essential (see Ashenfelter and Ehrenberg 1975; Ehrenberg 1973).[10]

The statutory provisions in Table 3—and others not shown there—reflect this view in qualifying strike rights of protective service workers more than others. Some laws indirectly prohibit police and firefighter strikes through the mechanism of court injunctions, while others formally bar them and substitute binding arbitration. Thus, the policy choice is not simply to support or oppose the right to strike; rather, public officials may adopt more selective policies between these polar positions.

The recent statutes giving even partial support for government employee strikes are most significant, as they indicate a general reappraisal of the relative costs of labor peace in public employment. That reappraisal is occurring at a time of growing fiscal constraints on government and at a time when American citizens are severely questioning their investments in public services. The result is pushing public sector bargaining and strike policies closer to those of industry rather than away from them. Thus the private sector bargaining model is not as inappropriate to—nor as closely followed by— government as has often been contended.

BARGAINING POWER AND ALTERNATIVE GOVERNMENTAL LABOR POLICIES

The public sector strike does not of course occur in a vacuum but is instead part of a larger labor relations dynamic. Too often discussions of strikes and strike policies proceed without proper regard for other, related aspects of collective bargaining and manpower utilization. To ignore them is to overlook other determinants of public union power while focusing too narrowly on a manifestation of such power—i.e. the strike.

Consider the role of supervisory and even middle management personnel in government. They typically do not represent their employer in collective bargaining, nor are they necessarily allied with him. Rather, they identify with and often support—if implicitly—the bargaining goals of employees whom they theoretically are responsible for supervising and managing. The relationship is not adversary or even arm's-length, as it is in the private sector.

Public supervisors and some managers identify with their subordinates for a number of reasons. Some of these inhere in the nature of government and cannot easily be altered; others can be changed. One important reform would be to amend public sector labor relations statutes to withdraw from supervisors and managers union representation and bargaining rights. (For a similar policy recommendation see Hayford and Sinicropi 1976.) At present, laws exclude only a few upper management and confidential employees, permitting others to organize and formally negotiate with their employers—which many have done, especially those employed in large city governments. And they are often represented by the same unions as their subordinates![11] This arrangement does not breed managerial independence and further complicates the boundary role occupied by public managers and supervisors. Removing them from representation and bargaining statutes would partially ameliorate these problems, though not to the degree achieved in the private sector when the 1947 Taft-Hartley Amendments excluded supervisors there from coverage of the Wagner Act.[12]

Similarly, personnel policies for public supervisors and managers should be reexamined. In brief, policies for personnel selection, compensation, job classification, and performance evaluation lump all employees together, thereby shading and sometimes eliminating distinctions between managers and their subordinates. These policies grew out of the largely successful effort—through civil service—to replace patronage with the merit system of public personnel management; but that should not prevent our recognizing problems with these policies, particularly with the large-scale growth of unionism and collective bargaining in government. (On this point, see Lewin and Horton 1975; Lewin 1976a.)

Several policy initiatives would distinguish public managers and supervisors from other government workers. They include raising managerial compensation; creating dual salary structures and broader use of merit pay; reducing reliance on promotion from within and expanding use of lateral entry to intermediate and upper-level jobs; creating multiple job classification plans within individual governments; and evaluating managerial personnel for their performance.

None of these policy changes by itself is likely to promote a radically new sense of management identification in government, but together they should foster sharper distinctions between managerial and non-managerial emloyees and lessen managers' identification with their subordinates. Thus, with such management reforms, unionized public employees would exercise greater caution in using militant tactics, and especially the strike.

In both the public and private sectors, a strike's effectiveness depends largely on the importance of unionized labor to the "production" and delivery of the service in question. As Marshall noted long ago, union power varies, among other things with the availability of substitutes for it.[13] While in labor-intensive public services technology is not particularly suitable substitute, nonunion labor may be. Removing organization and bargaining rights for public managers and supervisors—along with modifying personnel policies pertaining to them—helps create a source of nonunion labor which may be substituted to deliver public services during a strike. Moreover, the additional costs of such nonunion labor are small since public supervisors and managers are salaried and generally not subject to overtime pay provisions.

Substitutes for union labor need not be drawn solely from within the government experiencing a strike. They may come from other public jurisdictions. For example, the State of California presently is training a several thousand member police force to temporarily replace striking local government police (see *Los Angeles Times,* April 12, 1976). Similarly, multiemployer bargaining may provide a source of substitute labor, though this bargaining structure is as yet only rarely used in government. (For a generally pessimistic view of the prospects for multiemployer bargaining in the public sector, see Feuille et al. 1976). Another possibility is subcontracting with the private sector not only during strikes but also as an alternative to costly publicly operated services. Interestingly, these sources of substitute labor may involve both union *and* nonunion employees. The key point is that, to the extent that their costs do not surpass the cost of simply taking a strike, they are alternative sources of labor to government. If public officials and managers actively cultivate these sources, as well as reform governmental labor relations and personnel policies, they will have a potentially effective counterweight against the power of organized public employees, and they can mitigate the consequences of government work stoppages, if not totally eradicate them.

Finally, we must consider public policy toward government employee strikes in relation to union security arrangements. Most public sector labor statutes do not sanction the agency or union shop—or of course the closed shop—although the issue is being litigated in a number of places. Yet the principle of exclusive representation—as widespread in public as in private sector labor relations—imposes on labor organizations the duty to represent all employees in the bargaining unit whether or not they are members of the union.[14] It is not surprising, therefore, that public labor leaders pursue union security provisions, while critics decry the restrictions on individual freedom that result from "compulsory unionism." What *is* surprising, perhaps, is that this objective remains more elusive than attainable.

Public sector labor organizations for which union security is not much of an issue—police, firefighters, sanitationmen, teachers—typically enroll members of a single occupation and have a history of tradition, custom and circumstance that results in very large proportions of dues-paying members. Other labor organizations—especially such multi-occupational ones as the American Federation of State, County and Municipal Employees (AFSCME) and the Service Employees International Union (SEIU)—have more diverse internal interests—i.e. more constituencies—and proportionately fewer dues-paying members. Hence, they are major supporters of union security arrangements in government, but have not been very successful getting these provisions incorporated into public sector labor statutes.

The critical aspect of union security provisions—more precisely, of union dues—is that payments made in connection with them are the principal means of financing strikes. Thus, public labor policies that do not sanction the union shop, agency shop, or other forms of union security may act to constrain public employee strikes. Conversely, to the extent such policies exacerbate internal union conflicts and leadership instability, they may promote strikes.

The analysis presented here does not offer a clear policy implication on this issue. Some governments will oppose all forms of union security provisions, others only some forms, and still others will trade them off for alternative bargaining objectives—such as the exclusion of managerial and supervisory personnel from union representation. Thus, on this dimension of labor relations—as on many others—public employers will behave much like their private sector counterparts.[15]

SOME CONCLUDING THOUGHTS

The economic environment of the American public sector—especially state and local government—has changed dramatically in a short period. Whereas it expanded continuously in the 1960s and early 1970s, since then government has suffered major economic and financial problems, especially in large northeastern cities, most notably New York City. But the problems are by no means confined to them. Personnel layoffs, postponed or eliminated capital construction projects, and service reductions are now widespread in state and local government (see Schlosstein 1975), and they will be counterbalanced only partially by a sustained economic recovery from the 1974-1975 recession.

Mounting economic difficulties have changed the political climate within which public sector labor relations take place. In the new climate, the access of organized public employees to the political process diminishes; the support of politicians and the public for unionism and collective bargaining in government declines; the commitment of management to a hardline negotiating approach increases; and a more vigorous search is pursued for alternatives to public services.

The climate also contributes to reappraisal of legislative frameworks for public sector labor relations, especially strike prohibitions and substitute impasse procedures. Thus, the objective of labor peace is being questioned for the extent to which it is achievable and for the costs of doing so. At a preliminary level at least, the reassessment is generating growing support for broadened if not unqualified public employee strike rights—and for more restricted use of contract arbitration in government.

These developments suggest that public sector labor relations are not totally immune from market forces, as advocates of the government-as-monopolist thesis contend. In responding to the financial difficulties presently confronting them—including laying off personnel, resisting wage increases and in some cases imposing absolute wage cuts, searching for alternatives to union labor, emphasizing productivity, upgrading the quality of management, and reducing some services—public officials and managers are reacting much the same way as operators of private business who face adverse economic circumstances.

During the period of economic expansion when the "first generation" of public sector collective bargaining developed in the United States, governments appeared to occupy monopoly positions in their respective jurisdictions, and organized public employees seemed freely able to exercise their power. In the "second generation" of bargaining that is now evolving, the limits to union power are both more operative and visible as governmental decisionmakers respond in various ways to "consumer" demands for reduced expenditures, stable—if not lower—tax rates, and improved management.[16]

If a stronger market connection to government services exists than is generally recognized, then the rationale supporting an alternative public bargaining model is correspondingly weakened.[17] As we have seen, public sector bargaining statutes and policies are not simply mirror images of private sector labor legislation. To the contrary, most of them assume—as reflected in anti-strike and impasse procedure provisions—that government does have unique characteristics. But as the economic environment of government becomes more constrained, as the costs of labor peace are reassessed, and as governments revise their management and manpower utilization policies, public sector strikes will be treated less as events always to be prohibited and more as events whose consequences must be weighed against other bargaining outcomes. (A similar point is made by Aaron 1975.)[18]

Public sector bargaining and strike policies will more closely approximate those of industry not because the latter are necessarily "correct," but because government cannot entirely escape from the discipline of the market. Ironically, the most significant aspect of public employee strikes may be helping citizens and elected officials to understand this reality.

X

UNION LEADERS AND PUBLIC SECTOR UNIONS

AFL-CIO
GEORGE MEANY, *President*

National Labor Relations Act, 1935: governmental and farm worker exclusion. Public employees and the states. Public vs. private sector unions. The process of collective bargaining. The steel industry. Voluntary vs. compulsory arbitration.

The United States Congress, like any other human institution, has made its share of blunders over the years. In the field of labor-management relations, one of the most grievous was the singling out of farm workers and government workers for exclusion from the protection of the National Labor Relations Act of 1935.

By that action the Congress trampled on the principle of equal justice under law. It relegated large numbers of free and equal human beings to a category of second-class citizenship. It armed agricultural operators with weapons to keep migrant workers in a state of peonage. It authorized state and local governments to outlaw collective action by employees seeking redress of grievances.

165

As a result, forty years later America has an underclass of ill-housed, ill-fed, ill-educated, and shamefully exploited farm workers who are not participants in American society but victims of it. It has a class of government workers who perceive themselves to be excluded from the mainstream of American economic life, who feel themselves at the mercy of petty tyrants whose tyranny is upheld and enforced by unjust laws enacted in the name of the "public interest."

It should come as no surprise that in recent years both farm workers and government workers have begun to rebel. They marked time for decades as they watched workers in private industry, working through their unions, improve their living standards and upgrade their lives and the lives of their children both economically and socially. It has become increasingly clear to them that what makes the difference is collective action, and they have moved in increasing numbers to assert the right to collective action that is enjoyed by other workers and that is the right of all free men and women. They are rebelling as much against their second-class citizenship as against inequities and injustices on the job.

The farm workers have succeeded in persuading the California legislature that there is no way to stabilize labor relations in the fields except through union organization and collective bargaining. California's "Little NRA" is still poorly administered and inadequately enforced, chiefly because of the legislature underfunding the agency. But that situation will improve and the California experience will be extended to other states. The farm workers will continue their efforts until justice is achieved for migrant workers in every corner of the United States.

Just as confidently, I can make the same forecast for government workers. At every level of government the drive for equal rights is well under way, and before many years have passed I am sure that collective bargaining will be the norm in the vast majority of federal departments and agencies and in the states and counties and cities and school districts.

The reason for this confidence is simple: It is the common sense way to do business, and common sense wins in the long run.

Public employees are the largest bloc of workers in the national work force and one of the largest blocs of union members. About three million federal, state, and local employees are members of thirty-two AFL-CIO unions. The full organizing potential is about thirteen million and growing.

While collective bargaining is authorized in the federal sector as a result of presidential executive orders, it has no statutory base. What one president grants another can rescind. So it is obvious we want Congress to legislate and, to date, it has not. Only Postal Service workers so far have full collective bargaining rights. In most other agencies administrators "meet and confer" with their employees' unions, but anything approaching true collective bargaining is a rarity.

In the states the situation is in chaos.

Six states have authorized the limited right to strike. They are Alaska, Hawaii, Montana, Oregon, Pennsylvania, and Vermont (local employees only).

Fifteen states have authorized union shop and/or agency shop. This provision is required by law in three states —Hawaii, Minnesota, and Rhode Island (for state employees). The remaining eleven states make this provision negotiable. They are Alaska, California (just teachers), Kentucky (just fire fighters), Maine (university employees only), Massachusetts, Michigan, Montana, Oregon, Vermont (local employees only), Washington, and Wisconsin. One state, Pennsylvania, provides for maintenance of membership.

Twenty-four states have mandatory comprehensive bargaining laws for all public employees, both state and local. They are Alaska, California, Connecticut, Delaware, Florida, Hawaii, Iowa, Kansas, Maine, Massachusetts, Minnesota, Montana, Nebraska, New Hampshire, New Jersey, New York, North Dakota, Oregon, Pennsylvania, Rhode Island, South Dakota, Vermont, Washington, and Wisconsin. Two states, Indiana and Missouri, exclude police and fire fighters only. Michigan excludes certain categories of civil service workers.

Two states have mandatory comprehensive bargaining laws for state employees only. These are Illinois and New Mexico.

One state, Nevada, has a comprehensive bargaining law only for local employees.

Clearly, this situation makes no sense. Inequities and injustices are inevitable, and so are frustration, anger, and resentment on the part of the workers. One of the side effects of denying collective bargaining procedures and the right to strike to public employees is apathy, favoritism, and incompetence at human relations on the part of public administrators. It is easier to deny or ignore grievances when there is no formal need to resolve them. It is easier to wrap oneself in the flag and take refuge behind no-strike laws than to struggle to reach fair agreements when the unions are deliberately weakened by law.

The number of strikes in private industry has been declining, simply because industrial managers have been learning to listen to workers, to negotiate fair agreements, to resolve grievances. The number of strikes in schools and other public services has been growing, simply because public administrators have not learned to do these things and have been under no pressure to learn.

In recent years a great many federal, state, and local agencies have begun to contract-out to private employers work that previously had been done by government employees, work such as street, park, and building maintenance, trash collection, and similar tasks. In many cases the same workers have continued to do the same work in the same buildings, only drawing their paychecks from a different source.

These workers serve the same public, but they are free to organize unions, negotiate contracts, pursue grievances, and strike, if necessary, while their fellow workers still on government payrolls are not.

Such anomalies vividly point up the arbitrariness with

which public employees are discriminated against, and they further increase the resentment public employees feel.

Public perception of the rights of public employees has changed dramatically. Back in the middle 1930s even Franklin D. Roosevelt, who was clearly a friend of workers, stated flatly that there was no right anywhere for public employees to strike at any time.

The theory was that government workers enjoyed a degree of tenure and job stability that other workers didn't have, and that well-administered civil service rules would ensure justice on the job.

The theory doesn't hold water. Workers in private industry, if they belong to unions, have no less job security than civil servants. They can't be fired without going through grievance procedure and arbitration. If they are forced to strike, they make job security and protection against reprisals the first condition of settlement.

But even more important, through the collective bargaining process they have a voice in helping to set their own wages and working conditions. They help design the conditions under which they work. They have a forum at which they can discuss their goals and problems. They can reach compromises and settle disputes through give and take with their own employers, rather than having to rely on the understanding and goodwill of a civil service commission or some other third party.

So I don't see that government employees have any real advantages over workers in private industry. But I see disadvantages so great that it's no wonder that public employees find them intolerable and find union representation so necessary.

The usual argument for depriving government employees of the right to collective bargaining is that they might exercise the right to strike, and that the public might suffer inconvenience or something more serious as a result.

In the first place, I don't see that a public body has any greater right to enslave human beings than a private one. I take it that the rights to life, liberty, and the pursuit of happiness include the right to withhold your labor. And I believe that right takes precedence over anybody else's right to enjoy the fruits of that labor.

If it is tyranny to compel a human being to work against his will for the private profit of another, it is tyranny to compel anybody to labor against his will for the convenience of a public that feels entitled to services or protection on the cheap.

But the public, insofar as its wishes find direct expression rather than being interpreted by editorialists and other self-anointed spokesmen, does not lay down such tyrannous conditions. Public employees who are forced to strike receive a great deal of support from the public. The ordinary man or woman in the street usually shows much more understanding and sympathy for the strikers than for city hall or the school board. They don't resent the workers who are driven to the picket line; they resent the officials who refuse to go to the bargaining table.

And that is why laws forbidding public employees to strike do not work. Ordinary Americans recognize tyranny when they see it. They are not greatly moved by the fracture of an unpopular law, as we saw during Prohibition, nor of an unjust law, as we have seen in the case of New York's old Condon-Wadlin law and countless other cases of class legislation.

It ought to be clear by now that free men and women will not quietly permit themselves to be legislated into second-class citizenship. No law yet written has ever successfully forced Americans to work under conditions they find intolerable. None ever will.

But in seeking the right to collective bargaining, public employees are not pursuing strikes as a goal. Nobody enjoys a strike. Strikes are painful and expensive for all concerned, and sensible unions and sensible managements do everything in their power to avoid them.

Collective bargaining, like the idea of democratic government, is based on consent and acceptance. It assumes that two parties to a dispute can reach a reasonable agreement that both parties can live with. It assumes that workable compromises, fair and just to both sides, can be reached by the exercise of reason through give and take at the bargaining table.

Ultimately, it assumes that not merely a grudging accommodation but real harmony is possible.

It is not a perfect instrument. It rests on the somewhat fragile foundation of mutual confidence and good faith among human beings. But like all democratic institutions it has the great virtue of strengthening its own foundation as it is exercised.

It is a tool for reasonable people who believe in democracy and who do not insist that their side is the only one that has a right to life, liberty, and the pursuit of happiness. It won't work for people who say "take it or leave it" or who submit "non-negotiable demands."

It is a tool for flexible people who set reachable goals and who are willing to make and keep firm agreements for specific periods of time and then reexamine their goals, weigh changing conditions, modify their agreement, and move forward for another period of time.

Collective bargaining, as it has grown and evolved in the United States, is the most effective instrument the mind of man has so far devised for reaching mutually agreeable solutions to the natural and unavoidable conflicts of interest between employers and employees. And strikes and lockouts are a normal and natural and necessary part of the collective bargaining process. They are the last resort.

But it is necessary to preserve the right to that last resort. Unless the real possibility of a strike exists, unless both sides are constantly aware that serious consequences may flow from misjudgments and breaches of faith, bargaining is a charade—an exercise in futility.

Every year upward of 100,000 separate labor-management agreements are negotiated in this country, more than 98 percent of them without friction and without a moment's lost working time. In the 2 percent in which strikes or lockouts do take place, the total of lost working time amounts to a great deal less than the time lost because of the common cold. Last year it added up to around 0.2 percent of all scheduled working time, which is a ridiculously small price to pay for freedom.

Even so, unions and managements work tirelessly to reduce that lost time still further. We would like very much to eliminate every work stoppage, and we have been making some real progress.

In the steel industry, to take an outstanding example, strikes have been conditionally eliminated by an early negotiations system in which the United Steelworkers and the companies strive to reach agreement on all issues before the expiration of the old agreement. They work against that date as a deadline after which all unresolved issues will pass for disposition into the hands of impartial arbitrators, selected in advance, whose decisions, for better or worse, will be final and binding on both parties throughout the coming contract term.

Of course that agreement works because it is voluntary. Both sides agreed to it. Neither forced the other to do so and no third party, especially the government, was involved at all.

So far, that system, in that industry, has been completely successful in preserving the peace with minimal infringement on freedom. The possibility of a strike or lockout is still present, though it has been moved a little further down the road. Any time either party feels that arbitration has worked against its best interests, it is free to abrogate the arbitration agreement before the next negotiations. So far, both the workers and employers have been satisfied. With the end of the stockpiling that used to precede steel bargaining as a hedge against a possible strike, production schedules have been smoothed out and pre-contract overtime and post-contract layoffs have been eliminated.

That system, or some variation of it, is applicable in many industries and in public service as well, provided it meets the crucial test of free, mutual agreement by both employers and employees.

The success of voluntary arbitration in settling disputes unresolved at the bargaining table is based on the fact that such arbitration is itself a product of the collective bargaining process. It is not imposed by some outside authority against the will of either party.

And this is the rock against which the notion of compulsory arbitration has been shipwrecked every time it has been tried. The hasty, ill-conceived legislation with which Congress tried to break strikes in the airline and railroad industries only succeeded in making matters worse. In any guise, under any name—"mediation to finality," "final-offer" arbitration, or what have you—compulsory arbitration has been perceived by employers as an out that makes real bargaining unnecessary and by employees as a tool of tyranny that makes bargaining meaningless.

Collective bargaining is a two-handed tool that won't work unless both parties want it to work, and that goes for arbitration as well.

There are those who argue that collective bargaining is all very well in "non-critical" public services such as schools and sanitation departments, but that some substitute for the strike must be found in the areas of law enforcement, fire protection, and hospital services.

That would be fine if such a substitute could be found, but so far none has been found. There are no shortcuts and no substitutes for the bargaining table and mutual freedom of contract.

And compulsory arbitration—the favorite proposal of certain editorialists—just will not work because it is an abrogation of freedom. The crucial difference between voluntary and compulsory arbitration is the difference between freedom and its denial.

Fairly long experience convinces me that the best, surest and, indeed, only way to secure stability in labor-management relations in any area, including government service, is through the normal pattern of free negotiations on every aspect of wages and working conditions.

I firmly believe that the sooner Congress acts to grant all public employees the same rights their fellow workers in the private economy have had since 1935, the better off the country will be.

AFSCME
JERRY WURF, *President*

The growth and goals of public employee unions. History of AFSCME. The Memphis strike, 1968. Collective bargaining and legislation. Private and public sector unions vs. government sovereignty. Impasse resolution and management organizations. Solving the problems of public service: financial alternatives.

Public employee unionists have a singularly modest goal, but some observers have called it revolutionary. Their goal is to reach a day when it will be possible for representatives of public employees everywhere to sit down with public officials as equals, and negotiate a fair contract covering wages, hours, and working conditions. When that day arrives, public employees will be freed from arbitrary management authority, and the delivery of public services will be freed from political manipulation. We have made progress, but we have a long way to go.

During the 1960s, as the scope and size of public service and the public work force grew, a revolution began which brought collective bargaining in one form or another to dozens of states and cities around the country. It remains to be seen whether that revolution will continue under the pressures of the 1970s and reach fulfillment as part of the American governmental system.

SPECTACULAR GROWTH

By the mid-1970s public employee unionism passed one signpost of growth, with remarkable, if little noted, implications for the futures both of public service and the labor movement.

According to U.S. Labor Department figures, more than 51 percent of state and local government employees are unionized. In contrast, among workers in private industry—whose rights to collective bargaining are, for the most part, guaranteed by federal law—only 29 percent belong to unions.

Our union, the American Federation of State, County and Municipal Employees, has enjoyed spectacular growth. From fewer than a quarter of a million members in 1964, AFSCME has grown to nearly 750,000 members in 1976. In most state and local governments, unions operate without the benefit of union security laws or agreements requiring workers to contribute to the union representing them. AFSCME members pay dues, for the most part, on a voluntary basis in order to support the union and to have it work on their behalf.

AFSCME is not the only organization to participate in the rapid growth of public employee unionism. The National Education Association, once a professional organization of teachers that eschewed trade union activities, has embraced collective bargaining and conducts aggressive organizing drives and—when necessary—authorizes strikes. With more than 1.8 million members today, the NEA has far outpaced the growth of the AFL-CIO's American Federation of Teachers.

Within federal employment, the American Federation of Government Employees, AFL-CIO, and the postal unions have also experienced substantial growth. So have several independent federal employee unions.

The growth of trade unionism in public employment has exceeded the growth of the entire labor movement in recent years. For example, during the period 1970-1972 government employees' unions signed up an additional 143,000 members, while all other American unions grew by only 50,000. In other words, the growth in public employee unionism has offset a net loss in membership among workers in private industry. Largely for this reason, a number of unions from private industry have begun organizing public employees.

Meanwhile, the tide of public employee unionism has swept

along many traditional independent civil service groups in its wake. Occasionally, public officials have simply recognized these associations—whose purposes originally encompassed social activities or insurance programs—as bargaining agents for their employees. In so doing, the employers were taking advantage of the lack of legal protections for the public workers' right to choose their own bargaining agents. On the other hand, these associations sometimes have responded to their members' desire for legitimate collective bargaining and have begun to function as trade unions. Several state employee associations, including those in Hawaii, Rhode Island, and Iowa, have voted to affiliate with AFSCME.

AFSCME had its beginnings in 1932 with a group of Wisconsin state employees who came together to defend the civil service system in that state against the threat of a resurgent patronage system that would have subjected hirings and promotions to political favoritism. They founded the Wisconsin State Employees Association, which eventually joined with other state and local government employee groups to become in 1936 the American Federation of State, County and Municipal Employees, chartered by the American Federation of Labor.

Over the years, the union made full collective bargaining one of its goals, moving away from the restrictive concept of civil service as a panacea for public employees. At present, we have more than two thousand agreements with different levels of public management—states, counties, special districts, hospitals, and charitable agencies.

We've come a long way, and it hasn't been easy. In state after state, governors aspiring to strengthen or reinstate political patronage have attempted to crush public employee unionism. In several southern communities, workers who had the audacity to seek union recognition were confronted with the full fury of the conservative local establishment.

One of the more difficult tests of the will of public employees occurred in Memphis in 1968. A mayor named Loeb refused to bargain with the union representing sanitation workers in that city. He provoked a strike in which workers who had very little were required to make great sacrifices for themselves and their union. Dr. Martin Luther King gave his life in support of that strike.

Today, our union has a strong bargaining relationship with the City of Memphis. Our strength there does not derive from any legal recognition of public employees' rights, nor from the friendliness of the local political and economic establishment. It is derived from the power and unity of public employees.

In Memphis and elsewhere, we've taken the worst public management has thrown at us—and we're still there.

WHY PUBLIC EMPLOYEE UNIONISM?

When I addressed the United States Conference of Mayors in 1967, I declared: "Public employees and collective bargaining have engaged in sporadic flirtations with each other for decades. It is no longer a flirtation. It is a marriage. And it will endure."

Public employee unionism and collective bargaining express impulses that are fundamental to the American spirit. American life promises men and women a voice in the nation, their communities, and their conditions on the job.

Through collective bargaining, public employees have found a way to meet their employers at the bargaining table and negotiate the terms of their employment. Collective bargaining is not just a wage increase, or another paid holiday, or a better pension plan. It is a process which transforms begging—which is not a very noble act—into negotiations. It confers dignity, not charity.

Even if public officials were endowed with absolute wisdom (and lately, most Americans have come to suspect differently), a system of unilateral labor relations would still be unsatisfactory. Like most Americans, public employees want to be part of the decisionmaking process when the decisions affect them.

THE LEGAL TANGLE

Public employee unions exist more in spite of the laws than because of them. Because public workers are denied federal protection in their efforts to organize and bargain with their employers, we deal with a maze of inadequate state collective bargaining legislation and employer-dominated "civil service" systems.

Twenty-six states now have laws recognizing some sort of collective bargaining for public employees. Nineteen states have comprehensive laws mandating broad-scope collective bargaining for local government workers. Several other states provide less comprehensive protections of public employees' rights. In many jurisdictions, collective bargaining exists without any substantive authority—on an *ad hoc* basis.

Some of the state laws work well. Others hardly work at all. One thing characterizes each of them—and that is the consistently inferior rights granted to public workers in comparison to the rights guaranteed other American workers under the National Labor Relations Act.

At its 1970 Convention, our union made an important decision. We decided that it makes much more sense to seek relief through a federal law governing state and local government labor-management relations than to dribble out our lives trying to convince the states to establish impartial labor relations mechanisms.

PUBLIC AND PRIVATE SECTORS —
WHERE'S THE DIFFERENCE?

Laws in this country underscore the difference between workers in government and private industry, although in most other advanced industrial democracies such distinctions are less significant.

Labor relations in the public service have not escaped the grasp of the outmoded doctrine of government sovereignty. This doctrine cloaks the decisions of public officials with a veil of absolute public authority. It gives the public official the right to act without consulting anyone—except possibly his own conscience.

This doctrine—which has its roots in the Old World—bears more than an accidental resemblance to what our forefathers rebelled against in 1776. It views power as an end in itself—to be hoarded by the rulers, not shared with those subject to public authority. Collective bargaining involves an equitable sharing of power, and it is consistent with a trend in American history towards restricting arbitrary authority and enhancing the rights of ordinary citizens.

Over the years, the distinctions between the public and private sector have been blurred—not so much by trade unionists as by the most vigorous opponents of public employee unionism. These corporate officials and public officials are eager to shift the responsibilities for providing services back and forth from government to private industry. They'll turn over unprofitable operations, such as mass transit, to public agencies while farming out other public services, such as health care for the aged, to private for-profit contractors.

It seems there is one criterion for deciding whether an enterprise should be public or private. That criterion is not who can best perform the service. It is profitability.

But while traditional distinctions between the public and private sectors have been erased, one gap remains: the chasm between the earnings of workers in private industry and public service.

Traditionally, the earnings of public employees lagged behind those of workers in private industry. Their earnings still lag behind private industry, although substantial gains have been made during the past twenty years. According to recent figures from the U.S. Department of Commerce, average earnings for state and local government employees—including teachers—lag behind average earnings for employees in transportation by $3,000; in electric, gas, and sanitary service industries by $2,300; in mining by $2,000; in communications by $1,400; and in contract construction by $1,200.

ALTERNATIVES TO STRIKES

Rational discussion of labor relations in public employment has been paralyzed by a preoccupation with the emotional issue of strikes.

Years of experience in public employment have taught us that the absence of legislation recognizing public employees' rights, and the existence of repressive legislation prohibiting strikes, do not prevent strikes. In fact, exactly the opposite has been true—such a legal climate fosters an unyielding and hostile attitude by both labor and management.

The first realistic step towards restraining conflict is to enact legislation that fully provides public employees with the right to engage in collective bargaining. Any such law must be administered impartially and must contain procedures designed to bring about agreement.

When collective bargaining reaches an impasse, there need not be a strike or a surrender by either side. What is needed is a mutually acceptable route for resolving the impasse. AFSCME has suggested for some time that we favor the use of voluntary binding arbitration in impasses. But we find public officials resisting this peaceful alternative to strikes.

AFSCME recently endorsed compulsory binding arbitration in emergency public safety services. Our proposal would give fire fighters and police officers access to fair mechanisms for reaching resonable settlements of labor disputes. It would eliminate the danger that communities could suffer from the disruption of vital services.

But we have met intransigent opposition to binding arbitration from management organizations—the National League of Cities, the U.S. Conference of Mayors, the National Governors Conference, and the National Association of County Officials. Apparently, these organizations fear sharing power with public employees, fear letting an impartial third party enter into labor relations—in short, fear reasonableness more than they fear strikes.

PUBLIC EMPLOYEES AND PUBLIC SERVICES

Public employees as a class—and there are 12.3 million of us in state and local government alone—have a stake in making government work better. Once public employees are assured a voice in their working conditions, once unions such as ours need not be preoccupied with mere survival, we will be able to work with public officials to improve public services. And there is room for improvement.

In a rational system, the people decide—after free discussion—what services a society should provide its citizens. Once these decisions are made, the delivery of these services should be insulated from political manipulation. Professional administrators should provide the expertise to deliver these services, and a rational tax structure should provide the revenue.

In large measure, such a system prevails in most other advanced industrial democracies, such as the Scandanavian nations and West Germany. But the United States has a way to go. There should be a thorough overhaul of mechanisms for financing public service.

Our state and local governments derive 72 percent of their revenues from sales and property taxes. These taxes take their biggest bites from the incomes of those who can least afford to pay and their smallest bites from those who can best afford to pay. During periods of prosperity, revenues from these taxes grow at a slower rate than the economy. During periods of high unemployment, revenues from sales and property taxes take a dive.

The states should raise a greater share of their revenues from progressive income taxes. Ten states have no income taxes at all, including Connecticut, the state with the highest per capita income in the nation. In Pennsylvania, Massachusetts, and Ohio, income taxes do not raise much money and the rate structures are not progressive.

There are many ways in which the federal government can

help state and local governments to provide the financial wherewithal for public service. In times of national economic recession, states and cities with high unemployment rates take a severe fiscal beating. Tax revenues decline, demands for public service increase—and their budgets are caught in a terrible bind. Our union helped devise the idea of "countercyclical" federal financial assistance to state and local governments suffering severe unemployment rates. The aid would enable them to provide a constant level of public service, avoiding layoffs of public employees and increases in taxes.

Other proposals have been advanced for easing the financial crisis of state and local governments. AFSCME has supported the concept of federal subsidies for the interest payments on municipal bonds in return for an end to the tax exemption on subsidized debt issues. There should be an increased federal assumption of the cost of health care and social welfare programs.

Another step towards improving public service would be entrusting administrative duties to a corps of professional public managers who would interface with the elected officials. This is the practice in most Western European nations, and public service there is better for it.

Better trained managers would be helpful, but we also need a whole new attitude towards public service. There are many professionally trained managers—city managers, county managers, and agency heads—in public service. But instead of professionalizing the politicians, the public officials end up politicizing the managers.

Essentially, public employees seek a voice in the delivery of higher quality—and more equitably financed—public services. This is a reasonable goal. And we will achieve it.

XI

ECONOMICS, POLITICS, AND COLLECTIVE BARGAINING: THE CASE OF NEW YORK CITY

RAYMOND D. HORTON
Professor of Business, Columbia Business School
Staff Director, Temporary Commission on City Finances

New York City finances and municipal union influence. Labor relations in prosperity—in scarcity. Financial and political revolution: special city and state agencies. Salaries vs. employment and unemployment. Implications of collective bargaining for unions, management, political processes. The dynamics of public sector labor relations in a distributive and a redistributive environment.

During the second half of the 1960s when the public economy of New York City was strong, the city's labor relations process changed dramatically and organized civil servants came to dominate the collective bargaining process. However, steadily deteriorating local government finances in the first half of the 1970s changed the process again and reduced municipal union influence significantly by 1975. These de-

velopments suggest that the state of public sector labor relations and the distribution of influence over the collective bargaining process may be highly dependent on changing
economic conditions.

It is possible, of course, that the political economy of New
York City may be unique, and that what transpires there may
not be relevant to persons studying or shaping labor relations
in other governments.[1] While many other urban governments
grew rapidly during the 1960s—and, as a result, experienced
significant advances in public employment, unionization, collective bargaining, and pay levels—none apparently suffered
as severe a contraction as New York City in the first half of the
1970s. Comparative research now in progress should clarify
whether or to what extent public sector labor relations in New
York City is unique.[2]

LABOR RELATIONS AMIDST
ECONOMIC PROSPERITY

The rapid changes that took place in City labor relations particularly after 1965 occurred when the local government
economy was strong, and when the citywide economy was
strong—if, in retrospect, not fundamentally sound. The
strength of the City government economy does not mean its
fiscal or managerial policies also were sound. It was strong,
rather, in the sense that there was growing demand for local
government services and—more important—rapidly increasing revenues to finance them.

To illustrate the expansion of the local public economy,
Table 1 compares growth rates of three key local government
economic indicators for five-year periods between 1950 and
1970. Between 1965 and 1970 operating expenditures of the
City government increased at an extremely high average annual rate of 15.6 percent. During the 1960-1965 period the
rate of increase also was high, 9.4 percent, at least when compared to the 1955-1960 annual growth rate of 6.4 percent. The

TABLE 1. Average Annual Rates of Increase of
Selected New York City Economic Indicators from
1950 to 1970

Five-Year Periods	Expenditures		Intergovernmental Aid		Employment	
	Current $	Constant $	Current $	Constant $	FT	FT + PT
1950-1955	7.3%	5.3%	2.7%	0.7%	n/a	n/a
1955-1960	6.4	4.1	10.0	7.6	1.9	0.7*
1960-1965	9.4	7.7	18.5	16.7	4.2	3.9
1965-1970	15.6	10.3	22.6	17.0	3.0	5.0

*Data for period include only 1958, 1959, and 1960.
Sources: Expenditure and intergovernmental aid data computed from data in
Report of the Comptroller, fiscal years 1950-1951 through 1970-1971; full-
time employment data computed from data in *Report of the Department of
Personnel*, 1955 through 1970; full-time and part-time employment data
computed from data provided by New York State Department of Labor.

1950-1955 rate was 7.3 percent. Table 1 also shows that adjusting for inflation, real increases exhibited a similar pattern.

State and federal aid played an important role in the growth
of local government expenditures in the 1960s. Between 1960
and 1965 intergovernmental aid increased at an average annual
rate of 18.5 percent; in the next five-year period the rate increased to 22.6 percent. Employment in the City government
appears to have increased much more rapidly in the 1960s than
in the previous decade, although longitudinal employment
data are difficult to derive because of almost constant changes
in methods of accounting for employment. Using full-time
employment data, Table I shows that annual rates of increase
for periods 1960-1965 and 1965-1970 were 4.2 percent and 3
percent, respectively, compared to 1.9 percent during the
1955-1960 period. Employment figures that include part-time

as well as full-time employees also show rapid growth during the 1960s and a much slower rate during the 1950s.

Major Developmental Factors

Perhaps the most important factor underlying the rising influence of municipal unions during the 1960s was the growth of local government employment and unionization.[3] Between 1960 and 1970 full-time employment in the City government rose 43 percent, and civil service union membership increased almost four-fold. By 1970 roughly three-quarters of the City's workers were union members, compared to approximately one-third in 1960, and over 90 percent of the City's employees were represented by a civil service union for collective bargaining purposes.

As one observer noted, the rise of municipal unions coincided with the decline of the Democratic Party in New York City (Lowi 1967). Because of the large number of workers they represented and their growing organizational strength, by the mid-1960s municipal unions were among the most influential political interest groups in New York City. This fact did not go unnoticed by the City's elected leaders, particularly the two persons who served as mayor during the decade—Robert F. Wagner, Jr., and John V. Lindsay.

Wagner, who served three terms as mayor from 1954 to 1966, introduced collective bargaining in 1958, though it was not until 1960 that City officials actually promulgated the rules governing collective bargaining. He proved to be a tough, skillful negotiator who personally dominated the collective bargaining process until his last year in office. Wagner carefully limited the scope of bargaining to salaries and a few fringe and leave benefits. He also maintained political control over mediation panels convened to assist the resolution of disputes. Wagner maintained this practice until 1965, when an independent impasse panel settled a 28-day strike by welfare employees.

The years 1965 and 1966 represent a critical transition point in the City's labor relations. The panel created to settle the welfare strike not only did so on terms more favorable to the union than to the City but also recommended that a tripartite panel be formed to reevaluate the City's entire labor relations system. In November 1965 Lindsay was elected mayor, defeating Abraham D. Beame. Lindsay took office on January 1, 1966, and on that day the City's transit workers began a 13-day strike they subsequently won almost unconditionally. The combination of two major strikes lost by the City, creation of the tripartite panel that led to review of Wagner's labor relations program, and Lindsay's election and early experience with the transit strike all helped to produce a new labor relations climate within the City government.

Lindsay's labor relations attitudes and skills were different from Wagner's. [Cf. Chapter VI in which Douglas discusses their differences in considering how political leadership styles and attitudes affect labor relations outcomes.] During Lindsay's first term, the rules of the game changed dramatically. After losing the politically atmospheric transit strike, Lindsay decided quickly that the informal, highly political labor relations of the Wagner years should be reformed by instituting a more formal system which would involve less participation by the mayor, administration by "impartials" rather than "interested" parties, and tripartite impasse procedures. The panel charged with reviewing Wagner's program embraced Lindsay's views, and its recommendations were enacted. Whereas Wagner's political instincts led him to active involvement in all facets of municipal labor relations, Lindsay's did not, particularly after a series of major civil service strikes from 1966 to 1968. Thus during Lindsay's two terms in office, mayoral delegation of labor relations authority became organizationally and politically institutionalized.

Lindsay's early and open desire to reduce the growing union influence in City politics had been a key factor in the labor unrest between 1966 and 1968, but by 1969 the mayor's position was altered by the (perhaps accurate) perception that his reelection chances depended on two important political resources largely controlled by municipal union leaders—labor peace the year before the campaign and labor support during the campaign:

> Labor peace was restored temporarily to New York City in 1969, a year that saw both a mayoral election and contract negotiations with the major unions. There is considerable evidence to suggest that Lindsay and the leaders of the major unions perceived and then realized a mutuality of interest in this combination of events. No major strikes occurred; major unions which had opposed Lindsay's election in 1965 supported him in 1969; and unions did extremely well at the bargaining table. (Horton 1971:687.)

While this brief description of the Wagner-Lindsay years emphasizes political rather than economic considerations—the growing size and organizational strength of civil service unions, formal rule changes and informal strategies that reduced the mayor's influence over collective bargaining, and electoral politics—the essentially cooperative political relationship that emerged eventually between City Hall and municipal unions would not have been easy or perhaps even possible absent the favorable economic condition of the local government at the time. The immense revenue flow into the City treasury made it relatively easy to buy, so to speak, labor peace and labor support without important prejudice to the resource interests of other political interest groups.

Resources were abundant for several reasons. In addition to intergovernmental aid, local revenues were growing rapidly during this period because of tax-rate and economic base increases. Finally, the City's substantial borrowing capacity and—closely related to its ability to borrow—its ability to obfuscate financial facts through complex budgetary and accounting techniques, also contributed to the impression if not the reality that money was not in short supply.

In this environment it is not surprising that economic constraints on management in collective bargaining were not fully operative. Amidst economic prosperity, cooperative political relationships between City Hall and municipal unions were relatively easy to realize.

Labor Relations Outcomes during the 1960s

While analyzing political strategies, organizational growth, and institutional change is useful in establishing *prima facie* evidence of political change, the best evidence of change comes from examining actual decisions rather than the process by which they are reached. By analyzing collective bargaining and other labor relations decisions during the 1960s, particularly after 1965, a strong case can be made that the major redistribution of labor relations influence occurring during that period was related closely to the strong expansion of the local public economy.

Table 2 relates wage increases for patrolmen during the 1960s to cost of living increases and to those in private sector wages in New York City. Public-private wage comparisons always pose difficult empirical, methodological, and conceptual problems. Patrolmen were selected for analysis because their wage gains during the 1960s were similar to the gains made by a representative cross section of City employees. This is because uniformed employee negotiations, usually police negotiations, historically have played a key role in establishing bargaining patterns in the City's parity-laden compensation structure (Schoolman 1976).

Between 1960 and 1975, base pay of patrolmen—excluding two supplemental wage benefits, paid holidays, and the night-shift differential, which are tied to base pay and are received by all patrolmen—rose 173.6 percent, compared to a 90.8 percent increase in the local consumer price index. When the two supplemental benefits are included, wages of patrolmen rose 195.7 percent, or more than twice the local inflation rate.[4]

Between 1960 and 1974, the last year for which data are available on average wage gains in the private sector, private workers' wages rose only 105.6 percent. In addition to illus-

TABLE 2.   Average Annual Rates of Wage Change of Patrolmen
Compared to Private Sector workers in
New York City from
1960 to 1975

Period	Current $		Current $	
	Patrolman	Private Worker	Patrolman	Private Worker
1960-1965	6.4%	3.5%	4.8%	2.0%
1965-1970	8.3	6.2	3.4	1.4
1970-1975	7.8	6.4	0.8	(0.4)
1960-1975*	7.5	5.3	3.0	1.1

*Private employee wage data available only through 1974.
Sources: Data for patrolmen are computed from data from New York City
Office of Labor Relations; data for private workers are computed from
data from New York State Department of Labor.

trating the wage relationships between patrolmen and private
workers, Table 2 illustrates the harsh effect of inflation on real
wages in New York City. Over the entire period, private
workers' real wages rose at an average annual rate of only 1.1
percent; and real wages in the private sector actually have declined since 1970.

But real wages for patrolmen—and most other City
employees—increased despite unusually high inflation rates
after 1970. In each of the five-year periods, the annual average
rate of pay increase for patrolmen exceeded the corresponding
increase for private workers by more than 2 percentage
points—suggesting that different market forces affected the
wage determination process in the two sectors.

When improvements in fringe and retirement benefits are
considered, a more complete understanding is possible of the
scope of City employee collective bargaining gains during the
decade—again, particularly after 1965. In 1963 the City first
introduced through collective bargaining a fringe benefit
known as the union welfare fund, essentially a health benefit
plan that supplements the City's basic health insurance plan.

In 1966 the City moved to full financing of the basic health plan, picking up 100 percent of its costs.

In addition, several major retirement benefits were negotiated between 1965 and 1970. A twenty-year retirement benefit was granted to sanitationmen in 1967, transit workers in 1968, and teachers in 1970. Citywide employees received a twenty-five-year retirement benefit in 1968 and a twenty-year plan in 1970—the latter not approved by the state legislature in 1971, precipitating an unsuccessful strike by City workers that brought the trend toward negotiated pension liberalization to a halt. In 1968 a new retirement benefit, union annuity funds, was provided to uniformed employees and teachers. In 1970 transit workers negotiated a pension plan fully paid for by the employer.

When negotiated improvements in wages, fringe benefits, and retirement benefits during the 1965-1970 period are examined—not to mention expansion of the scope of bargaining to include civil service rules, work rules, and even, in some instances, public policies (see Horton 1973)—it is generally agreed that the negotiating gains of organized City workers were markedly different than in previous years. That other state and local government employees in the U.S. also enjoyed substantial benefit increases during the same period—in some instances, like Chicago, without formal collective bargaining rights—strengthens the inference that the generally expansive economies of state and local governments influenced substantially the development and outcomes of public sector labor relations during the 1960s (see Lewin 1976d).

LABOR RELATIONS AMIDST SCARCITY

Compared to the 1965-1970 period, Table 3 shows that the local public economy in New York City was a disaster area from 1970 to 1975. Whereas operating expenditures increased at an annual average of 15.6 percent in the second half of the 1960s, the rate of increase fell about a third to 10.2 percent

TABLE 3. Average Annual Rates of Change of
Selected New York City Economic Indicators from
1965 to 1975

Five-Year Periods	Expenditures		Intergovernmental Aid		Employment	
	Current $	Constant $	Current $	Constant $	FT	FT+PT
1965-1970	15.6%	10.3%	22.6%	17.0%	3.0%	5.0%
1970-1975	10.2	3.0	8.9	1.8	(2.2)	0.9

Source: For 1965-1970 period, same as Table 1; 1975 expenditure and intergovernmental aid data computed from data in 1976-1977 Executive Budget;
1975 full-time employment data are derived from data from the New York
City Bureau of the Budget; 1975 full-time and part-time employment data
are derived from data provided by New York State Department of Labor.

between 1970 and 1975. In constant dollars, expenditures increased an average of only 3 percent a year from 1970 to 1975,
compared to 10.3 percent over the previous five years.

State and federal aid also increased more slowly in the
1970s than in the 1965-1970 period. In the later five-year
period intergovernmental aid grew an average 8.9 percent a
year, which, adjusted for inflation, amounted to only 1.8 percent in real growth. This compared to 22.6 percent average
annual growth—or 17 percent real growth—in the 1965-1970
period.

The same pattern is evident in employment. After increasing 3 percent a year between 1965 and 1970, full-time employment fell at an annual rate of 2.2 percent over the
1970-1975 period. Part-time and full-time employment increased an average 5 percent a year from 1965 to 1970, but
less than 1 percent between 1970 and 1975. In 1975 alone,
full-time plus part-time employment fell 11.2 percent, and
full-time employment fell 12.9 percent.[5]

The three-year financial plan under which the City now is

operating calls for expenditure reductions of $379 million in fiscal year 1977 below the fiscal year 1976 level, and an additional $483 million reduction in fiscal year 1978. It is likely that local government expenditures will continue to fall throughout the remainder of the decade, and employment in the City government almost certainly will continue to decline sharply.

Unlike the 1965-1970 period, no dichotomy existed between the local public economy and the overall New York City economy. The economy of New York City failed to recover from the national recession of 1969-1970 and, to complicate matters, the 1974-1975 recession coincided with the initial contraction of the City government. Between 1969 and 1975 New York City lost 522,000 jobs, almost 14 percent of its 1969 total.[6] The adversity of New York City's economic condition was such that during the first half of the 1970s it is estimated that its population declined by at least 400,000 persons, or more than 5 percent. By the mid-1970s the private and public economies of New York City were in serious disrepair.

The City's political leadership, including municipal union leaders, was either slow to appreciate or unwilling to address the significance for municipal labor relations of the City's changing economic condition. As late as 1974 City employees were able to negotiate two-year contracts raising wages 14 percent—8 percent in the first year and 6 percent in the second—and introducing a cost-of-living adjustment. In 1975 the Patrolmen's Benevolent Association sought to break its long-standing pay parity relationship with firemen by seeking a 19.4 percent salary increase instead of the 6 percent second-year increase negotiated between the firefighter's union and the City. In an arbitration on that issue, the police union strongly contested the City's defense that for financial reasons it was unable to pay more than the 6 percent increase negotiated with all other City workers. One month later, in March 1975, the City was unable to sell its securities publicly, and default was imminent.

The Financial and Political Revolution

Without access to money markets, the City would have been unable to maintain its operations or avoid default on its obligations. In June 1975 the state created a special agency, the Municipal Assistance Corporation (MAC), and empowered it to sell obligations, the proceeds of which were to be used to finance short-term City debt and pay operating expenses through September 1975. The City's sales and stock transfer tax receipts were made available in amounts necessary to service the MAC debt. The legislation creating MAC also required the City in ten years to eliminate over $700 million in operating expenses accumulated in its capital budget in the decade after 1965. While MAC was able to convert an extraordinary amount—more than $2 billion—of the City's short-term debt into its own long-term debt and to provide an additional $1.8 billion for the City's operating expenses, the market for MAC's obligations did not last long.

In the fall of 1975 the financial revolution produced a political revolution. While the legislation creating MAC imposed certain limits on City budgeting and accounting practices, MAC itself was conceived as a financing rather than governing instrument. In September 1975 the state legislature passed the Financial Emergency Act, creating the State Emergency Financial Control Board (EFCB), a seven-man body headed by Governor Hugh L. Carey and also including Mayor Beame, the City and State comptrollers, and three private businessmen who were appointed by Governor Carey. The EFCB was given substantial authority to intervene in the management of the City government. The Financial Emergency Act also required the creation of a three-year financial plan designed to produce a balanced budget in fiscal year 1978.

The creation of MAC and to a much greater extent the EFCB effectively increased the political influence of state and private actors at the expense of City officials. Two months after the Financial Emergency Act, in November 1975, the City again was on the verge of default. New bankers were required and new bankers emerged—though none enthusiastically—including the federal government, pension funds of municipal workers, and holders of City notes. A complicated financing scheme was worked out which once more enabled the City to avoid default: a three-year moratorium was declared on the payment of nearly $2 billion of maturing short-term City debt; the federal government agreed to provide up to $2.3 billion in seasonal loans; and trustees of the five City pension funds agreed to purchase $2.5 billion of City and MAC bonds. Thus the municipal unions assumed a central financing role in the City.

Labor Relations Outcomes

The first significant impact of the City's fiscal problems on labor relations occurred several years before the events of 1975 and were not registered on salaries. Indeed, as Table 2 indicated, salaries—though not real wages—continued to increase between 1970 and 1975 at rates similar to the 1965-1970 period. The first major impact of economic scarcity was on employment. In 1970 a selective attrition policy was announced that resulted, by 1973, in substantial manpower reductions among firemen, police, sanitationmen, and teachers. Faced with the choice of moderating employment and paying larger wage increases, collective bargaining participants chose the latter option. (For a more detailed discussion of this period, see Horton 1974.) This course persisted until 1975, indicating that civil service unions still dominated City officials in the collective bargaining process. From all viewpoints other than that of municipal unions, the "rational" labor relations policy would have been to attempt to moderate labor cost increases and, through gradual employment growth, expand public services. Between 1970 and 1975, however, both employment and services were restricted by wage and benefit increases resulting from collective bargaining.

The second major labor relations impact resulting from the City's increasing financial problems was in the area of pensions. In June 1971 a strike by City employees was called in an unsuccessful attempt to pressure the state legislature into ratifying a liberalized pensions program negotiated in the previous year by the largest City employee union. Shortly thereafter, the state legislature created the Permanent Commission on Public Employee Pension and Retirement Systems to assist it in evaluating retirement benefits of government employees. In 1973 certain pension reforms recommended by the Permanent Commission were enacted that reduced retirement benefits for employees hired after 1973. In addition, a three-year ban on pension bargaining was imposed. In sharp contrast with the 1965-1970 period, no major liberalization of City employee pension benefits occurred between 1970 and 1975. In 1975 certain pension benefits of City workers again were reduced. In 1976 the City announced its intention to withdraw from the social security system, a move designed to save the City more than $250 million annually.

It was not until 1975 that the fiscal crisis began to affect salaries of New York City workers. In 1974, as noted earlier, City employee unions negotiated a two-year contract calling for an 8 percent pay increase in fiscal year 1975 and a 6 percent increase, plus a cost-of-living adjustment, in fiscal year 1976. In September 1975 most of the City's major civil service unions entered into wage deferral agreements with the City under which all or part—depending on an employee's salary level—of the fiscal year 1976 salary increase was postponed for one year. In addition to the wage deferral agreement, various unions agreed to reductions of $8 million in previously negotiated welfare fund payments. In November 1975 the Financial Emergency Act imposed a wage freeze for one year that could be extended by the EFCB if deemed necessary to preserve the integrity of the three-year financial plan. However, the Act does provide that cost-of-living adjustments may be paid to those workers whose unions previously entered into wage deferral agreements with the City.

It is not hard to predict precisely what effect the financial crisis and the EFCB's authority to approve or disapprove collective bargaining contracts will have on salaries in particular and labor relations in general. The first two major contracts negotiated after the EFCB was created, one with teachers and the other with transit workers, were disapproved initially as in violation of the wage freeze. Municipal union leaders faced a seemingly impossible situation by 1976—although this condition was not limited to municipal union leaders, so precarious was the City's financial position. If union leaders aggressively sought and successfully realized salary or cost-of-living adjustments beyond the City's extremely limited ability to pay, default and bankruptcy were likely.

Bankruptcy probably threatens local government employees more directly than any other class of persons in New York City. First, existing contractual benefits, including possibly even retirement benefits that for the most part are protected against diminution by the New York State Constitution, would be subject to revision in a bankruptcy proceeding. Second, a default would place the pension funds of municipal workers in some jeopardy. The decision reached by municipal union leaders in 1975 to invest pension funds heavily in City securities greatly increased the danger posed by default, though at the time the alternative of almost immediate default was unattractive for the first reason noted above. Third, default and bankruptcy probably would lead to wholesale dismissals of City workers, particularly those not involved in the delivery of so-called "essential" services.

Given these conditions and the gloomy prospects for an economic recovery in New York City at least for several years, it is almost certain that the real wage gains realized by civil servants in the 1960s will be substantially if not entirely eliminated during the 1970s. It is likely also that fringe and retirement benefits of City workers will be reduced, with the savings thereby realized perhaps providing one means of granting limited wage increases. In all likelihood, the municipal labor relations process in New York City will change as dramatically in the 1970s as it did in the 1960s.

IMPLICATIONS FOR THE FUTURE
OF COLLECTIVE BARGAINING

Five years of labor relations amidst increasing prosperity and
five years amidst increasing scarcity permit some tentative
conclusions about the nature and future of the collective bargaining process in New York City. Several trends or developments rooted in economic decline appear to be important, not only in explaining the changes that occurred between
1970 and 1975 but in predicting future public sector labor relations developments. To repeat an initial observation, the labor
relations experience of New York City may not be repeated in
other state and local governments, possibly because New York
City's economic and political circumstances may be unique or
because the New York City experience may prompt adaptive
responses elsewhere.

Important Union Implications

First, declining employment and union membership—related
products of economic scarcity—appear to pose serious organizational problems for civil service unions. To the extent government employment declines, the political influence of government unions will also likely decline. Further, employment
declines that reduce union membership reduce union income.
This cycle raises the possibility that civil service unions will
face organizational retrenchment problems not unlike those
experienced by contracting governments.

Second, severe economic conditions like those in New York
City may tend to blur the goals and strategies of municipal
union leaders. Prior to the City's fiscal collapse in 1975, there
appeared to be no—or at least few—economic and organizational constraints substantial enough to force union leaders to
moderate the traditional claims union leaders make on behalf
of their constituencies. Beginning in 1970, wage increases
were partly financed through savings realized by reduced employment, but this trade-off appeared to have no major effect

on collective bargaining demands or outcomes until 1975.

In 1975 the wage deferral agreements explicitily indicated an important strategic goal change by union leaders and, presumably, union members: union bargaining objectives accepted wage reductions to protect civil service jobs. But a more important factor contributing to the goal ambiguity of municipal union leaders is the financial role they assumed by agreeing to invest City employee pension funds in New York City bonds. By the mid-1970s the goals of civil service union leaders were more ambiguous than in the 1960s, again, because of the City's changing economic circumstances.

Important Management Implications

At the same time a fiscal crisis tends to blur the goals of union leaders, it also tends to bring more sharply into focus the labor relations goals of public officials. Throughout most of the decade after 1965, public officials in New York City found it difficult to reconcile their managerial responsibilities with their political interests in collective bargaining. That they so frequently pursued their political interests to the detriment of their managerial interests seems best explained by the fact that resources, generally speaking, were adequate enough to satisfy union demands without sacrificing the basic interests of other political interest groups in New York City. But when the financial crsis emerged full-blown in 1975, and the City's many political interest groups finally realized that resources available for public allocation were scarce, public officials found it easier to reconcile their managerial and political interests in more forcefully contesting municipal union demands.

A second important management implication is that the fiscal crisis has increased the influence of state officials in City labor relations. Because elected state officials have statewide constituencies, they have relatively fewer political incentives

than do New York City politicians to seek cooperative relationships with City employees. To the extent that federal officials become involved in the labor relations process to protect
national interests, another managerial layer will be operative,
even less susceptible to municipal union influence.[7]

Third, a fiscal crisis appears to promote better integration of
collective bargaining with other management functions such as
budgeting and financial planning. During the late 1960s and
early 1970s collective bargaining in New York City was relatively isolated from other central management processes.
Again, this resulted from the relative economic prosperity of
the period. However, as conservation of scarce financial resources grew increasingly important in the 1970s, earlier tendencies toward isolated resolution of labor disputes gave way.
The experience in New York City also suggests that periods of
economic scarcity will tend to reduce the importance of collective bargaining formalism and quasi-independent labor relations agencies such as New York City's Office of Collective
Bargaining.

Important Process Implications

The New York City experience raises anew some important
and interesting theoretical considerations of a broader nature.
First, the thesis that changing economic circumstances produce important changes in public sector labor relations suggests that political processes generally and collective bargaining in particular should not be conceived of either in static or
highly generalized terms. Changing economic conditions
caused two major political transformations in New York City
labor relations in the decade after 1965. If economic conditions indeed are influential in shaping local public sector labor
relations processes, it is likely that city, state, and regional
economic differences will contribute to the diversity of city,
state, and regional public sector labor relations.

Second, theoretical understanding of the dynamics of public
sector labor relations may be advanced by distinguishing col-

lective bargaining in a *distributive* political environment from bargaining in a *redistributive* environment. (For a theoretical analysis of the impact of distributive and redistributive decisions on the nature of political processes, see Lowi 1964*a*.) While all political acts are redistributive in the broad sense that they impose political costs on some groups and create political benefits for others, the New York City experience suggests that economic prosperity promotes a distributive model of collective bargaining, while economic scarcity is associated with a redistributive model.

Between 1965 and 1970 collective bargaining was regarded as but one political subprocess in a larger political system wherein resources were considered susceptible to almost infinite distribution. That is, the gains of one group were not necessarily considered in terms of the losses to another. However, from 1970 to 1975 the redistributive potential of collective bargaining became increasingly obvious to all groups, including organized civil servants. No longer were resources viewed as capable of being easily distributed to one group without hurting the perceived interests of another. By 1975 civil servants realized that wage increases meant increased layoffs, and the public understood that wage increases meant reduced services.

During a period of economic scarcity, it may be that collective bargaining in the public sector functions more like the (assumed) competitive model of private sector bargaining than it does during a period of economic prosperity.

XII

CONCLUSION: THE CURRENT POLITICAL CONTEST

A. H. RASKIN
Labor Columnist, New York Times

Public unions and municipal survival. A two-way street in public labor relations. Changing public sentiment. San Francisco 1975-1976. Washington backlash. Are things improving? New York 1976: "They don't have the wallop we have." Other recent rip-offs. A question of productivity. Right to strike and compulsory arbitration. Openness and public opinion.

The second half of the 1970s is a watershed period for the unions representing governmental employees at all levels, and particularly so for those in the nation's beleaguered cities. After fifteen years of meteoric growth and impressive economic gains based on a combination of politics and muscle, the civil service unions must learn to coexist constructively with their governmental employers in a framework of permanent austerity.

That shift is inescapable, though it may come painfully in big cities where entrenched unions have become accustomed

203

to converting strikes and strike threats into extra money in
their members' paychecks—money the community originally
insisted it did not have and could not get. Citizen
revulsion—that healthiest of correctives in a democracy—is
signaling an imminent end to further retreat by civic authorities into appeasement.

The clearest signals have come from New York City and
San Francisco—the two cities that traveled furthest both in
fostering a hospitable climate for unionization of public employees and in surrendering whenever unions controlling vital
services clubbed them through abuse of the power the community had helped them acquire. These copyright holders in
all that was best—and worst—in the municipal approach to
labor relations are now putting padlocks on their overtaxed
treasuries and discovering that "no" can be a supportable answer if officials and citizens are resolute enough.

It would be preposterous, however, to suggest that a full
turn in relationships has already been made in those two cities
or in government generally. Indeed, it is doubtful that it will
stay made at all if the transformation must depend on substitution of governmental arbitrariness for union arbitrariness. That
would simply put things back where they were before unionism penetrated the civil service.

TOWARD A TWO-WAY STREET
IN PUBLIC LABOR RELATIONS

If public sector labor relations are to become a two-way street,
traffic must flow in both directions, with mutual benefits for
the public and those who work for it. Many of the worst sins at
the bargaining table have been committed by management,
sometimes out of desire for political advantage, sometimes out
of cowardice, but most often out of ignorance or incompetence. Obviously, in a democracy no one can provide insurance against the inadequacy of elected officials. But it is in-
contestable that the quality of the public's representatives—not
only in collective bargaining but in day-to-day supervision in

every level of government—is essential if a new foundation of trust is to be established in union relations and if heightened productivity is to play its proper role in trimming the blubber from the bureaucracy without forcing abandonment of indispensable services.

The same public outrage that has brought the embattled unions to heel in many cities represents the best foundation for hope that municipal managers will begin to assume the monumental responsibilities they must discharge. No longer are the citizens ready to roll over and play dead in the face of union exactions. Yet neither will they forgive administrators who destroy the foundation for cooperation by giving the unions double-talk on the true state of governmental finances or on the options available for meeting civic needs with minimal injury to employee welfare. The viability of the cities is questionable enough without building frustration in unionists convinced it is time to jettison confrontation methods imported into the civil service from the private sector.

THE CHANGE IN PUBLIC SENTIMENT

San Francisco 1975-1976

The inappropriateness of the transplant from the private sector is made graphic by a close-up look at the 1975-1976 developments that turned San Francisco from the most union of union towns into a community as rabidly dedicated to breaking a strike as any citadel of the open shop in the Southern textile belt. The reversal in sentiment surfaced in August 1975, when most of San Francisco's police officers and firemen struck because they wanted a larger pay increase than the Board of Supervisors was willing to approve.

A month before the walkout Mayor Joseph L. Alioto, attending a somber annual conference of the United States Conference of Mayors in Boston, had eclipsed all his colleagues in gloom about the plight of the cities and about the need for firmness in holding the line against unreasonable demands by

unionized municipal employees. He was particularly emphatic
in calling on the assembled mayors to save their communities
from disaster by being tough in police and fire strikes. His
prescriptions included mandatory dismissal for all strikers in
public safety jobs. "In those emergency categories, you simply cannot fool around with a strike," Mayor Alioto said.

But he forgot all his brave words when his own police force
and firemen struck. He spurned a request by the Board of
Supervisors that he ask Governor Edmund G. Brown, Jr., to
assign state troopers to patrol the city—a move that would
have given its 670,000 people more security at the same time
that it strengthened the community's leverage at the bargaining
table.

Instead, the mayor "mediated" the pay dispute by giving
the strikers twice as much as the supervisors had
authorized—the unions' full 13 percent demand, subject only
to an October 15 effective date as against July 1. When the
irate municipal legislators vetoed the pay boost, Alioto
blandly proclaimed a state of emergency and put it into effect
all by himself. His excuse, as relayed by aides, was that all
San Francisco labor was poised for a general strike and that the
deferred pay boost was a small price for rescuing the city from
that calamity. Amnesty for all the strikers was another part of
the price.

There was not much the voters could do to Mayor Alioto to
show how deeply they resented his capitulation; he had already
announced his decision to retire at the end of his term December 31. But the November election did give the electorate
an opportunity to demonstrate their wrath and to seal the door
against future raids on municipal funds by the unions and their
protectors at City Hall. By top-heavy margins, San Franciscans modified the parity formulas on which the unions had
relied to push up wages beyond those prevailing in other
California cities. They revoked the mayor's power to declare
an emergency and to act without sanction by the supervisors.
They also authorized dismissal of police and firefighters involved in future strikes.

The only consolation the civil service unions could take from the election results was that the Democratic candidate to succeed Alioto, George Moscone, nosed out the underdog, a conservative Republican named John Barbagelata, who had sparked much of the supervisors' opposition to the old mayor. The unions had backed Moscone, even though he campaigned on a promise to keep union demands under restraint.

The first test came at the end of March of this year when the supervisors voted to cut the salaries on 1,900 craft employees on the ground that they were excessive under the newly established standards. The protested rates ran from $17,300 a year for laborers to $24,100 for electricians. In other California cities the same jobs carried salaries ranging from $9,200 to $18,650. For maintenance craftsmen with year-round employment in private industry, the range was from $14,900 to $20,500.

The supervisors' insistence on bringing the municipal craft salary schedule into line with the rates in private industry brought a strike in defiance of an injunction. It had the immediate effect of cutting off service on the city-operated buses, trolleys, and cable cars and it brought a renewal of the general strike threats that had thrown Alioto into a tailspin. But Mayor Moscone refused to panic, and Harry Bridges—the venerable firebrand who had led the general strike that began on the San Francisco waterfront in the early days of the New Deal—lost little time in letting it be known that he had no intention this time of involving his longshoremen in a general strike.

Indeed, four-fifths of the unionized workers in the civil service stayed on the job along with the rest of the San Francisco work force. As for the bulk of the city's population, it rallied behind the supervisors, even to the point of organizing volunteer crews to clean up downtown streets in place of the striking streetsweepers. In dozens of interviews citizens endorsed the "get tough" policy toward the strikers. Their reasons went beyond the humiliation they felt over Alioto's surrender or their resentment against skyrocketing municipal taxes. They did not want San Francisco to follow New York City into near bankruptcy, a mendicant reduced to begging Washington and the state for emergency handouts.

"Labor's day of running San Francisco is over," said Quentin L. Kopp, president of the Board of Supervisors, at the end of the strike's first week. "What started it was New York. That scared people." (Cf. Chapter XI.)

In the end, after thirty-nine days of strike, it was the unions not the city that ran up the white flag. The supervisors had voted to put on the referendum ballot in a special June election two propositions which the unions considered poison. One would have confirmed and made irrevocable the pay cuts the supervisors were demanding, a total rout for the craftsmen. The other would have required the automatic dismissal after a hearing of any city worker who shall "instigate, participate in or afford leadership to a strike or engage in any picketing activity in furtherance of such a strike" against the city or county.

As an alternative to putting these propositions before the voters, the supervisors offered to go along with a formula that would let a fact-finding committee decide how much the craftsmen should get if they returned to work immediately. The panel was to include five representatives of the supervisors and five of the unions, but a dispute developed over who would be chairman. Mayor Moscone had frequently expressed the view that the supervisors were right and the unions wrong, and the head of the plumbers' union objected to having him as impartial chairman on those grounds.

But whatever the union reservations on that score, they were as nothing to the fears of what would happen if the electorate were given another chance to record its distaste for civil service unions. With the supervisors adamant on going ahead with the referendum unless an elected official headed the fact-finders, the strikers bowed less than forty-eight hours before the deadline for eliminating the two propositions from the June ballot. Splits within the unions' own ranks had made their defeat unavoidable; in the past it had always been divisions within the city's elected officialdom on which the unions had counted for victory.

Growing Resistance

A similar tide of community conviction that unions have been getting too much in collective bargaining and giving too little in job performance is noticeable throughout the country. And nobody is noticing it more than mayors and other elected officials, including many who owe their election to labor support. "There is a growing resistance to increased taxes and, since most of what cities do is service, that means a growing resistance to increased wages," is the way John J. Gunther, executive director of the United States Conference of Mayors, puts it. "The most that people are willing to let civil service workers do is keep pace with the cost of living and often they don't even want to go that far."

The same tide is running at the state level. Governor Hugh Carey of New York, heavily backed with money and manpower by the public employee unions in his victorious 1974 campaign, denied the state's 180,000 organized workers half of the 6 percent wage raise recommended by an official factfinding panel for 1975 and gave them no increase at all this year. Another prime favorite of the civil service unions, Connecticut Governor Ella T. Grasso, has turned into a pariah in their eyes as the result of her unsuccessful effort to ram through the legislature a requirement that state employees work five hours extra a week without more pay. "She's a traitor to the people who elected her—working people, labor, consumers," says the regional head of the American Federation of State, County and Municipal Employees.

A far more sweeping assault on civil service unions has been initiated in Virginia by Governor Mills E. Godwin, never noted as pro-labor. He has directed the state's attorney general to seek a court judgment declaring that contracts between unions and state or local governmental agencies are illegal. Nearly a third of Virginia's public school teachers are currently covered by bargaining agreements with their school boards. Similar pacts cover thousands of police officers, firefighters, and other civil servants in Virginia communities rimming the District of Columbia. But the state has specifically delegated authority to localities only for collective bargaining affecting public transit lines, and the governor hopes that will provide a handle for upsetting the pacts now in force in other agencies.

Washington Backlash

In the federal realm it is scarcely surprising to see public employees with few open champions in a year when Democratic presidential candidates are vying with the Republican incumbent, President Ford, and his challenger, Ronald Reagan, in "running against Washington." Last year the Civil Service Commission and the Office of Management and Budget recommended that the President raise federal salaries by 8.66 percent to meet the legal requirement that government pay scales be comparable to those in private industry. Mr. Ford, in line with his determination to fight inflation by holding down federal spending, put through an increase of only 5 percent. It went unchallenged by the Democratic Congress, despite anguished screams from the civil service unions. In this election year, the same procedure seems likely to be repeated. The politicians have decided there are more votes lost than gained by giving money to public employees.

The backlash against government unions has made an orphan of what originally was to have been one of organized labor's "must" bills in Congress this year. That bill was designed to mandate federal minimum standards for the states and localities on recognition of unions and procedures for collective bargaining. These would parallel the rules covering private employees and would include both a right to strike and authorization for agency-shop agreements under which all civil service workers would have to pay the equivalent of union dues, whether or not they actually joined.

The bill's supporters on Capitol Hill walked away from it under the combined incubus of the San Francisco police and fire strike and the collapse of New York City's credit—a development which most Congressmen ascribed to botched labor relations and prodigality at the bargaining table even more than to years of Ponzi-like budget manipulation by the city's elected leaders. An abortive effort to breathe life back into the bill was made by Jerry Wurf, president of the 700,000-member American Federation of State, County and Municipal Employees, at the biennial convention of the AFL-CIO in San Francisco last October.

The Wurf initiative took the form of a plea to the general labor movement to take the bill's reluctant sponsors off the hook by endorsing an amendment that would exclude police, fire and other public safety workers from the right to strike. His proposal envisaged compulsory arbitration of police-fire disputes and voluntary arbitration for other essential employees. Though Wurf has done plenty in his own right to foster the public impression of labor arrogance, his sensible plea for moderation as the only means of getting the embalmed measure out of the legislature morgue earned him a round of denunciations from the rest of the union fraternity. "I hope I will never see the day that the AFL-CIO, sitting in convention, will ask Congress to impose compulsory arbitration on anybody, anywhere, at any time," roared George Meany, the federation's eighty-one-year-old president.

That left the legislation still inanimate. But the absence of any prospect that Uncle Sam will order bargaining nationwide has not stopped unions from making continued progress in getting statutory go-aheads at the state and local levels. Connecticut, Indiana, Maine, New Hampshire, Utah, and Washington did pass comprehensive new public sector bargaining laws in 1975, despite the chill in public sentiment toward the fruits of such laws. California went part of the way with a law encouraging unions and collective bargaining in the public schools and community colleges, but it did not pass a similar law for all public employees.

THE GROWTH OF PUBLIC UNIONS

The reality is that the civil service unions remain the fastest growing section of the labor movement. In the face of mass layoffs of public employees, pay freezes, and community hostility, they continue to enroll members. If anything, adversity makes civil servants conscious for the first time that the job security which supposedly distinguishes their employment from jobs in industries organized for profit is largely illusory. That consciousness, combined with the fact that thirty-seven states now have bargaining laws, encourages unionization for all the reasons outlined in Robert Nisbet's chapter (II). Unions in the public sector therefore can be expected to keep growing, no matter how sharp the contraction in civil service payrolls.

The growth has already been phenomenal, especially by contrast with the static course of most union membership. In the federal service a total of 1.2 million workers, or 59 percent, is now unionized. This is more than double the 25 percent ratio of unionists in the overall nonagricultural work force. In state and local employment, the official figures lag by a couple of years, but even as of 1974 the Census Bureau recorded 4.7 million of the 9.2 million state and local employees, or 51 percent, as members of unions or associations. Two years earlier the ratio had been only 41 percent. That meant membership had grown by a quarter in that brief span. And the federal figure does not include the postal service, with more than a half-million unionized employees.

The postal service is a disaster area, its postage rates and its deficits astronomic, the quality of its service abysmal. Its unions can scarcely be blamed for all or even most of its deficiencies, but it is clear that these cannot be corrected without union cooperation. In a sense, the reorganization of the old Post Office Department into what was supposed to become a self-supporting, quasi-private corporation was itself a union product. The postal strike of March 1970—the first major violation in any federal agency of the doctrine that no legal right exists to strike against the government—broke the impasse between the White House and Congress over creation of an independent unit to deliver the mail on a pay-as-you-go basis. The settlement, which encompassed the outlines of the reorganization as well as protective features for the postal employees, was personally negotiated by George Meany and Richard M. Nixon—two chiefs of state dealing on terms of equality against a backdrop of illegality.

In the same way that nothing can change for the better in the postal service unless the unions concur, it is fatuous to think that New York City can dig itself out of its fiscal morass if it has to contend with foot-dragging or outright conflict by its unions. An unresolved question even now is whether the city's officials are adequately aware of the necessity for building a new relationship free of the old-line political concessions and capitulations. The rest of the country's mayors may see New York as a monstrous example of everything that needs avoiding in terms of union relations, but there are disturbing indications even at this late date that the message has not got through to many in high places within the city's own administrative structure.

FUTURE PROSPECTS: ARE THINGS IMPROVING?

New York 1976: "They don't have the wallop we have"

The negotiations for a New York subway and bus agreement last March were a ghastly case in point. Governor Carey had just got through telling the state employees they would get nothing because the state had nothing to give. What's more, he made the union of state employees swallow that bad news. The city was preparing to tell its police, fire, sanitation, and general unions the same thing when their contracts expired June 30. The Transit Authority, with a big deficit despite federal, state, and city subsidies, was in no position to do any better than the state or city. Indeed, on the basis of past increases, a strong argument could be made that transit employees were less entitled to a raise than any other state or city employee group.

Aware of all these pressures, the Transport Workers Union decided to content itself with a liberalization of the cost-of-living escalator it had established two years before. That was moderate by comparison with the contract gains negotiated in earlier years, but it exceeded the city's capacity to pay when viewed as a pattern-setter for the other unions. The city's fiscal experts estimated that it would boost municipal labor costs by $225 million to $375 million over its two years, thus wrecking Mayor Beame's austerity budget.

The official explanation by the Transit Authority for breaching the pay freeze was that the union had promised productivity improvements which would offset all of the extra cost; but it quickly became clear that the contract guaranteed the escalator pay increases regardless of whether productivity went up or down. The private explanation, as given by one ranking transit official, was the classic one—the one that had contributed so substantially to dragging New York to the lip of bankruptcy: "We were negotiating with a cannon to our head. If they walk out, they bring the city to its knees." It was just such a concern that stopped Mayor Beame from repudiating the pact on the night it was written. He knew it would impose an intolerable, fresh burden on his precariously balanced budget for the next three years, but when his advisers warned him that rejection of the accord would mean a strike, with all the risk of a costlier settlement at its end, he took refuge in a mealy-mouthed statement that he could neither embrace nor spurn it until its implications had been further studied. Six weeks later that study still was being conducted by the city's fiscal Seeing Eye dog, the Emergency Financial Control Board.

How much rode on the outcome of the review board's analysis was quickly disclosed by Senator William Proxmire of Wisconsin. Under ordinary circumstances what the senator thought of a New York labor settlement wouldn't be worth the 50-cent price of a subway token. But in his role as chairman of the Senate Banking Committee, his opinions of the city's fiscal integrity are of critical importance whenever it goes to

Washington, tin cup in hand. Proxmire lost no time in pronouncing the transit settlement "a tragic mistake," one that cast so much doubt on the constancy of New York's determination to live within its insufficient means that it placed in peril its right to continued help from the federal government.

Point was given to his comment in mid-May when the full membership of the Senate Banking Committe subscribed to a report urging that Washington "seriously consider" terminating its $2.3 billion in annual seasonal loans if the city failed to maintain its three-year wage freeze. The report cited the transit agreement as a troublesome example of the type of regression it feared. Application of the beefed-up escalator to all union contracts, in line with a tradition of "me too" settlements, could wipe out any chance of repayment of the federal loans, the committee declared. The Transit Authority *ex post facto* redoubled its efforts to get from the union productivity commitments explicit enough to reassure both the state-city fiscal monitors and the senators that the pact made under the club of a strike threat would not actually cost anybody anything.

Matthew Guinan, president of the TWU, had made it all clear even before the pact was initialed. Asked why his members should get more money this year when state employees had accepted the need for signing without a raise, his reply was terse: "They don't have the wallop we have." That cynical maxim seemed destined to prevail until late in May after San Francisco held firm. Following the Golden Gate settlement, the Emergency Financial Control Board and Mayor Beame's financial advisers dug in on a hard line and convinced the transit union they would not budge from it even if it meant putting the city through a strike.

Once that message got through, the union folded. It went along with an imposed formula curtailing payments under the escalator and making any payments at all contingent on audited proof of productivity improvements sufficient to finance the extra costs without exceeding the budget or reducing service. Other cutbacks in the original plan also were ordered, all aimed at bringing down the total bill for wages and pensions.

New York City employees thus received a tangible stake in making city operations more efficient without ripping the corset of fiscal constraints within which New York had to live.

Guidelines were established for contracts still in negotiation with other city unions. The guidelines stipulated that no agreement could provide for cost-of-living increases or any other form of pay boost unless "funded by independently measured savings realized, without reduction in services, through gains in productivity, reductions of fringe benefits, or through other savings or other revenues approved by the board." And that was not all. The guidelines required that each agreement contain a mechanism for savings in pension costs or other fringe benefits.

The transit union submitted to this ukase with scarcely a whimper, but other municipal unions with contracts still unsigned started muttering defiance. Some talked of strike. Most recognized, however, that a new weapon might be needed if the TWU, long the fiercest tiger in the union zoo, could no longer scare City Hall by threatening to stop the subways and buses. Victor Gotbaum, head of the 125,000-member District Council 37 of the American Federation of State, County and Municipal Employees, hinted that the billions of dollars in union pension funds might become the club which labor employed to clobber the city into punching holes in the guidelines.

If the control board and the mayor balked at genuine collective bargaining, he warned, the unions might balk at investing promised money from these reserves in municipal bonds, thus plunging the city into bankruptcy. This revised version of *East Lynne*—the flint-hearted union banker foreclosing on an impecunious metropolis—failed to take into account the damage civil service workers themselves might suffer as front-line casualties in such a fiscal debacle. As these lines are written, it is still too early to tell who will blink first in the June 30 showdown over the guidelines—the city or the unions.

There are still plenty of appeasers left in City Hall. Moreover, union muscle on the picket lines or at the bond loan window is not the only kind of clout New York's politicians defer to. Unlike San Francisco's officialdom, they are still not sure they can stand up against union pressure without paying a high price at the polls. How potent the union influence remains in the state legislature at Albany was illustrated twice in April.

Other Recent Rip-Offs

The first episode involved passage—in the face of energetic objections by Mayor Beame and a veto by Governor Carey—of a bill lobbied through by the United Federation of Teachers, a union with a Ph.D. in politics. The bill, ostensibly directed at assuring equal treatment for the schools in budget cuts, would have had the effect of forcing the city to give them $140 million more than they were scheduled to get. It would also trigger demands for similar "equality" of treatment by police, fire, and every other service with a political constituency. Haggling is still going on about ways to neutralize the measure now that it is on the statute books.

Meanwhile the New York City police and fire unions sneaked a so-called "heart" bill through the Republican State Senate and the Democratic Assembly, though two prestigious fact-finding groups had pronounced all such measures rip-offs the public could not afford. The bill would classify all heart ailments suffered by policemen or firemen as automatically service-connected, with the victim entitled to retirement on full pension regardless of age. Dozens of such "retirees" in their twenties or thirties hold full-time jobs as security officers in industry.

BACK TO FUNDAMENTALS:
THE NEED FOR INCREASED PRODUCTIVITY

It is plain from all this that the public cannot count on everything to straighten out in civil service union relations simply because it is tired of paying the bill for over-generous settle-

ments made to avert strikes or to end them. The problems of
civic decay are too pervasive and the need for positive union
action to alleviate and eradicate them too great to justify hope
that anything lasting will be achieved by a policy that begins
and ends with "hang tough."

A good starting point on trying to reform relationships on
mutually beneficial lines is to stress the theoretical point of
enacting statutes to encourage unionization of the civil service.
The preambles of almost every state bargaining law and all
federal executive orders on dealing with unions contain decla-
rations comparable to the one in New York's Taylor Law. It
states that the law's purpose is "to promote harmonious and
cooperative relationships between government and its employees and to protect the public by assuring, at all times, the
orderly and uninterrupted operations and functions of government." It is easy to argue that this is garbage, a collection of
pieties belied by everything that has happened under im-
primatur of the statute or in defiance of it.

The difficulty with all such cavalier statements is not that
they are untrue. On the contrary, the reason we are in such a
sad state is that these laws have become passports to victimiza-
tion of the community at least as often as they have contributed
even marginally to building a more efficient, more dedicated,
better qualified civil service. But that does not lessen the de-
sirability of trying to achieve the virtuous purposes that underlie them. That is essential if only because so much of government is the people who work for it and so much of the cost of
government is paying for their services.

Last year federal, state, and local salaries came to $175 bil-
lion, more than one-fifth of the whole flow of wages in the
economy. Almost half of the federal outlay on goods and services goes for wages. The proportion is even higher at the state
and local level, where the need for budget balance is most
pressing. Fifty-seven percent of state and city spending is accounted for by payroll.

The survival of the cities and eventually of all government,
given the mounting rebelliousness of the taxpayer, depends on

getting more and better service for every dollar of wage investment. That is the only alternative to a downward spiral in which every economy simply aggravates the community's downhill slide by making it less livable. Thus, one of the country's leading bankers—John R. Bunting, chairman and chief executive officer of the First Pennsylvania Corporation—warns that cutbacks being made in New York, Philadelphia and certain other cities might, with the perspective of time, be considered as absurd and counterproductive as Herbert Hoover's efforts to halt the Great Depression by balancing the budget.

> At a time when unemployment is in double digits in these cities, we are raising taxes drastically, reducing the number of city workers and decreasing, if not eliminating, city capital spending. The result is to "lock in"—indeed, to make permanent in our major cities—the recession from which the rest of the country seems to be emerging.

Bunting's suggested cures—mandatory federal aid through revenue-sharing whenever a city's unemployment exceeds 6 percent and a $50,000 exemption from local property-tax assessments on new building—do not require consideration here. There is undisputed merit, however, to the view that layoffs can destroy a city, not save it, if they are all made through curtailment of the protections, the services, and the amenities that determine the safety and quality of urban life. Only by combining vastly improved municipal management with unstinting union cooperation based on a conviction of need and good faith is it possible to let go large numbers of workers while providing all essential services—perhaps even in superior fashion. Experiments in worker participation both in this country and West Europe hint at the potentialities for city-saving along this line.

Productivity is the lever for freeing civil servants of the unpalatable prospect of one contract after another in which all the bargaining centers on how much they are to give up. It is also the instrument for rescuing the cities from a steady deterioration in services as a result of the reductions in spending that are intended to halt the flight of private industry and of the middle class. The problem is to develop trustworthy yardsticks for measuring improved productivity so that there are demonstrable benefits for communities and public employees to share. With requisite ingenuity on the part of the Transit Authority and the Emergency Financial Control Board, the much-criticized New York transit agreement could become a bellwether in the movement toward such efficiency generators.

THE RIGHT TO STRIKE AND COMPULSORY ARBITRATION

I have always been something of an absolutist on the need for maintaining a rigid ban against strikes in government. I still believe that in principle a strong case can be made for differentiating between public and private employees in this regard, even though I recognize the fuzziness these days of the boundary lines between what is public and what is private. I see little purpose to opening up a general right to strike in the public sector and then providing that certain groups be excluded on the basis of essentiality. It is precisely these groups—police, fire, hospital, sanitation, and in some situations transit—that cause the worry when they strike. The others can stay out forever and never be missed.

But, basically sound as I consider the no-strike concept in government, it is silly to deny that it has been and will continue to be widely disregarded if only a blanket statutory prohibition sustains it. That converts the real key to preventing disruptive strikes into one based on the community's capacity for creating both fundamental relationships and auxiliary peace mechanisms adequate to make unionists and their leaders feel there is no need for striking—and good reason not to.

Compulsory arbitration provides one useful alternative where all efforts at direct negotiation and conciliation have failed. Twenty-two states now have final and binding arbitration in some form—mostly in police and fire disputes. New York City has a law making arbitration the end of the line for all disputes that cannot be resolved within its Office of Collective Bargaining, an apparatus under tripartite control. Unfortunately, the future of compulsory arbitration is cloudy in New York and many other places, not because the unions are unhappy with it but because public administrators, caught in the budget squeeze, are unwilling to let neutrals devoid of either fiscal expertise or operational responsibility make decisions that may upset their spending plans.

In view of organized labor's atavistic objection to compulsory arbitration as a stifler of free collective bargaining, it is interesting how few cases require arbitration. In New York City, for example, only eight cases went from impasse panels to compulsory arbitration in the fifty-two months since the bargaining law was changed to establish finality in dispute-resolution. And every one of these eight cases resulted in unanimous affirmation of the recommendations made by the impasse panel. In the light of that record, there seems plentiful warrant for urging other communities to follow New York City in establishing arbitration machinery.

But the current administrative trend is away from arbitration, not toward it. New York's proposed substitute would be to have the City Council, the municipal legislative arm, make the final decision in deadlocks after it had held a public hearing. The council, based on past performance, is indecisive to the point of spinelessness—and painfully susceptible to union political pressure. The community will have to be watching over it if sneak deals of the kind the unions regularly float in Albany are not to become the mode once a detour from arbitration is made. Whether the battered metropolis can stand a return to politicized decisionmaking on the civil service labor front is almost a self-answering question. It can't.

But even if mayors and governors do not kill compulsory arbitration as a slur on their ability to rule, it is likely the courts will do it for them. Thus, South Dakota's Supreme Court struck down last year a law prescribing arbitration in police and fire impasses. It held that the statute constituted an illegal delegation of legislative power in violation of the state constitution. Michigan's Supreme Court split two-to-two on the constitutionality of a similar law, and other challenges to arbitration's legality await decision in many areas. If the principle is struck down, it will be harder than ever to avoid showdowns on the picket line as the court of final appeal in bargaining stalemates.

THE NEED FOR RESISTANCE—AND ITS PROBLEMS

In those circumstances the community has no choice except to stand and fight against union unreasonableness, as San Franciscans did last April. It is only realistic, however, to note that cities and their elected officials have few weapons to draw upon other than determination when muscle replaces reason and civilized procedure in basic departments. That handicap was well-stated by Mayor Harry E. Kinney of Albuquerque, New Mexico, after his community had staggered through a nine-day police strike in July 1975. "Mayors just don't have the tools to counter the force of strong unions," he said. "They are helpless even in the face of an illegal strike."

The National League of Cities endeavored to correct this power imbalance at its meeting in Miami Beach last December by exploring the feasibility of a plan under which mayors faced with strikes in their emergency services could call on neighboring communities for assistance. The obvious flaw in any such plan is that the cooperating mayors might find themselves strikebound if they ordered their own police and firefighters to break another community's strike. The National Guard remains a better bet in such situations; yet few mayors choose even to ask for assignment of Guard units, fearful that labor will interpret their action as waving the bloody shirt.

THE NEED FOR OPENNESS

That brings us back to those two old but little-applied weapons—public opinion, now coming into its own for the first time; and education of union leadership and rank and file in the fiscal facts of the urban disaster, also now moving apace. There remains, however, a vexing disposition shared by professional negotiators on both sides to treat everything that happens in collective bargaining as part of a secret cabal about which neither the general public nor the workers directly involved should know anything until the talks have reached agreement or failure. By that time, of course, it is too late for the community to do anything but applaud or deplore.

One salutary by-product of Watergate and its chamber of horrors has been a general awakening to the evils spawned by this conspiratorial approach to any aspect of governmental business. Since the fate of the cities is now so largely dependent on what happens in collective bargaining, it is imperative that the process cease being a private game for a little company of insiders and become part and parcel of open government.

Florida, a pioneer in the trend toward "sunshine laws," since the end of 1974 has required that all negotiations involving state and local agencies be conducted in a goldfish bowl. The experts warned that this would destroy confidential communication and substitute table-pounding and exercises in demagogy by both union and management spokesmen, but a survey by the United States Conference of Mayors and the National League of Cities indicated that the law had worked reasonably well in producing settlements at the same time that it gave the public access it had never had before.

The new California law covering collective bargaining for teachers contains a novel public notice section, intended to serve essentially the same purpose as the Florida sunshine law. It requires that the community be informed of what the union is asking and what the school board is offering so that parents, taxpayers, and other interest groups can register their views before everything is irretrievably signed and sealed. The initial positions must be set forth at a public meeting and made matters of public record, and no formal negotiations can start until the community has had a reasonable opportunity to analyze and comment on them. New subjects introduced during the contract talks must be made public within twenty-four hours. So must all votes within the school board on issues presented in the talks.

PUBLIC OPINION AND
THE BATTLE FOR MUNICIPAL SURVIVAL

The happiest attribute of the evolving relationship in government, with the cities in the forefront, is that the public has shown that it cares. If the initial mood is restrictive—even punitive—toward unionized civil servants, it reflects both past abuses of power and the desperateness of the battle for municipal survival.

The need now is for mutuality of action to adjust to a prolonged and often excruciating period of belt-tightening. This is not something unions are good at. They are still devoted to the Samuel Gompers creed of "more" and it is hard to wrench them away from the pursuit of that goal in an inflationary period when unions in the private sector are still bringing home double-digit pay increases. But it is clear that many union chiefs in the government field are adjusting their sights and are helping to persuade their rank and file that preserving their jobs and preserving their communities is more important than transitory gains in wages and fringe benefits. In New York City the unions have invested more heavily than any bank in keeping the municipality solvent by lending $3.7 billion in pension fund reserves to prevent default. That puts their old-age protection as well as their immediate jobs on the line.

Imagination and reciprocal trust are essential ingredients in making civil service bargaining function in accordance with its stated aims. Public officials will have to know what their communities require; they will have to convince their unions that they genuinely want cooperation, not mere submission, in meeting those needs. The unions cannot be expected to come as whipped dogs, but neither can they be allowed to come as overlords. That is the challenge for bargaining in the second half of this decade and the last quarter of this century.

POSTSCRIPT

A. LAWRENCE CHICKERING
Executive Director, Institute for Contemporary Studies

Reviewing the terms of discussion. The place of experts: lawyers, industrial relations specialists, economists. Strategies of bargaining. Understanding the broader issues. Rediscovering social trust and public spirit.

The cities are going broke, and following New York's experience a national debate has been touched off on the control and responsibility of public unions. This book, however, reveals limitations in the terms of debate which may inhibit current efforts to moderate union demands.

Discussions of public sector labor relations usually reflect the concerns of those involved day-to-day in bargaining or in its study. Lawyers concentrate on the "rights" of public employees, industrial relations experts on mechanics and strategies, and economists on wage comparisons or on larger economic influences.

So it is with contributors to this book who are regarded as labor relations experts. As lawyers, Kheel, Wellington, and Winter deal with rights. Kheel (Chapter I), one of the country's best-known labor mediators, stresses the refinement of bargaining rights and argues that the major difficulty in pub-

225

lic labor relations is the failure to define those rights adequately. Wellington and Winter (Chapter IV) emphasize the differences between the rights of public and private unions to bargain and strike. They are more concerned than Kheel about the recent growth of union power, but their mode of analysis is similar.

Economists have made important contributions in studying the earnings of different classes of workers, as well as the relationship between local economies and bargaining outcomes—all of which are attracting increased public attention. Public reaction to the recent San Francisco strike showed the depth of resentment felt by ordinary union workers to $17,000 public streetsweepers and to public plumbers who make $35,000 or more including overtime. A general strike for that?

These are the extreme cases which are well known. In Chapter VIII, Daniel Orr presents evidence on wage differentials which is little known. In 1966 average public employee wages began rising faster than wages in private industry; by 1973—the most recent year for which complete data are available—earnings of government workers at all levels exceeded private earnings by an average of about 10 percent, exclusive of pensions and fringe benefits (which increase the differential).

Wurf (Chapter X) gives conflicting figures, which he attributes to the Department of Commerce without specific citation. Repeated efforts to get clarification of these figures through his office strengthened our initial suspicion that no effort was made to analyze the many relevant variables. While Wurf's lack of rigor may be understandable under the circumstances, Meany's persistent stress on labor's solidarity is less easy to understand in the face of evidence that some (public) workers are enjoying high standards of living at least in part at the expense of lower-paid workers. This point is particularly important because awareness of wage differentials within the labor movement—and the willingness of labor leaders publicly to acknowledge them—may help moderate public union demands.

Lewin (Chapter IX) and Horton (Chapter XI) apply economic analysis in another way. They argue that although the
unions may be out of control, the solution to runaway unions
—which originated in order to mitigate the market's injustice
—is at hand; and the solution ironically is the market itself.
No longer able to afford their prodigal ways, cities have
begun to shop for alternatives, and market discipline is thus
about to bring the unions to heel.

STRATEGIES OF BARGAINING

The mechanics of labor relations and bargaining do suggest
some solutions. Lewin notes the anomaly of permitting
government-employed supervisors to bargain collectively. In
addition to eliminating one source of substitute labor during a
strike, this practice also eliminates independent government
representation, raising the serious question on which side of
the bargaining table government supervisors and managers sit.
This could be corrected by legislation, along with related problems.

Wellington, Winter (Chapter IV), and Lipset (Chapter VII)
note the vulnerability of governments that results from their
monopoly position. Unlike private business, when a strike of
public employees occurs the absence of practical substitutes
puts instant and unusual pressure on the employer-govern-
ment. The only recourse is to develop alternatives, especially
for essential services such as police and fire protection. Lewin
notes that such alternatives—as in subcontracting—often involve the use of other union members.

A vital tactical question involves the strike. While Wellington and Winter feel that no right to strike exists in the public
sector, Lewin raises an important economic question: Can we
afford a policy committed to an absolute strike ban? He says
not. According to his analysis, we can hold costs down only if
we are willing to permit strikes—and win some, as recently in
San Francisco. Avoiding strikes is too expensive. We can't
afford it.

Public opinion is the critical element in all public labor disputes, because negotiating officials will bargain according to

their perception of the public mind. Raskin (Chapter XII) stresses openness in bargaining to encourage public interest and participation. The public stood firm in the San Francisco strike because the facts were clear and open, and the Board of Supervisors was therefore able successfully to rally general support of its position.

Whatever the importance of tactical considerations, they represent only part of the story.

EQUITY AND EQUALITY

In the introductory chapter, Kheel notes that a major, largely unrecognized issue in the disastrous 1966 New York transit strike was the shrinking pay differentials between skilled and unskilled workers resulting from across-the-board increases in preceding contracts. Lipset discusses this problem in noting an important tension between equality and achievement which underlies public sector labor relations.

An increasing emphasis on equality is evident in all Western countries; yet even in nations conspicuously dedicated to egalitarianism—Sweden and Israel, as well as the Communist states including China—strong pressures continue to push for differential rewards and inequality. When the balance shifts too far toward equality, some union activity may press for greater wage differentials, against the normal union tendency to pursue that equality. Moreover, Lipset argues that when the balance shifts, corruption tends to appear in surprisingly diverse cultures and political systems—often with government acquiescence—as the better educated and more highly skilled seek to reinstate the differential rewards they feel they deserve.

Although achievement and equality are important, they are influenced by deeper social and traditional values which are discussed by Nisbet (Chapter II), Mansfield (Chapter III), and Douglas (Chapter VI).

REDISCOVERING SOCIAL TRUST
AND PUBLIC SPIRIT

If Lewin and Horton are correct that economic adversity will bring public unions under control, the prospect of mounting hardship and unemployment in our cities may provide a solution. But broader questions remain unanswered.

Douglas argues that the dominant problem in the older cities of the northeast and the Pacific Coast involves *social order* and *social trust*. It is a problem born from the coexistence of immensely diverse cultures and social and ethnic groups, and is not easily settled by talk of "rights" or "equality" or values rooted in individual interest. Without strong group allegiances, no "rights" can make most people *feel* equal and secure in the older cities; the *sense* of protection depends on the group.

The social structure of the older cities explains the strength of their public unions, which have taken over the function of preserving a fragile order that formerly belonged to political machines. This explains how, by including the unions in his administration, Mayor Daley has been able to maintain municipal services in Chicago while avoiding fiscal collapse. As mayor of New York, Lindsay did the opposite; he sought to attack the city's traditional social structure through the "politics of disintegration." In attempting to "rationalize" collective bargaining, Lindsay introduced an adversary dimension which so destroyed social trust that it could be restored only by immense payoffs. At the end of the 1960s Lindsay and a few others were symbols of idealism in our culture, while Daley was—and continues to be—a symbol of the worst in American politics. Yet New York collapsed economically while Chicago remains solvent.

Understanding social trust is essential to explain the rise of public unions. Genuine trust is based on informal agreement; formal contracts appear when trust is gone. In Chicago "bargaining" is done informally and granting "rights" to Chicago unions would only reduce their sense of participation in the

social and political life of the city. In New York the unions sit
with their "rights" across the bargaining table in negotiations
governed by elaborated and rationalistic bargaining procedures; and lacking a sense of participation, they have battered
their adversary into submission.

Social trust is the key to peaceful labor relations. The experience of New York City shows that formal rights and bargaining procedures may only undermine social trust and increase enormously the price of restoring it.

REVISITING THE 1960s

Nisbet and Mansfield consider social trust from different per-
spectives but end on almost identical notes. Through historical
sociology, Nisbet notes that when trust in the central state is
strong, the smaller associative communities—family, church,
township, labor union, and corporation—tend to be weak.
When the small communities are strong, allegiance to the state
weakens. From these assumptions he argues that the rise of
public unions results from the decline of confidence in political government.

Mansfield reaches the same conclusion from the perspective
of political philosophy. He notes that the prestige of public
employment depends on public spirit, and that public spirit is
discouraged by the traditional liberal emphasis on individual
interest as the legitimating basis for creation of the state. Solving the problem of public unions, he argues, depends on rediscovering public spirit in liberal society; and that rediscovery
must ultimately depend on the esteem in which the government is held by its citizens.

The chapters by Nisbet and Mansfield are important to an
understanding of public employee unions as well as to the possibilities for containing them. We can see this by recalling the
circumstances surrounding their explosive growth.

The key date is 1966. Lewin tells us that public union
strikes increased from an average of 29 per year before 1966 to
319 since—an eleven-fold increase. Orr notes that 1966 was

the year when public union wages began to grow faster than wages in the private sector. Nineteen sixty-six was also the first year after the outbreak of race riots, widespread urban disorder, and the sharply increased U.S. commitment in Southeast Asia—all of which led to rapidly declining confidence in government.

In such times social trust became impossible. During that period the social authority of government at every level weakened to such a point that by mid-1968 serious people were asking if the country had not grown ungovernable.

The collapse of public confidence and spirit not only eliminated the prestige of public employment; public employment in some respects became a reviled and hated symbol. By the end of the 1960s policemen, once guardians of the public peace, were widely condemned as "pigs" and symbols of oppression. During the riots firemen were frequently shot at by snipers. And the Vietnam debacle destroyed the prestige of the armed services. Under the the circumstances, perhaps the best way to understand the phenomenon of public unions is by understanding that a man requires more pay to be a "pig" than to be a policeman.

In such a climate, it is little wonder that public spirit turned to unionism. The situation recently seems to have improved; but tension and distrust are still evident in public attitudes toward politicians and toward government in general. Nineteen seventy-six indicates our increasing difficulties in returning an incumbent President to office—a chilling symbol of instability in this bicentennial year.

Public unions may be helping to destroy our major cities, but their strength reflects a deeper dilemma. It remains to be seen whether the problem can be solved without a major change in public attitudes toward government, and therefore toward the concept of public service.

This volume reflects a deep concern with the techniques and mechanics of bargaining, the legal and economic relationships between unions and municipalities, and the rights and responsibilities of government employees and the public they serve.

But the long-term future of public sector labor relations may ultimately depend on the restoration of social trust and public spirit.

NOTES

III. Harvey C. Mansfield, Jr.: "The Prestige of Public Employment"

[1]Wellington and Winter 1971:36-38.
[2]Petro 1974:25-165.
[3]Wellington and Winter 1971:24, 167; Petro 1974:136.
[4]A recent example is the British Labor government's budget of April 1976, in which the provision for a tax cut was made conditional upon trade union acceptance of a 3 percent limitation on wage raises.
[5]Locke 1960:2:139; Hobbes 1909:chaps. 18, 21.
[6]Tocqueville 1960:2, part 2, chap. 5.

IV. Harry H. Wellington and Ralph K. Winter, Jr.: "The Limits of Collective Bargaining in Public Employment"

[1]Kheel 1969:931, 942.
[2]U.S. Industrial Commission 1902:844.
[3]See, for example, testimony of Louis D. Brandeis on January 23, 1915, in U.S. Commission on Industrial Relations 1916: 8:7657-81.
[4]See generally Wellington 1968:215-38.
[5]See, for example, U.S. Industrial Commission 1902:800:

It is quite generally recognized that the growth of great aggregations of capital under the control of single groups of men, which is so prominent a feature of the economic development of recent years, necessitates a corresponding aggregation of workingmen into unions, which may be able also to act as units. It is readily perceived that the position of the single workman, face to face with one of our great modern combinations, such as the United States Steel Corporation, is a position of very great weakness. The workman has one thing to sell—his labor. He has perhaps devoted years to the acquirement of a skill which gives his labor power a relatively high value, so long as he is able to put it to use in combination with certain materials and machinery. A single legal person has, to a very great extent, the control of such machinery, and in particular of such materials. Under such conditions there is little competition for the workman's labor. Control of the means of production gives power to dictate to the workingman upon what terms he shall make use of them.

[6]The use of the term monopsony is not intended to suggest a labor market with a single employer. Rather, we mean any market condition in which the terms and conditions of employment are generally below those that would exist under perfect competition.

[7]There is by no means agreement that monopsony is a significant factor. For a theoretical discussion, see Machlup 1952:333-79; for an empirical study, see Bunting 1962.

[8]See Reynolds 1961:18-19. To the extent that monopsonistic conditions exist at any particular time one would expect them to be transitory. For even if we assume a high degree of labor immobility, a low wage level in a labor market will attract outside employers. Over time, therefore, the benefits of monopsony seem to carry with them the seeds of its destruction. But the time may seem very long in the life of any individual worker.

[9]See U.S. Congress 1964:§ 1, 29 U.S.C. § 151.

[10]The monopsony justification views collective bargaining as a system of countervailing power—that is, the collective power of the workers countervails the bargaining power of employers. See Galbraith 1952:121ff. Even if the entire line of argument up to this point is accepted, collective bargaining nevertheless seems a crude device for meeting the monopsony problem, since there is no particular reason to think that collective bargaining will be instituted where there is monopsony (or that it is more likely to be instituted there). In some circumstances collective bargaining may even raise wages above a "competitive" level. On the other hand, the collective bargaining approach is no cruder than the law's general response to perceived unfairness in the application of the freedom of contract doctrine. See Wellington 1968:26-38.

[11]Compare, e.g., Simons 1944 with Lester 1947.

[12]Rees 1962:194-95. Also see Johnson and Mieszkowski 1970.

[13]U.S. Council of Economic Advisers 1967:119.

[14]Ibid.:119-34. See generally Sheahan 1967.

[15]See Lewis 1963 and earlier studies discussed therein.

[16]See generally Dunlop 1944:28-44; Friedman 1951:204; Rees 1962:50-60.

In Ross (1948:76-93) the argument is made that the employment effect of a wage bargain is not taken into account by either employers or unions. One reason given in support of this conclusion is the difficulty of knowing what effect a particular wage bargain will have on employment. But the forecasting difficulty inheres in any pricing decision, whether it is raising the price of automobiles or of labor, and it certainly does not render the effect of an increase on the volume purchased an irrelevant consideration. Uncertainty as to the impact of a wage decision on employment does not allow union leaders to be indifferent to the fact that there is an impact. If it did, they would all demand rates of $100 per hour.

Ross's second argument is that there is only a loose connection between wage rates and the volume of employment. It is not clear what he means by this assertion. It may be a rephrasing of the uncertainty argument. Presumably he is not asserting that the demand curve for labor is absolutely vertical; although proof of that phenomenon would entitle him to the professional immortality promised by Professor Stigler (1966:24), the unsupported assertion hardly merits serious consideration. But if the curve is not vertical, then there is a "close connection" since the volume of employment is by hypothesis affected at every point on a declining curve. Probably he means simply that the curve is relatively inelastic, but that conclusion is neither self-evident, supported by his text, nor a proposition generally accepted on the basis of established studies.

[17]U.S. Bureau of the Census 1971: Table 1; ibid. 1964: Table 1.

[18]See U.S. Industrial Commission 1902:805; Summers 1962:273, 275.

[19]For the "early" history, see Spero 1948.

[20]See, for example, New York 1966:9-14.

[21]See Chamberlain 1948:94.

[22]This is surely one reason that might explain the widely assumed fact that public employees have fallen behind their private sector counterparts. See Stieber 1967:65, 69.

[23]See Taylor 1967:617, 623-25.

[24]The cost increase may, of course, take some time to work through and appear as a price increase. See Reese 1962:107-9. In some oligopolistic situations the firm may be able to raise prices after a wage increase without suffering a significant decrease in sales.

[25]*Steele v. Louisville & Nashville Railroad Co.,* 323 U.S. 192 (1944).

[26]The pressure is sometimes resisted. Indeed, the United Mine Workers has chosen more benefits for less employment. See generally Baratz 1955.

[27]See Cohany 1966:510-13; Bernstein 1961:131-57.

[28]And the law would protect him in this. Indeed, it would protect him if he were moved by an antiunion animus as well as by valid economic considerations. See *Textile Workers Union of America v. Darlington Manufacturing Co.,* 380 U.S. 263 (1965).

Of course, where fixed costs are large relative to variable costs, it may be difficult for an employer to extricate himself.

[29]This does not mean that collective bargaining in the private sector is free of social costs. It means only that the costs are necessarily limited by the discipline of the market.

[30]See generally Dahl 1961. On interest group theory generally, see Truman 1955.

[31]See, for example, Sayre and Kaufman 1960:366-72.

[32]See Moskow 1966:79-86.

[33]This is based on the reasonable but not unchallengeable assumption that the number of significant employers in a labor market is related to the existence of monopsony. See Bunting 1962:3-14. The greater the number of such employers in a labor market, the greater the departure from the classic case of the monopsony of a single employer. The number of employers would clearly seem to affect their ability to make and enforce a collusive wage agreement.

[34]Organized parent groups, for example. Compare the unsuccessful attempt of the New York City Board of Education to reduce the employment of substitute teachers in the public schools in March 1971. *New York Times,* March 11, 1971, p. 1.

[35]See generally Dorfman 1967.

[36]In the private sector what is involved is principally resource allocation rather than income redistribution. Income redistribution occurs to the extent that unions are able to increase wages at the expense of profits, but the extent to which this actually happens would seem to be limited. It also occurs if unions, by limiting employment in the union sector through maintenance of wages above a competitive level, increase the supply of labor in the nonunion sector and thereby depress wages there.

[37]In the private sector the political question was answered when the National Labor

Relations Act was passed: the benefits of collective bargaining (with the strike) out-weigh the social costs.

[38]The fact that American unions and management are generally economically oriented is a source of great freedom to us all. If either the unions or management decided to make decisions about the nature of services provided or products manufac-tured on the basis of their own ideological convictions, we would all, as consumers, be less free. Although unions may misallocate resources, consumers are still generally able to satisfy strong desires for particular products by paying more for them and sacrificing less valued items. This is because unions and management generally make no attempt to adjust to anything but economic considerations. Were it otherwise, and the unions—or management—insisted that no products of a certain kind be manufac-tured, consumers would have much less choice.

[39]The major qualification to these generalizations is that sometimes unions can generate more support from the membership for certain demands than for others (more for the size of the work crew, less for wage increases). Just how extensive this phenomenon is, and how it balances out over time, is difficult to say; however, it would not seem to be of great importance in the overall picture.

[40]Dahl 1956:145.

[41]Ibid.:124-25.

[42]See, for example, Spero 1948:1-15.

[43]Strikes in some areas of the private sector may have this effect, too. See below.

[44]Contrast the situation in the private sector (Livernash 1963:10, 15):

management cannnot normally win the short strike. Management can only win the long strike. Also management frequently tends, in fact, to win the long strike. As a strike lengthens, it commonly bears more heavily on the union and the em-ployees than on management. Strike relief is no substitute for a job. Even regular strike benefits, which few unions can afford, and which usually exhaust the union treasury quite rapidly (with some exceptions), are no substitute for a job.

[45]A vivid example was provided by an experience in New Jersey. After a twelve-hour strike by Newark firefighters on July 11, 1969, state urban aid funds, originally authorized for helping the poor, were diverted to salary increases for firemen and police. See *New York Times,* August 7, 1969, p. 25. Moreover, government decision makers other than the mayor (for example, the governor) may have interests different from those of the mayor, interests that manifest themselves in pressures for settlement.

[46]Consider also the effect of such strikes on the fabric of society. See, for example, Mayer 1969.

[47]Kaufman 1963:127-28.

[48]Polsby 1963:135.

[49]Dahl 1956:145.

[50]Sometimes this is so because of the nature of the endeavor—national defense, for example—and sometimes because the existence of the governmental operation neces-sarily inhibits entry by private entities, as in the case of elementary education.

[51]Marshall 1920:383-86.

VI. Jack D. Douglas: "Urban Politics and Public Employee Unions"

[1]For a stunning contrast between the human and social functions of the machine

and the moralist/rationalist critique, compare Denise Tilden Lynch's 1928 description of *Boss Tweed* and Edwin O'Connor's real-life description of a Boston boss in *The Last Hurrah*.

[2]The classic statements of this analysis are found in Dahl 1961; Banfield 1961a; Banfield and Wilson 1967; Wilson 1966; Lowi 1964b.

[3]For classical analyses of political machines see Gosnell 1924, 1967; Banfield and Wilson 1967; Mandelbaum 1965.

VII.   Seymour Martin Lipset: "Equity and Equality in Public Wage Policy"

[1]For a discussion of different sociological approaches to inequality and stratification, see Lipset 1968. For a review of the empirical research on different aspects of inequality in the United States see idem. 1976.

[2]For a review of Soviet sociological analyses of stratification see Lipset and Dobson 1973:114-85. It is difficult to compare the range of Soviet incomes with those in Western societies, particularly because of the situation among people at the top. Elite salaries and incomes in rubles are seemingly less than those of people in comparable positions in Western society, and the range of income differences between the bottom and top also appears to be less. But there are problems in making comparisons, because Communist societies lack a graduated income tax structure, and because they reward people in elite positions with a variety of nonmonetary forms of income such as access to special stores, special vacation facilities, control over automobiles which are given to executives, special pension rights, and a variety of other services not easily measured (Matthews 1975).

Equally unmeasurable in comparing the two types of societies is the variation in power relationships. The most striking formal difference between capitalist and communist systems are in the distribution's extreme: capitalism produces extremely rich people with a great deal of investment capital, communism does not (Wiles and Markowski 1971:344).

[3]An interview with President Tito, "We Must Have a Vanguard and United Party," *Vjesnik* (Zagreb), October 8, 1972, as translated in the Yugoslav magazine *Socialist Thought and Practice*, 49 (August-December 1972), pp. 8-9, 11, 12-13, 21.

[4]"Utopia's Dark Side," *Newsweek*, May 3, 1976, p. 39.

[5]For a detailed theoretical analysis of the impact of a concern for vote maximization on wages in the public sector see Reder 1975.

[6]"On Implementation of New Academic Salary Structure," testimony presented by United Professors of California before the Faculty and Staff Affairs Committee of the CSUC Trustees on December 8, 1972, p. 1. For the comparable position by the NEA affiliate see "CCUFA to Act: Duplicity Ends CSUC Salary Talks," *The California Professor*, 7 (December 1972), pp. 1,4. For the UPC's report on the way they claim to have killed the proposal with the help of the California labor movement, see "UPC-Labor-Demo Coalition Rolls Back Salary Scheme," *The UPC Advocate*, 3 (February 1973), pp. 2-3.

[7]"A Position Paper on Tenure," Council of New Jersey State College Locals AFT, 1972. For a more detailed discussion of this issue, see Ladd and Lipset 1973:72-81. I have drawn on this monograph here.

[8]"The Real Meaning of Turmoil in Communist China. Interview with A. Doak Barnett," *U.S. News and World Report*, April 26, 1976, p. 33.

VIII. Daniel Orr: "Public Employee Compensation Levels"

[1]That is, the greater the elasticity of substitution between capital and labor.

[2]Lewis (1963) sets forth numerous case studies in which unionization has in varying degrees been successful.

[3]Rees (1963) uses this simple model of worker displacement to estimate the social costs of unions. He finds that these costs ran approximately .15 percent of GNP in 1957.

[4]The work of John Nash, the most important of the bargaining theorists, is critically summarized in Luce and Raiffa 1958.

[5]I use the word "generates" and not "collects" since the data are a product of an elaborate system of projections and estimates based on sampling information. The principal data source is *The National Income and Product Accounts of the United States, 1929-65* (Washington, D.C.: U.S. Government Printing Office, 1966); these accounts are updated annually in *The Survey of Current Business* (July issues, 1967-74). The 1975 update had not appeared as of April 1976.

[6]In Smith (1974) there is a review of earlier work by Ronald Oaxaca, Robert Hall, and Stephen Perloff, all of which discovers systematically higher wages in government employment.

[7]Aggregate data published by the U.S. Department of Commerce (source cited in Table 1) does not disclose that "fringe benefits" are a great deal higher in public employment than private. However, those data run only through 1973; they are compiled by a complex sampling and estimation technique, and estimation methods have not been changed since 1965. Consequently, undetected gains in the government sector may have occurred. Since 1966, biennial changes in the annual value of "fringe benefits" to the worker are:

	1966	1968	1970	1972	1973
Government	459	635	817	1,074	1,198
Private	545	732	877	1,110	1,253

IX. David Lewin: "Collective Bargaining and the Right to Strike"

[1]The New York State statute followed closely the recommendations of the Governor's Committee on Public Employee Relations, which was headed by the late George W. Taylor, professor at the University of Pennsylvania and noted authority on private sector industrial relations. The 1962 Presidential Executive Order was patterned after the report of the President's Task Force on Employee-Management Relations in the Federal Service whose chairman was Arthur Goldberg, formerly General Counsel to the United Steelworkers of America and also Secretary of Labor. Both Taylor and Goldberg advocated prohibitions on and substitutes for the strike in public employment.

[2]Contract arbitration does exist in major league baseball, and was partially incor-

porated into the 1973 steel industry labor agreements. However, most private sector employers and union leaders strongly oppose the practice.

[3]Unless otherwise indicated, all data in this section are from U.S. Department of Labor 1976: passim. For an early accounting of government work stoppages, see Ziskind 1940.

[4]Interestingly, of the 210 educational strikes recorded in 1974, only 133 or 63 percent involved teachers (U.S. Department of Labor 1976:6). The strikes of noninstructional employees in education deserve further attention and analysis.

[5]The limitations of this particular study are underscored by Stieber 1975:178-82.

[6]These conclusions are based on field research conducted by Lewin, Horton, and Kuhn 1977. For further analysis of municipal labor relations in Chicago, see Lewin 1976c.

[7]This argument is more fully developed in Horton 1975:497-507. In New York City municipal government over the 1968-1975 period, it was primarily the small, less-powerful public employee unions that used impasse procedures and pursued arbitrated settlements. See Schoolman 1976.

[8]The same may be said of governmental wage-setting processes. See Lewin 1974a:149-55; Fogel and Lewin 1974:410-31; Lewin 1974b:473-85.

[9]The governors of several large states—California, New York, Wisconsin, and Illinois—as well as the mayors of large and medium-size cities, recently have adopted policies that reduce or at least impede the political access of organized public employees. For popular expressions of this developing political climate, see "Public Employees Lose Leverage," *Business Week,* December 22, 1975, p. 15; and "Public Employee Unions Hit Tough Going as Strikes, New York's Ills Stir Opposition," *The Wall Street Journal,* December 12, 1975, p. 34. The strike of San Francisco's municipal workers over mandated wage cuts, unsettled as of the date of this writing, is one that the public has shown its willingness to take. It has not rushed to the support of a quick settlement.

[10]Sanitation services are also relatively essential, especially in the northeastern and midwest regions.

[11]New York City and Los Angeles are but two examples of municipalities in which local government employees and supervisors are represented by the same unions, though they are enrolled in different bargaining units. Interestingly, New York City's municipal labor relations system, in which collective bargaining is well-entrenched, is considerably more developed than in Los Angeles, whose city and county governments operate under "meet and confer" statutes. See Lewin 1976b.

[12]Between 1935 and 1947, then, private sector supervisors (and even managers) possessed union representation and collective rights. That is no longer true, of course, but employers may voluntarily recognize and bargain with such personnel (though few of them actually do so).

[13]This is but one of four major determinants of the elasticity of demand for union labor, as identified by Alfred Marshall. The more inelastic the demand, the greater a union's bargaining power. A cogent summary of the Marshallian analysis is contained in Rees 1962:69-73.

[14]This is a practice virtually unique to the American industrial relations system. It is easy but unwise to overlook that fact when discussing public sector labor relations. See Bok 1971:1394-1463.

[15]In this instance, behaving like the private sector means that governments will

display diverse rather than uniform labor practices. For more on this theme, see Horton, Lewin, and Kuhn 1976:497-516.

[16]The terminology "first" and "second generation" bargaining has been coined by Professor Thomas A. Kochan of Cornell University in a communication to the author.

[17]For an earlier and more fully developed statement of this position, see Lewin 1973:309-21. Moreover, recent empirical studies reveal only a limited ability of public employee unions to make relative wage gains, even during a sustained employment expansion in government. These studies are summarized in Lewin 1976d.

[18]Of course, the incidence of strikes is closely related to the state of the economy. Even with broadened public employee strike rights, therefore, the volume of government work stoppages can be expected to decline as fiscal constraints on the public sector continue to mount.

XI. Raymond D. Horton: "Economics, Politics, and Collective Bargaining: The Case of New York City"

[1]For two recent comparative studies indicating that New York City's fiscal problems, while extreme, may not be unique, see Muller 1975, and Clark et al. 1976.

[2]The author and two Columbia University Graduate School of Business colleagues, Professors James W. Kuhn and David Lewin, are engaged in a comparative study of public sector labor relations conducted under the auspices of the Columbia University Conservation of Human Resources Project and supported by the Ford Foundation and U.S. Department of Labor. For a preliminary study describing the central concerns of the larger study, see Horton, Lewin, and Kuihn 1976:497-516.

[3]Unless otherwise noted, the material in this subsection is drawn from Horton 1973: chapters 1-5. This study focussed primarily on the 1965-1970 period, emphasizing the politics of the municipal labor relations process.

[4]Base pay of patrolmen rose from $6,381 in 1960 to $17,458 in 1975. Including the supplemental wage benefits—holiday and night-shift differential pay—wages rose from $6,479 in 1960 to $19,156 in 1975.

[5]The New York State Department of Labor reported that full-time and part-time employment fell from 438,900 in January 1975 to 389,000 in January 1976, a decline of 49,300. Data from the New York City Bureau of the Budget show a full-time employment drop from 294,522 to 256,370 during the same period.

[6]Data from U.S. Department of Labor, Bureau of Labor Statistics, Middle-Atlantic Regional Office, show total nonagricultural employment in New York City at 3,797,000 in 1969 and 3,275,900 in 1975. The 1975 employment total is lower by almost 200,000 jobs than in 1950.

[7]For an example of federal awareness of the importance of the labor relations issue to the City's financial problems, see *Statement of William E. Simon, Secretary of the Treasury, before the Senate Committee on Banking, Housing, and Urban Affairs,* April 1, 1976, pp. 16-20.

BIBLIOGRAPHY

Aaron, Benjamin. 1975. Procedures for Settling Interests Disputes in the Essential and Public Sectors: A Comparative View. In *Collective Bargaining in the Essential and Public Service Sectors*, ed. Morley Gunderson. Toronto: The University of Toronto Press.

Adler-Karlsson, Gunnar. 1970. *Functional Socialism*. [Canadian title: *Reclaiming the Canadian Economy*.] Toronto: Amansi Press.

Ashenfelter, Orley C., and Ehrenberg, Ronald G. 1975. The Demand for Labor in the Public Sector. In *Labor in the Public and Nonprofit Sectors*, ed. Daniel S. Hammermesh. Princeton, N.J.: Princeton University Press.

Banfield, Edward C. 1961a. *Political Influence*. New York: Free Press.

———, ed. 1961b. *Urban Government*. Glencoe, Ill.: Free Press.

———, and Wilson, James Q. 1967. *City Politics*. Cambridge, Mass.: Harvard University Press.

Baratz, M. 1955. *The Union and the Coal Industry*. New Haven, Conn.: Yale University Press.

Barnett, A. Doak. 1973. More Thoughts Out of China: There Are Warts There, Too. *The New York Times Magazine* (April 8, 1973), pp. 103-4.

Ben David, Joseph. 1970. Professionals and Unions in Israel. In *Integration and Development in Israel*, ed. S. N. Eisenstadt et al. New York: Praeger.

Ben Rafael, Eli. 1976. Higher Education in Israel. Unpublished ms., School of Education, Hebrew University, Jerusalem.

Bernstein, I. 1961. The Growth of American Unions, 1945-1960. *Labor History* 2.

Bok, Derek C. 1971. Reflections on the Distinctive Character of American Labor Laws. *Harvard Law Review* 84 (April).

———, and Dunlop, John T. 1970. *Labor and the American Community*. New York: Simon and Schuster.

Bunting, R. 1962. *Employer Concentration in Local Labor Markets*. Chapel Hill, N.C.: University of North Carolina Press.

Burton, John F., Jr., and Krider, Charles E. 1975. The Incidence of Strikes in Public Employment. In *Labor in the Public and Nonprofit Sectors*, ed. Daniel S. Hammermesh. Princeton, N.J.: Princeton University Press.

Carter, Barbara. 1964. New York City—Can It Be Governed? *The Reporter Magazine* (January 30, 1964).

Chamberlain, N. 1948. *The Union Challenge to Management Control*. New York: Harper.

Clark, Terry Nichols, et al. 1976. How Many New Yorks? The New York Fiscal Crisis in Comparative Perspective. Unpublished ms. Research Report No. 72, Comparative Study of Decision-Making, University of Chicago.

Cohany, H. 1966. Trends and Changes in Union Membership. *Monthly Labor Review* 89.

Curtis, Michael, and Chertoff, Mordecai, eds. 1973. *Israel: Social Structure and Change*. New Brunswick, N.J.: Transaction Books.

Dahl, Robert A. 1956. *A Preface to Democratic Theory*. Chicago: University of Chicago Press.

———. 1961. *Who Governs? Democracy and Power in an American City*. New Haven: Yale University Press.

Derber, Milton. 1973. Histadruth and Industrial Democracy. In *Israel: Social Structure and Change*, ed. Michael Curtis and Mordecai Chertof. New Brunswick, N.J.: Transaction Books.

Dorfman, R. 1967. *Prices and Markets*. New York: Prentice-Hall.

Douglas, Jack D. 1971. *American Social Order*. New York: Free Press.

———. 1974. *Defining America's Social Problems*. Englewood Cliffs, N.J.: Prentice-Hall.

———. 1975. Going Broke the New York Way. *New Society* (December 1975).

Dunlop, J. 1944. *Wage Determination Under Trade Unions*. New York: Macmillan.

Ehrenberg, Ronald G. 1973. The Demand for State and Local Government Employees. *American Economic Review* 53 (June).

Eisenstadt, S. N., et at., eds. 1970. *Integration and Development in Israel*. New York: Praeger.

Feuille, Peter. 1975. *Final Offer Arbitration: Concepts, Developments, Techniques*. Chicago, International Personnel Management Association.

———; Juris, Harvey; Jones, Ralph; and Jedel, Michael Jay. 1976. Multiemployer Bargaining among Local Government. In *Proceedings* (February 1976), Industrial Relations Research Association.

Fogel, Walter, and Lewin, David. 1974. Wage Determination in the Public Sector. *Industrial and Labor Relations Review* 27 (April).

Friedman, M. 1951. Some Comments on the Significance of Labor Unions for Economic Policy. In *The Impact of the Union*, ed. D. Wright. New York: Harcourt.

Galbraith, John Kenneth. 1952. *American Capitalism: The Concept of Countervailing Power*. New York: Houghton Mifflin.

Garbarino, Joseph W. 1973. Creeping Unionism and the Faculty Labor Market. In *Higher Education and the Labor Market*, ed. Margaret Gordon. New York: McGraw-Hill.

Gleason, Bill. 1970. *Daley of Chicago*. New York: Simon and Schuster.

Goodstadt, Leo. 1973. *China's Search for Plenty. The Economics of Mao Tse-tung*. New York: Weatherhill.

Gosnell, Harold F. 1924. *Boss Platt and His New York Machine*. New York: Russell & Russell.

———. 1967. *Machine Politics: Chicago Model*. Chicago: University of Chicago Press.

Gotbaum, Victor. 1972. Collective Bargaining and the Union Leader. In *Public*

Workers and Public Unions, ed. Sam Zagoria. Englewood Cliffs, N.J.: Prentice-Hall.

Gottehrer, Barry. 1969. Urban Environment: New York City. In *Social Intelligence for America's Future,* ed. Bertram M. Gross. Boston: Allyn & Bacon.

Gras, Alain. 1972. Social Scientists and Other University Teachers in Sweden. *Social Science Information* 11 (December 1972).

Gross, Bertram M., ed. 1969. *Social Intelligence for America's Future.* Boston: Allyn & Bacon.

Gunderson, Morley, ed. 1975. *Collective Bargaining in the Essential and Public Service Sectors.* Toronto: The University of Toronto Press.

Hammermesh, Daniel S., ed. 1975. *Labor in the Public and Nonprofit Sectors.* Princeton, N.J.: Princeton University Press.

Hancock, M. Donald. 1972. *Sweden: The Politics of Postindustrial Change.* Hinsdale, Ill.: The Dryden Press.

Hayes, Frederick O'R. 1972. Collective Bargaining and the Budget Director. In *Public Workers and Public Unions,* ed. Sam Zagoria. Englewood Cliffs, N.J.: Prentice-Hall.

Hayford, Stephen L., and Sinicropi, Anthony V. 1976. Bargaining Rights Status of Public Sector Supervisors. *Industrial Relations* 15 (February).

Hobbes, Thomas. 1909. (1951). *Leviathan.* London: Oxford University Press.

Horton, Raymond D. 1975. Arbitration, Arbitrators and the Public Interest. *Industrial and Labor Relations Review* 28 (July).

———. 1973. *Municipal Labor Relations in New York City: Lessons of the Lindsay-Wagner Years.* New York: Praeger.

———. 1971. Municipal Labor Relations: The New York City Experience. *Social Science Quarterly* 52 (December).

———. 1974. Productivity Bargaining in the Public Sector: Caveat Emptor. In *MBO and Productivity Bargaining in the Public Sector,* ed. Chester A. Newland et al. PERL Series No. 45. Chicago: International Personnel Management Association.

———, Lewin, David, and Kuhn, James E. 1976. Some Impacts of Collective Bargaining on Local Government: A Diversity Thesis. *Administration and Society* 4 (February).

Johnson, H., and Mieszkowski, P. 1970. The Effects of Unionization on the Distribution of Income: A General Equilibrium Approach. *Quarterly Journal of Economics* 539.

Johnston, T. J. 1962. *Collective Bargaining in Sweden.* Cambridge, Mass.: Harvard University Press.

Kaufman, Herbert. 1963. Metropolitan Leadership. In *Community Power and Political Theory,* by N. Polsby. New Haven: Yale University Press.

Kemerer, Frank R., and Baldridge, J. Victor. 1975. *Unions on Campus.* San Francisco: Jossey-Bass.

Kheel, Theodore W. 1969. Strikes and Public Employment. *Michigan Law Review* 67.

Komarovsky, Mirra, ed. 1957. *Common Frontiers of the Social Sciences.* Glencoe, Ill.: Free Press.

Kravis, Irving. 1973. A World of Unequal Incomes. *The Annals* 409 (September 1973).

Kugler, Israel. 1969. Unionism: A New Instrument for Faculty Governance. *ISR Journal* 1 (Summer).

Labedz, Leopold. 1959. *Sociology and Communism 1957-1958*. London: Soviet Survey.

Ladd, E. C., Jr., and Lipset, S. M. 1973. *Professors, Unions and American Education*. Berkeley, Cal.: Carnegie Commission on Higher Education.

Lester, R. 1947. Reflections on the Labor Monopoly Issue. *Journal of Political Economy* 55.

Lewin, David. 1973. Public Employment Relations: Confronting the Issues. *Industrial Relations* 12 (October).

⸻. 1974*a*. Aspects of Wage Determination in Local Government Employment. *Public Administration Review* 34 (March-April).

⸻. 1974*b*. The Prevailing Wage Principle and Public Wage Decisions. *Public Personnel Management* 3 (November-December).

⸻. 1976*a*. Collective Bargaining Impacts on Personnel Administration in the American Public Sector. *Labor Law Journal* 27 (July) forthcoming.

⸻. 1976*b*. Local Government Labor Relations in Transition: The Case of Los Angeles. *Labor History* 17 (Spring).

⸻. 1976*c*. *Mayoral Power and Municipal Labor Relations: A Three-City Study*. New York: Graduate School of Business, Columbia University.

⸻. 1976*d*. Public Sector Labor Relations: A Review Essay. *Labor History* 17 (Fall) forthcoming.

⸻, and Horton, Raymond D. 1975. The Impact of Collective Bargaining on the Merit System in Government. *The Arbitration Journal* 30 (September).

⸻, Horton, Raymond D., and Kuhn, James W. 1977. *Manpower Utilization and Collective Bargaining in Local Government*. Forthcoming.

Lewis, H. Gregg. 1963. *Unionism and Relative Wages in the United States: An Empirical Inquiry*. Chicago: University of Chicago Press.

Lindsay, John V. 1969. *The City*. New York: W. W. Norton.

Lipset, S. M. 1963. *The First New Nation*. New York: Basic Books.

⸻. 1976. Equality and Inequality. In *Contemporary Social Problems*, ed. Robert Merton and Robert S. Nisbet. 4th ed. New York: Harcourt, Brace, Jovanovich.

⸻. 1968. Social Class. In *International Encyclopedia of the Social Sciences*, ed. David Sills 15:296-316. New York: Macmillan Co. and Free Press.

⸻, and Dobson, Richard B. 1973. Social Stratification and Sociology in the Soviet Union. *Survey* (Summer).

⸻, and Trow, Martin. 1957. Reference Group Theory and Trade Union Wage Policy. In *Common Frontiers of the Social Sciences*, ed. Mirra Komarovsky. Glencoe, Ill.: Free Press.

Liss, L. F. 1973. The Social Conditioning of Occupational Choice. In *Social Stratification and Mobility in the U.S.S.R.*, trans. and ed. Murray Yanowitch and Wesley A. Fisher. White Plains, N.Y.: International Arts and Sciences Press.

Livernash, E. 1963. The Relation of Power to the Structure and Process of Collective Bargaining. *Journal of Law and Economics* 6 (October).

Locke, John. 1960 (1690). *Two Treatises of Government*. Cambridge: Cambridge University Press.

Lowenberg, J. J. 1973. Histadruth: Myth and Reality. In *Israel: Social Structure and Change*, ed. Michael Curtis and Mordecai Chertoff. New Brunswick, N.J.: Transaction Books.

Lowi, Theodore J. 1964*a*. American Business, Public Policy, Case-Studies, and Political Theory. *World Politics* 16 (June).

———. 1964*b*. *At the Pleasure of the Mayor: Patronage and Power in New York City, 1898-1958*. New York: Free Press.

———. 1967. Machine Politics Old and New. *The Public Interest* 9 (Fall).

Luce, R. D., and Raiffa, Howard. 1958. *Games and Decisions*. New York: John Wiley and Sons.

Machlup, F. 1952. *The Political Economy of Monopoly: Business, Labor and Government Policies*. Baltimore, Md: Johns Hopkins Press.

Maltzev, G. V. 1974. Social Justice and Human Rights in Socialist Society. *Sovetskoye Gosudarstvo i Pravo* 11 (November 1974), abstracted in *The Current Digest of the Soviet Press* (June 4, 1975).

Mandelbaum, Seymour J. 1965. *Boss Tweed's New York*. New York: Wiley.

Margolin, Leo J. 1969. Negotiated Increases Put CUNY Professors at Top Pay. *The Christian Science Monitor* (October 22, 1969).

Marshall, Alfred. 1920. *Principles of Economics*. 8th ed. New York: Macmillan.

Matthews, Mervyn. 1975. Top Incomes in the USSR: Towards a Definition of the Soviet Elite. *Survey* 21 (Summer).

Mayer, M. 1969. *The Teachers Strike: New York, 1968*. New York: Harper and Row.

Merton, Robert K., and Nisbet, Robert S., eds. 1976. *Contemporary Social Problems*. 4th ed. New York: Harcourt, Brace, Jovanovich.

Meyerson, Martin, and Banfield, E. C. 1961. A Machine at Work. In *Urban Government*, ed. E. C. Banfield. Glencoe, Ill.: Free Press.

———, and Wilson, James Q. 1955. *Politics, Planning and the Public Interest*. Glencoe, Ill.: Free Press.

Miller, Zne L. 1968. *Boss Cox's Cincinnati: Urban Politics in the Progressive Era*. New York: Oxford University Press.

Mortimer, Kenneth P., and Lozier, G. Gregory. 1972. *Collective Bargaining: Implications for Governance*. University Park, Pa.: Center for the Study of Higher Education.

Moskow, M. 1966. *Teachers and Unions*. Philadelphia: Wharton School of Finance and Commerce, University of Pennsylvania.

Muller, Thomas. 1975. *Growing and Declining Urban Areas*. Washington, D.C.: The Urban Institute.

New York. 1966. *Governor's Committee on Public Employee Relations, Final Report*. Albany: State of New York.

O'Connor, Len. 1975. *Clout: Mayor Daley and His City*. Chicago: Regnery.

Okun, Arthur. 1975. *Equality and Efficiency*. Washington, D.C.: The Brookings Institution.

Pack, Howard. 1973. Income Distribution and Economic Development: The Case of Israel. In *Israel: Social Structure and Change*, ed. Michael Curtis and Mordecai Chertoff. New Brunswick, N.J.: Transaction Books.

Parkin, Frank. 1972. *Class, Inequality and Political Order*. New York: Praeger.

Perloff, Stephen. 1971. Comparing Municipal, Industry and Federal Pay. *Monthly Labor Review* 94 (October 1971).

Petro, Sylvester. 1974. Sovereignty and Compulsory Public-Sector Bargaining. *Wake Forest Law Review* 10.

Polsby, Nelson W. 1963. *Community Power and Political Theory.* New Haven, Conn.: Yale University Press.

Prybyla, Jan S. 1975. A Note on Incomes and Prices in China. *Asian Survey* 15 (March).

Raskin, A. H. 1972. Politics Up-Ends the Bargaining Table. In *Public Workers and Public Unions,* ed. Sam Zagoria. Englewood Cliffs, N.J.: Prentice-Hall.

Reder, Melvin W. 1975. The Theory of Employment and Wages in the Public Sector. In *Labor in the Public and Nonprofit Sectors,* ed. D. S. Hammermesh. Princeton, N.J.: Princeton University Press.

Rees, Albert. 1962. *The Economics of Trade Unions.* Chicago: University of Chicago Press.

———. 1963. The Effects of Unions on Resource Allocation. *Journal of Law and Economics* 5.

Reynolds, L. 1961. *Labor Economics and Labor Relations.* 3rd ed. New York: Prentice-Hall.

Richta, Radovan, et al. 1968. *Civilization at the Crossroads.* White Plains, N.Y.: International Arts and Sciences Press.

Riesman, David. 1973. Commentary and Epilogue. In *Academic Transformations,* ed. D. Riesman and V. Stadtman. New York: McGraw-Hill.

Ross, Arthur M. 1948. *Trade Union Wage Policy.* Berkeley, Cal.: University of California Press.

Royko, Mike. 1971. *Boss.* New York: E. P. Putnam.

Schlosstein, Ralph. 1975. State and Local Government Finances During Recession. *Challenge* 18 (July-August).

Schoolman, Mary M. 1976. A Functional Analysis of Impasse Arbitration Use in New York City, 1968-1975. Unpublished ms. New York: Graduate School of Business, Columbia University (April).

Schran, Peter. 1975. Institutional Continuity and Motivational Change: The Chinese Industrial Wages System, 1950-1973. *Asian Survey* 14 (November).

Sheahan, J. 1967. *The Wage-Price Guideposts.* Washington, D.C.: The Brookings Institution.

Sills, David, ed. 1968. *International Encyclopedia of the Social Sciences.* New York: Macmillan Co. and Free Press.

Simons, H. 1944. Some Reflections on Syndicalism. *Journal of Political Economy.*

Smith, Sharon P. 1974. Governmental Wage Differentials by Region and Sex. Working Paper No. 58, Industrial Relations Section, Princeton University (December).

———. 1976. Pay Differences between Federal Government and Private Sector Workers. *Industrial and Labor Relations Review* 29 (January).

Spero, S. 1948. *Government as Employer.* N.p.: Remsen.

Stieber, Jack. 1967. Collective Bargaining in the Public Sector. In *Challenges to Collective Bargaining,* ed. L. Ulman. New York: Prentice Hall.

———. 1975. Comments. In *Labor in the Public and Nonprofit Sectors,* ed. Daniel S. Hammermesh. Princeton, N.J.: Princeton University Press.

Stigler, G. 1966. *The Theory of Price.* 3rd ed. New York: Macmillan.

Summers, C. 1962. American Legislation for Union Democracy. *Modern Law Review* 25.

Taylor, G. 1967. Public Employment: Strikes or Procedures? *Industrial and Labor Relations Review* 20.

Teiwes, Frederick C. 1974. Before and After the Cultural Revolution. *The China Quarterly* 58 (April-June).

Tocqueville, Alexis de. 1960 (1835). *Democracy in America.*New York: Vintage Books.

Truman, D. 1955. *The Government Process: Political Interests and Public Opinion.* 3rd printing. New York: Alfred A. Knopf.

Tumin, Melvin M. 1966. Some Principles of Social Stratification: A Critical Analysis. In *Class, Status and Power,* ed. Reinhard Bendix and S. M. Lipset. New York: Free Press.

U.S. Bureau of the Census. 1964. *State Distribution of Public Employment in 1963.* Washington, D.C.

————. 1971. *Public Employment in 1970.* Washington, D.C.

U.S. Commission on Industrial Relations. 1916. *Industrial Relations.* Final Report and Testimony Submitted to Congress by the Commission on Industrial Relations, S. Doc. 415, 64 Cong. 1 sess (1916), 8:7657-81.

U.S. Congress. 1964. *Labor Management Relations Act.* Washington, D.C.

U.S. Council of Economic Advisers. 1967. *Economic Report of the President Together With the Annual Report of the Council of Economic Advisers.* January.

U.S. Department of Labor. 1976. *Work Stoppages in Government, 1974.* Bureau of Labor Statistics, Report No. 453. Washington, D.C.: Government Printing Office.

U.S. Industrial Commission. 1902. Final Report of the Industrial Commission. Washington, D.C.: Government Printing Office.

Wachtel, Howard M. 1973. *Workers' Management and Workers' Wages in Yugoslavia.* Ithaca, N.Y.: Cornell University Press.

Watson, Andrew. 1972. The Guides and the Guided. *The China Quarterly* 49 (January-March).

Wellington, Harry H. 1968. *Labor and the Legal Process.* New Haven: Yale University Press.

————, and Winter, Ralph K., Jr. 1971. *The Unions and the Cities.* Washington, D.C.: The Brookings Institution.

Wesolowski, W., and Slomozynski, K. 1969. Social Stratification in Polish Cities. In *Social Stratification,* ed. J. Jackson. London: Cambridge University Press.

Wheeler, Christopher. 1975. *White Collar Power. Changing Pattern of Interest Behavior in Sweden.* Urbana, Ill.: University of Illinois Press.

Wheelwright, E. L., and McFarlane, Bruce. 1970. *The Chinese Road to Socialism: Economics of the Cultural Revolution.* New York: Monthly Review Press.

Wiles, Peter, and Markowski, Stefan. 1971. Income Distribution under Communism and Capitalism: Some Facts about Poland, the UK, the USA and the USSR. *Soviet Studies* 22 (January).

Wilson, James Q. 1966. *The Amateur Democrat.* Chicago: University of Chicago Press.

Wollett, Donald H. 1971. The Status and Trends of Collective Negotiations for Faculty in Higher Education. *University of Wisconsin Law Review* 150.

Yanowitch, Murray, and Fisher, Wesley A., trans. and eds. 1973. *Social Stratification and Mobility in the U.S.S.R.* White Plains, N.Y.: International Arts and Sciences Press.

Zagoria, Sam, ed. 1972. *Public Workers and Public Unions.* Englewood Cliffs, N.J.: Prentice-Hall.

Ziskind, David. 1940. *One Thousand Strikes of Government Employees.* New York: Columbia University Press.

Zweig, Ferdynand. 1970. The Jewish Trade Union Movement in Israel. In *Integration and Development in Israel,* ed. S. N. Eisenstadt et al. New York: Praeger.